BORN IN TIBET

drawn by Sherab Palden Beru

MARPA THE TRANSLATOR
Father of the Ka-gyü School

Milarepa   Karmapa   Gampopa

Vajra Yogini   Mahakala
(Female Divinity)   *(The Protector)*

Overhead: Vajradhara Buddha with two Indian Gurus

BORN IN TIBET

by
CHÖGYAM TRUNGPA
The eleventh TRUNGPA TULKU

as told to
ESMÉ CRAMER ROBERTS

With Forewords by
THE SAKYONG MIPHAM RINPOCHE
and
MARCO PALLIS

Fourth Edition

SHAMBHALA
Boston & London
1995

To my Mother and motherland

Shambhala Publications, Inc.
Horticultural Hall
300 Massachusetts Avenue
Boston, Massachusetts 02115

9   8   7   6   5   4   3   2   1

1995 Edition

Printed in the United States of America on acid-free paper ⊗

Distributed in the United States by Random House, Inc.,
and in Canada by Random House of Canada Ltd

*The Library of Congress catalogues the 1985 edition
of this book as follows:*

Trungpa, Chogyam, 1939–
  Born in Tibet.
  Reprint. Originally published: Boulder, Colo.:
Shambhala, 1977, c1966.
  Includes index.
  1. Trungpa, Chogyam, 1939–   . 2. Lamas—China—
Tibet—Biography. I. Roberts, Esmé Cramer. II. Title.
BQ990.R867A33   1985   294.3'923'0924 [B]   85-8174
ISBN 1-57062-116-0 (1995 pbk.)
ISBN 0-87773-333-3 (1985 pbk.)
ISBN 0-394-74219-2 (Random House: 1985 pbk.)

FOREWORD TO THE 1995 EDITION

WHEN I think back upon my father's life, it amazes me how much he accomplished in such a short time. He was only forty-eight years old when he passed away, but within that time, the experiences he had and the people he encountered were as varied and rich as if he had lived for hundreds of years.

Often people would ask him how he was able to adapt to so many diverse cultures, and how he was able to deal with the tremendous hardships of his life. Always his answer would be that it was due to the rigorous traditional training and education that he received in Tibet while he was young. It might appear to the reader that the Tibet of Chögyam Trungpa's youth was medieval; it seems so distant from today's modern world, and so harsh. Ironically, however, it was that very training, with its simplicity and realness, that gave him the foundation that enabled him to relate with this modern world.

My father had two distinct roles in his life, corresponding with the periods of his life spent in the East and the West. During the first part of his life, since he was recognized as the incarnation of a famous teacher, people had high expectations of him. Many of the lamas and monks at the monastery were quite concerned that he be able to fit into his traditional role and continue the work of his predecessor. He very much had to fulfill the ambitions of the monastic community, as well as those of the lay people of his religion.

Once he left Tibet, his role was quite different—almost totally the opposite. In the West, very few people knew much about Buddhism as a whole, and they knew even less about the role of a lama, a spiritual teacher. People had little basis for any kind of expectations. In many ways, this was incredibly liberating for Chögyam Trungpa, and in fact it enabled him to become one of the most prominent Buddhist teachers of his time. His unique gift was that he was able to synthesize the ancient wisdom of Buddhism and transmit it to the West in a clear and concise way that was both meaningful and refreshing—so much so that a new generation of Western practitioners was born.

Born in Tibet is a unique book, one that I personally have always loved to read. It is not just a historical document, a book about

Tibetan culture, but it reveals many subtleties of what that life was actually like. It shows the spiritual development of teacher and disciple, and it illustrates the humanness that everyone possesses, regardless of culture, and the politics that come about from that.

Even though my father was not particularly a nostalgic person, he had tremendous pride in his Tibetan heritage, which he transmitted to me in various ways. Occasionally in the middle of the night, we would prepare bandit soup together. This was one of his favorite Tibetan delicacies, which was simply raw meat with hot water poured over it.

Knowing the tremendous hardships and challenges that confronted Chögyam Trungpa, and how he was able to overcome them through his courage, humor, and his faith in the spiritual disciplines of Tibet, I have always found this book inspiring. I hope that you too may be inspired by his example, and that this book will continue to benefit numberless beings.

THE SAKYONG MIPHAM RINPOCHE
25 November 1994
Karmê-Chöling

FOREWORD TO THE 1977 EDITION

STORIES of escape have always enlisted the sympathy of norma human beings; no generous heart but will beat faster as the fugitives from civil or religious persecution approach the critical moment that will, for them, spell captivity or death, or else the freedom they are seeking. The present age has been more than usually prodigal in such happenings, if only for the reason that in this twentieth century of ours, for all the talk about 'human rights', the area of oppression, whether as a result of foreign domination or native tyranny, has extended beyond all that has ever been recorded in the past. One of the side effects of modern technology has been to place in the hands of those who control the machinery of government a range of coercive apparatus undreamed of by any ancient despotism. It is not only such obvious means of intimidation as machine guns or concentration camps that count; such a petty product of the printing press as an identity card, by making it easy for the authorities to keep constant watch on everybody's movements, represents in the long run a still more effective curb on liberty. In Tibet, for instance, the introduction of such a system by the Chinest Communists, following the abortive rising of 1959, and its application to food rationing has been one of the principal means of keeping the whole population in subjection and compelling them to do the work decreed by their foreign overlords. Formerly Tibet was a country where, though simple living was the rule, serious shortage of necessities had been unknown: thus, one of the most contented portions of the world has been reduced to misery, with many of its people, like the author of the present book, choosing exile rather than remain in their own homes under conditions where no man, and especially no young person, is any longer allowed to call his mind his own.

Hostile propaganda, playing on slogan-ridden prejudice, has made much of the fact that a large proportion of the peasantry, in the old Tibet, stood in the relation of feudal allegiance to the great land-owning families or also to monasteries endowed with landed estates; it has been less generally known that many other peasants were small holders, owning their own farms, to whom must be added the nomads on the northern prairies, whose lives knew scarcely any restrictions other than those imposed by a hard climate and by the periodic need to seek fresh pasturage for their yaks and sheep. In fact all three systems, feudal tenure, individual peasant proprietorship and nomadism have always existed side by side in the Tibetan lands; of the former all one need say is that it naturally would depend, for its effective working, on the regular presence of the

7

landowner and his family among their own people; in any such case, absenteeism is bound to sap the essential human relationship, bringing other troubles in its train. In central Tibet a tendency on the part of too many of the secular owners to stop in Lhasa, with occasional outings down to India, had latterly become apparent and this was to be accounted a danger sign; further east, in the country of Kham to which the author belongs, unimpaired patriarchal institutions prevailed as of old and no one wished things otherwise. Of the country as a whole it can be said that, generally speaking, the traditional arrangements worked in such a way that basic material needs were adequately met, life was full of interest at every social level, while the Buddhist ideal absorbed everyone's intellectual and moral aspirations at all possible degrees, from that of popular piety to spirituality of unfathomable depth and purity. By and large, Tibetan society was a unanimous society in which, however, great freedom of viewpoint prevailed and also a strong feeling for personal freedom which, however, did not conflict with, but was complementary to, a no less innate feeling for order.

At the same time, it must not be supposed that the Tibetans had developed—or had any occasion to develop—an ideology of liberty of the type familiar in the West: a Tibetan experiences freedom (like any other desirable state, moreover) 'concretely', that is to say through his being rather than through its conceptual image in his thinking mind. The presence or absence of interference in his life tells him how far he is or is not a free man and he feels little need to call in abstract criteria for the sake of defining his own condition. By nature and habit he is 'down to earth', hence also his preference for an almost material phraseology when trying to express the most subtle metaphysical and spiritual truths; that is why our word 'philosophy' is but rarely appropriate in a Tibetan context. Whatever a Tibetan undertakes, he will do it wholeheartedly and when the wish to do that thing leaves him he will banish it just as completely from his thoughts. The same holds good for the religious life; by comparison with many of us, an average Tibetan finds contemplative concentration, with its parallel exclusion of irrelevant thinking, easy: the reader need not be surprised, when he comes to the description of the author's early training under various teachers, at the unswerving single-mindedness shown by one so young. In Tibet this is a normal attitude for one of his kind.

Another characteristic common to Tibetans of all types, not unconnected with the ones already mentioned, is their love of trekking and camping. Every Tibetan seems to have a nomadic streak in him and is never happier than when moving, on ponyback or, if he is a poor man, on foot through an unpeopled countryside in close communion with untamed Nature; rapid travel would be no travel, as far as this quality of experience is concerned. Here again, one sees how a certain kind of life helps to foster the habit of inward recollection as well as that sense of kinship with animals, birds and trees which is so deeply rooted in the Tibetan soul.

Tibetans on the whole are strangers to the kind of sophistry that in one breath will argue in favour of human brotherhood and of the irresponsible exploitation of all Man's fellow-beings in order to serve that interest reduced to its most shortsightedly material aspect. As Buddhists they know that all are in the same boat, tossed together on the ocean of Birth and Death and subject to a selfsame fatality. Therefore, for those who understand this truth, Compassion is indivisible; failure in one respect will, unfailingly, instil poison into everything else. This is not some abstruse idea reserved for monks or Lamas; people of the humblest degree are aware of it, though the Saints exemplify it more brightly. It is one of the great joys of being in Tibet to witness the results of this human attitude in the lack of fear displayed by bird and beast in all parts of the country. Admittedly most Tibetans, though averse to hunting or fishing, are meat eaters and could hardly be otherwise in a land of such prolonged winters where in any case the range of available foodstuffs is very limited. Nevertheless this fact is accounted a cause for regret; no one tries to prove that it is completely innocent and devoid of spiritually negative results. It is a common practice for people to abstain from the fruit of slaughter on certain days, as a kind of token of intent; while anyone who succeeds in keeping off meat altogether, as in the case of certain Lamas and ascetics, will invariably earn praise for doing so.

It is hard to believe that if such an attitude were more general the prospects of peace on Earth would not be that much brighter. If one wishes to pull up the taproot of war one has to seek it at a level for deeper than that of social or political events. Every Tibetan faithful to his tradition knows this plainly; it is only when he adopts the ways of our civilisation that he will begin to forget this truth, together with many other things.

* * *

It may perhaps now help the reader to be told something about the historical background of the present story, with particular emphasis on such events as affected conditions in eastern Tibet during the period just prior to the time when the author's personal narrative starts.

After the Chinese revolution of 1912, when the Manchu dynasty fell, the suzerainty the Emperor had exercised in this country (since 1720) was repudiated by the Tibetans; Chinese influence in Tibet had in any case been dwindling all through the nineteenth century. Not long before the fall of the Manchus, their last viceroy in the westerly Chinese province of Szechuan, Chao Erfeng, a hard and ambitious man, made an attempt (the first of its kind) to bring Tibet under direct Chinese administration; his troops occupied Lhasa in 1910. When the empire collapsed, however, giving way to a republic, the Tibetans rose and drove out the Chinese garrisons from the two central provinces of Ü and Tsang; Tibetan national independence in its latest phase dates from that time. Moreover, a further extension of the territory governed from Lhasa took place in 1918, when Tibetan forces succeeded in occupying the western part of Kham which thenceforth remained as a province of Tibet with its administrative centre at Chamdo, a place often referred to in the pages to follow.

The new Sino-Tibetan boundary consequently ran through the middle of the Khamba country, with people of Tibetan race, that is to say, dwelling on both sides of it; but paradoxically it was those districts that remained nominally under China that enjoyed the most untrammelled independence in practice. Occasional interference from neighbouring Chinese 'war-lords' apart, the local principalities, akin to small Alpine Cantons, which provided the typical form of organisation for a valley, or complex of valleys, in this region were left so free to manage their own affairs that people there must have been practically unconscious of, and equally indifferent to, the fact that, in the atlases of the world, their lands were coloured yellow as forming part of greater China. Under these conditions, which went back a long time, the Khambas had developed a peculiar sense of local independence which needs to be understood if one is to grasp the significance of many of the events mentioned in this book.

By comparison with the districts still attached to China, the part of Kham governed by Lhasa-appointed officials felt, if anything, less free; which does not mean, however, that the Khambas were lacking in loyalty to the Dalai Lama, as spiritual sovereign of all the Tibetan peoples: they were second to none in this respect. Only they did not see why an unbounded devotion to his sacred person need imply any willingness to surrender jealously treasured liberties at the bidding of others acting in his name. In their own country the Khambas much preferred the authority of their own chieftains ('kings' as the author describes them), personally known to everyone; laws or levies imposed from a distant centre was not a thing of which they could recognize the necessity, for their own valleys had always run their own affairs quite successfully on the basis of a self-contained economy and from their point of view nothing was to be gained, and much lost, by exchanging the old, homely arrangements for control by the nominees of a capital that lay in another province far to the west. Besides, some of the governors sent to Chamdo made matters worse by extorting from the local inhabitants more perquisites than what long established custom would sanction. When the Chinese invaded Tibet in October 1950 they were at first able to exploit these discontents in their own favour by saying they would put an end to the exactions of the Tibetan officials. It was not till afterwards that the clansmen of those parts realized, too late, that the change from capricious harassment to a meticulously calculated squeezing had not worked out to their advantage. It is hardly surprising that when eventually popular exasperation at Communist interference broke out in armed revolt it was the Khambas who bore the brunt of the patriotic movement and provided its most daring leaders.

It is hoped that enough has now been said by way of setting the stage for the Lama Trungpa's reminiscences: these are given with typically Tibetan matter-of-factness; he neither tries to feed the reader with opinions nor does he, for the sake of logical coherence, introduce information gathered after the event; the inevitable gaps in one man's experience are left, just as they were, unfilled. All the author does is to relate whatever he himself saw, heard and said; as each day brought its fresh needs and opportunities, he describes how he tried to act, adding nothing and omitting nothing—the Lama obviously has a most retentive memory for detail. Surely this way of presenting facts makes the documentary value of such a chronicle all the greater, illustrating, as it does, all the hesitations and uncertainties of a situation no one was prepared for, the doubts, the changes of plan, the conflicts of advice, out of which gradually grows the firm resolve, carrying out of which forms the second and most dramatic part of the book.

The first appearance of the Communists on what previously seemed like an idyllic scene is typical, it occurs almost casually: when they turn up one day people ask themselves what this means, but when nothing very unpleasant happens—none of the expected looting by the soldiers, for instance—everyone soon settles down again to his usual preoccupations. The soldiers pass on; the incident is half forgotten. It is only some pages later that one discovers them again, first just across the Tibetan frontier at Chamdo, and long afterwards in occupation of Lhasa, but how they got there one is not told. After a time one guesses that Tibet has capitulated, but is given few details simply because those actually involved in these events were often too cut off in their own locality to obtain a bird's eye view; we in England, watching the international scene from afar were, in some respects, better able to build up a general picture.

In fact, as the book shows, it was by no means easy for people in those remote districts immediately to form clear ideas about the nature of the new order in China. Moreover this also partly explains why the Tibetan Government itself, while the Communist threat was developing, was rather hesitating in its reactions; a temporizing policy, so often resorted to by small nations facing pressure from a great Power, may well have seemed preferable to crying Tibet's wrongs from the housetops regardless of consequences. The Lhasa government has been criticized, with a certain justice, for lack of initiative in face of a danger calling for swift decisions; but it is only fair to make considerable allowance for circumstances, material and psychological, that were inherent in the situation from the very start of the crisis.

The above remarks have somewhat anticipated on the sequence of events. The point I am trying to make is that it necessarily took some time before the author, young as he was, or his senior advisers were able to gather any precise impressions of what was to be expected under Communist rule. As the story unfolds we see an initial bewilderment gradually giving way to acute discomfort which in its turn becomes a sense of impending disaster. We hear that fighting has broken out in a certain valley, yet the adjoining valley may still be seemingly in enjoyment of its habitual calm, with every-one there intent on peaceful tasks—adding a wing to the local temple perhaps or preparing for the reception of a revered Spiritual Master. Eventually, however, the more wide-awake characters in the book begin to realize that this is no passing crisis: Tibet and its cherished way of life are facing a catastrophe without parallel in the past, one that no policy of 'wait and see' will enable one to live down. It is a time for far-reaching decisions if certain values, as well as one's own life, are to be preserved: here again, one is allowed to see into the conflict of outlook between those who cling to the belief that this trouble, like others before it, will blow over if only people will have the patience to sit tight and those others who think that their imperative duty is to carry whatever they can of Tibet's spiritual heritage to some place where the flickering spark can be rekindled in freedom; flight to India, the Buddha's native land, seems the only remedy left to them. These two much canvassed points of view become focussed, in this story, in the persons of the author himself and his elderly bursar, a well meaning man not wanting in devotion, but typical of the mentality that is for ever fighting shy of any solution that looks like becoming irrevocable. There is much pathos to be gathered from these repeated encounters between youthful virility ready to take the plunge and inbred caution for which 'stick to familiar ways and wait' is the universal maxim to fit every unprecedented emergency.

About the actual escape there is no call to speak here, except by remarking that at least one reader, while following this part of the story, has been repeatedly reminded of those young British officers of the late nineteenth century who found themselves launched by fate into positions of unusual responsibility at remote outposts of the Empire: one meets here the same readiness to take crucial decisions time and again, the same light-hearted spirit maintained over long periods of suspense and danger and, in more critical moments, a similar capacity for instilling courage into the timid and endurance into the weakly by the well turned appeal, the timely sally—all these qualities were displayed by the chief actor in this drama in a completely unselfconscious manner.

But after making this comparison, one still has to admit a certain difference, itself due to a very great difference in the respective backgrounds. This can be summed up in the fact that in the one case, aptitude for leadership rests on an acceptance of what are predominantly 'Stoic' loyalties and values—Marcus Aurelius would have shared them gladly—whereas in the other, it is from the heart of Contemplation that this strength is drawn forth; the centre of allegiance lies there, thus endowing whatever action has to be taken under pressure of necessity with an unmistakable flavour of 'inwardness'. It is the Lama who, speaking through the man, delivers his message and that is why, over and above its human and historical interest, this book has also to be treated as a Buddhist document in which much may be discovered by those who have the instinct to read between the lines. It is noticeable that whenever a pause in the action occurs there is an almost automatic withdrawal back into contemplation; the mind wastes no time in dwelling on its anxieties but finds within its own solitude, as well as in the stillness of Nature, the means of refreshment and renewal.

That a mind so attuned should harbour no enmity in return for injuries received seems only logical; in this respect the present history may well be left to speak for itself. Buddhism has always had much to say, not only about 'Compassion' as such, but also about what might be called its 'intellectual premises', failing which that virtue can so easily give way to a passional benevolence that may even end up in hatred and violence; this has been the persistent weakness of worldly idealists and of the movements they promoted. For Compassion (or Christian Charity for that matter) to be truly itself it requires its intellectual complement which is dispassion or detachment: a hard saying for the sentimentalists. Though feeling obviously has a place there too, it can never afford to bypass intelligence—as if anything could do that with impunity! This is a point which Buddhism brings out with implacable insistence: from its point of view Compassion must be looked upon as a dimension of Knowledge; the two are inseparable, as husband and wife. All this belongs to the basic tenets of the *Mahāyāna* or 'Great Way', of which the Tibetan tradition itself is an offshoot; Tibetan art is filled with symbolical delineations of this partnership. It is important for the reader to be made aware of the fact that these ideas pervade the entire background of the author's thinking, otherwise he will miss many of the finer touches.

It would be ungrateful to terminate this introduction to a remarkable book without some reference to the lady who helped the Lama Trungpa to put down his memories on paper, Mrs Cramer Roberts; in fact, but for her encouragement in the first place, the work might never have been begun. In interpreting what the Lama told her of his experiences she wisely did not try and tamper with a characteristically Tibetan mode of expression beyond the minimum required by correct English; in all other respects the flavour of the author's thought has been preserved in a manner that will much increase the reader's ability to place himself, imaginatively, in the minds and feelings of those who figure in the narrative; a more inflected style, normal with us, could so easily have covered up certain essential things. For the fine sense of literary discernment she has shown we all have to thank Mrs Cramer Roberts, as also for the unstinting devotion she brought to her self-appointed task.

MARCO PALLIS

ACKNOWLEDGEMENTS

This book was begun spontaneously as an authentic record of the wisdom and culture which existed in Tibet for so many centuries, and of the events of the last decade during which the Communists have destroyed everything its peace loving people held dear.

Living in East Tibet the author was a witness of these tragic happenings of which the world outside is largely ignorant.

We would like to offer our grateful thanks to Mr Gerald Yorke and Mr Marco Pallis for the great help that they have given us to bring the book to completion. Mr Yorke saw the script in its early stages, and not only introduced it to the publishers, but made many useful suggestions. Mr Pallis when consenting to write the foreword, devoted many weeks to the work of finally putting the book in order.

We also thank Lieut. Colonel F. Spencer Chapman and Major G. Sherrif for allowing us to use some of their Tibetan photographs.

CHÖGYAM TRUNGPA
ESMÉ CRAMER ROBERTS
February 1966
Oxford

The frontispiece and illustration No. 3 were specially drawn by the author's friend Sherab Palden Beru.

CONTENTS

ILLUSTRATIONS

ILLUSTRATIONS

ILLUSTRATIONS FOR THE 1977 & 1995 EDITIONS

How to pronounce Tibetan names and words
A simplified guide

It is obviously impracticable here to aim at the kind of accuracy that would satisfy an expert in phonetics: the use of numerous small additional signs, for instance, such as one finds in serious grammars, would complicate the issue too much for ordinary readers. Therefore one must try to limit oneself to whatever the Latin alphabet, coupled with a few rather rough and ready explanations, will give; in fact, a reasonable approximation can be obtained by this means, as is the case with most foreign languages; the reader should find no trouble in applying the following hints concerning Tibetan pronunciation:-

Vowel sounds : these include the five *open vowels*, A, E, I, O, U which should be sounded as in Italian: a final E should never be muted, it is open like the rest; the Tibetan name *Dorje* does *not* rhyme with 'George'; in French it would be written as 'Dorjé'.

To the above five should be added two *modified vowels*, Ö and Ü; these should be pronounced as in German.

These seven sounds give the complete vowel range.

Consonant sounds : here the problem of transcription is somewhat more difficult. The prevailing dialects of Central Tibet, where the capital Lhasa is situated, and of Eastern Tibet where the author belongs, contain a number of consonant sounds which, to a European ear, sound almost alike; there are, for instance, two kinds of K, two of T and so on. Short of using an elaborate system of diacritic marks, puzzling to a non-scholar, one is compelled to make do, in many cases, with a single letter where Tibetans would use two. The reader need not be troubled with these fine distinctions.

In the case of aspirated consonants such as KH, TH and so on *both* letters have to be sounded separately; they do not fuse to make an entirely new consonant as in the English word *the* for instance, or the Greek name *Thetis*. SH, CH should, however, be sounded as in English.

NB. There is no sound like our F in Tibetan: PH, whenever it occurs, follows the rule as above i.e. both letters are sounded as in *map house*.

Special attention must be drawn to combinations such as TR, DR in Tibetan: the author's name TRUNGPA is a case in point. The fact is that the R is not sounded independently; it only affects the preceding T or D by lending to it a slightly 'explosive' character. What one has to do, in these cases, is to press the tongue hard against the palate, while sounding T or D as the case may be; it sometimes helps to *think* of an R while so doing. (In Tibetan quite a number of such letters exist, such as GR, TR, BR, etc. which are all pronounced similarly; but obviously this aspect of the matter will only concern students of Tibetan who, in any case, will use the Tibetan alphabet).

NOTE ON GLOSSARY

The reader's attention is drawn to the list of Tibetan technical terms etc. at the end of the book, by referring to which he will be able to refresh his memory as to the meaning of any given term in case he has forgotten the explanation given by the author on its first appearance in the text.

For various titles indicating functionaries in a monastery see Appendix I.

CHAPTER ONE

FOUND AND ENTHRONED

My birthplace was a small settlement on a high plateau of north eastern Tibet. Above it, the celebrated mountain Pagö-pünsum rises perpendicularly to more than eighteen thousand feet, and is often called 'the pillar of the sky'. It looks like a tall spire; its mighty crest towers under perpetual snows, glittering in the sunshine.

Centuries before Buddhism was brought to Tibet, the followers of the Bön religion believed that Pagö-pünsum was the home of the king of spirits, and the surrounding lesser peaks were the abodes of his ministers. Myths linger on among the country folk, and these mountains have continued to be held in awe and veneration in the district.

The name of the place was Geje; it stands in a bare, treeless country without even bushes, but grass covered, and in the summer months the ground is bright with small flowers and sweet-smelling herbs whose scent in this pure air is thought to be curative; however, for the greater part of the year the whole land is under snow and it is so cold that the ice must be broken to get water. Two sorts of wild animals are peculiar to this province, the *kyang* or wild ass, and a kind of bison called a *drong*; both are found in herds of about five hundred each. The people live in tents made of yak's hair; the more wealthy have larger ones with several partitions, situated in the centre of the encampment, while the poorer peasants live on the fringes. Each village considers itself to be one large family, and in the individual family, the members from the oldest to the youngest live together and own their herds of yaks and sheep in common.

The fire, used for all domestic purposes, is always in the middle of the tent, and the shrine is in the far right hand corner with a butter lamp burning continually before a religious picture, or a set of the scriptures.

This northern area of East Tibet is called *Nyishu-tza-nga*, and

།དེ་སྐད་བཤད་ཅིང་རང་བཞིན་བཟང་པོ།།

།རྫུ་འཕྲུལ་ཆེན་པོ་ཐུགས་རྗེའི་གཏེར།།
།ལོ་འདབ་རྒྱས་ཤིང་འབྲས་བུ་སྨིན་པ་དང༌།།
།ཕན་བདེའི་དཔལ་ལ་རྒུན་པར་ཕུན་ཚོགས་བཀོད།།
།ཞི་བདེ་རྣམ་དཀར་ལས་ཀྱི་སྤྱན་འགུགས།།

I *Mount Pagö Pünsum*

has twenty-five districts; the name simply means twenty five. At one time it was under a king who gave the district where Geje is situated the special privilege of having its highlanders chosen for his bodyguard on account of their courage.

Geje was a small community of only about five-hundred people. My father, Yeshe-dargye owned a little land there; he met his future wife Tungtso-drölma when she was working for her relations, looking after the yaks and milking the females which are called *dris*. They had one daughter, but when a second child was already in her womb he left her, and she married again, this time a much poorer man who, when the child was born, accepted him as his son.

The night of my conception my mother had a very significant dream that a being had entered her body with a flash of light; that year flowers bloomed in the neighbourhood although it was still winter, to the surprise of the inhabitants.

During the New Year festival on the day of the full moon, in the Earth Hare year according to the Tibetan calendar (February 1939) I was born in the cattle byre; the birth came easily. On that day a rainbow was seen in the village, a pail supposed to contain water was unaccountably found full of milk, while several of my mother's relations dreamt that a lama was visiting their tents. Soon afterwards, a lama from Trashi Lhaphug Monastery came to Geje; as he was giving his blessing to the people, he saw me, who at that time was a few months old; he put his hand over my head to give me a special blessing, saying that he wanted me for his monastery and that I must be kept very clean and always be carefully looked after. Both my parents agreed to this, and decided that when I grew older I should be sent to his monastery, where my mother's uncle was a monk.

After the death in 1938 of the tenth Trungpa Tulku, the supreme abbot of Surmang, the monks at once sent a representative to His Holiness Gyalwa Karmapa, the head of the Karma-ka-gyu school whose monastery lay near Lhasa. Their envoy had to inform him of the death of the last abbot and to ask him if he had had any indication where his reincarnation would be found. They begged him to let them know at once should he obtain a vision.

Some months later Gyalwa Karmapa was visiting Pepung Monastery in the province of Derge in Kham, which is Tibet's eastern region. Jamgön Kongtrül Rinpoche, who had been a devoted disciple of the tenth Trungpa Tulku and lived at Pepung, also asked him not to defer giving any possible indication, for the monks of Surmang were feeling lost without their abbot and were eager that his reincarnation should be found without delay.

A vision had in fact come to Gyalwa Karmapa, who dictated a letter to his private secretary, saying that the reincarnation of the tenth Trungpa Tulku has been born in a village five days' journey northwards from Surmang. Its name sounds like two words *Ge* and *De*; there is a family there with two children; the son is the reincarnation. It all sounded rather vague; however, the secretary and monks of the Düdtsi-til Monastery at Surmang were preparing to go in search of the new abbot when a second sealed letter was received at the monastery. Rölpa-dorje, the regent abbot of Düdtsi-til, called a meeting, opened the letter and read it to the assembled monks. It said that Gyalwa Karmapa had had a second and much clearer vision: 'The door of the family's dwelling faces south; they own a big red dog. The father's name is Yeshe-dargye and the mother's Chung and Tzo; the son who is nearly a year old is Trungpa Tulku'. One senior monk and two others set off immediately to find me.

After five days' journey they reached the village of Geje, and called on all the more important families; they made a list of the names of those parents who had children of a year old, and returned to Düdtsi-til. The list was sent to Gyalwa Karmapa, who was still at Pepung. He found that the monks had merely taken names belonging to important families and said that they must go again and make further enquiries. On receipt of this message a second party of monks was sent to the village, which in the interval had removed to higher ground and changed its name to Dekyil: this time they called on every family and made a thorough search. In one tent they found a baby boy who had a sister and, as had been written in Gyalwa Karmapa's letter, the entrance faced south and there was a red dog. Also, the mother's name was Bo-chung, though her family called her Tungtso-drölma; thus her name confirmed Gyalwa Karmapa's vision, but the father's name was different from that in the letter, and this caused a great deal of confusion; yet they looked closely at the baby, for as soon as he had seen them in the distance he waved his little hand and broke into smiles as they came in. So the monks felt that this must be the child and gave him the gifts which Gyalwa Karmapa had sent, the sacred protective cord (*sungdü*) and the traditional scarf (*khata*); this latter the baby took and hung round

26

the monk's neck in the prescribed way, as if he had already been taught what was the right thing to do: delighted, the monks picked me up, for that baby was myself, and I tried to talk.

The following day the monks made a further search in another part of the village, then returned to say goodbye. As they made prostration before me, I placed my hand on their heads as if I knew that I should give them my blessing, then the monks were certain that I was the incarnation of the tenth Trungpa. They spoke to my mother asking her to tell them in confidence who had been my father. She told them that I was the son of her first husband Yeshe-dargye, but that I had always been known as the son of my step-father. This made everything clear to the monks, who immediately returned to Düdtsi-til. The news was taken to Gyalwa Karmapa who was sure that I, the child of Tungtso-drölma, was the eleventh Trungpa Tulku.

Gyalwa Karmapa was about to leave Pepung Monastery on a tour in which Surmang would be included, and the monks realized that if he was to perform the ceremony of my enthronement it was necessary to bring me there immediately. Kargyen, the senior secretary of Düdtsi-til, with a party of monks came to my native village of Dekyil to fetch me. He had to proclaim his mission to the whole area and to consult all the heads of the villages and the representatives of the people, since ordinarily it was expected that they would demand land or money. However, everyone was co-operative and modest and no-one asked for any gain for himself. Next, my parents had to be asked if they wished to live near Surmang, or would prefer to receive property in their own village. My parents decided that they would like to be given the land on which they lived; however, they told the secretary that at some future time they would be glad of permission to visit me at Surmang.

When these things were settled we set off, with both my parents travelling in the party, for they were anxious to see Surmang. My mother stayed on in a house near Düdtsi-til in order to look after me until I was five years old, but my stepfather returned to his village.

A messenger had been sent ahead to inform Düdtsi-til when we would arrive, and a great welcome was prepared. All the monks from Surmang and many from neighbouring monasteries assembled some five miles distant from Düdtsi-til to form a procession to escort me.

On that day the valley was misty, and a rainbow appeared in the sky forming an arch over the procession, but as we drew near the monastery the surrounding mists dissolved, and the low clouds spread like a canopy hiding us from distant onlookers.

At the monastery everything was in festival; all the monks were rejoicing. There were special ceremonies and a great feast was arranged. I have been told that, though I was only about thirteen months old at the time, I immediately recognized those monks in whom the tenth Trungpa Tulku had placed confidence, and that I behaved with the greatest decorum throughout the day and did not even cry once.

A few days later I was put through a test; pairs of several objects were put before me, and in each case I picked out the one that had belonged to the tenth Trungpa Tulku; among them were two walking sticks and two rosaries; also, names were written on small pieces of paper and when I was asked which piece had his name on it, I chose the right one. Now the monks were certain that I was the incarnation, so a letter was sent to Gyalwa Karmapa telling him the results of the examination and inviting him to officiate at my enthronement ceremony.

Every morning my mother brought me to the monastery and took me home with her in the evening. My earliest memory is being in a room with several monks who were talking to me, and I was answering them. I was told later that my first words were *Om Mani Padme Hum*; probably, I did not say them very correctly. When lamas came to visit me, I have been told that I used to clutch at their rosaries and try to imitate them. Every day that month, I held an audience and received visits from the friends and disciples of my past incarnation who took a great interest in me, and I always seemed to enjoy meeting people.

At the end of the month my enthronement ceremony was to take place, and so I was taken to the larger monastery of Namgyal-tse. This time, instead of the joyous informality with which I had been welcomed at Düdtsi-til, a procession came to escort me and everything was done with pomp and ceremony.

Gyalwa Karmapa arrived with some senior Lamas from Pepung; other people came from all parts of East Tibet: about one thousand Surmang monks and twelve thousand other monks and laity finally assembled. My monks were delighted, for this enthronement was to be one of the largest in living memory. There were several incarnate lamas already at Surmang including Garwang Tulku the regent abbot of Namgyal-tse. Rölpa-dorje the regent abbot of Düdtsi-til was appointed to act as my sponsor and give my responses at the enthronement. Both were regent abbots of their respective monasteries in the interregnum after the death of the tenth Trungpa and during my minority, and they remained so later when I was absent from Surmang.

Rölpa-dorje Rinpoche was the fifth incarnation of the great Rölpa-dorje, a contemporary of the fifth Trungpa Tulku, and he had been the teacher of *Taisitu* Chökyi-jungne in the early part of the eighteenth century; the latter was the second most important Lama in the Karma-ka-gyü school; *Taisitu* is a Chinese title. He had written many scholarly works and had revived the pictorial art of the 'Gabri school'. His teaching had been widely disseminated in Tibet, China and India.

My enthronement took place in the large assembly hall. The lion throne (*sengtri*), on which all *tulkus* are traditionally enthroned, stood at the further end of the hall on a dais. It was made of gilt wood, square in shape, with white lions carved on the sides which appeared to be supporting it. On the throne there were three cushions, red, yellow and blue, covered with two strips of brocade. A table was placed in front of it with all my seals of office. I was carried up the hall by the senior secretary of Düdtsi-til, escorted by a procession of the higher dignitaries. Rölpa-dorje Rinpoche stood at the foot of the throne, and my secretary handed me to him; he then mounted the dais and sat down in my place holding me on his lap and gave all the responses which should have come from me.

According to tradition, the service began with the rite of the primary *Upasaka* ordination, the entrance to the Buddhist Congregation. Gyalwa Karmapa cut my hair to symbolize a cutting away from the material, and entering the spiritual, life. Then the regent abbot spoke in my name.

'From today I take refuge in the Buddha.
From today I take refuge in the Dharma, (the Norm, embodied in the Doctrine)
From today I take refuge in the Sangha, (the Assembly or Church both earthly and heavenly).'

At the moment when he put the scissors to my hair there was a clap of thunder, sudden rain, and a rainbow appeared. This was thought to be very auspicious. After this I was given my personal name *Karma-tendzin-trinle-künkyap-pal-zangpo*: all monks of the Karma-Kagyü school are given the first name *Karma* after their founder; roughly translated the remaining words mean: 'the universal action of the holder of the Doctrine, the gloriously good'. Later that day I was given all the seals and official documents of the tenth Trungpa Tulku. Everyone came to receive my blessing and offered me ceremonial scarves. The incarnate lamas and heads of monasteries led the way, followed by monks and lay people; they presented me with robes and many other gifts.

After a few weeks Gyalwa Karmapa Rinpoche left for his own centre close to Lhasa, and the senior *tulkus* from Pepung, after escorting him half way, likewise returned to their monastery.

The Umbrella of Protection

CHAPTER TWO

THE FOUNDING OF SURMANG

FOR my life as the eleventh Trungpa Tulku to be understood, it is necessary to know the history of the Ka-gyü school to which the Surmang monasteries belonged. The basic teaching was introduced into Tibet by Marpa the Translator, a great adept. He made three journeys to India under most difficult conditions to study with Naropa and other Indian Buddhist *gurus* and brought back many precious teachings which he translated from the Sanskrit. He was one of the leading scholars of what is known as the New Translation Period. Milarepa, later to become one of Tibet's greatest saints, became his chief disciple to whom he handed over the spiritual authority to carry on his work. Milarepa's poems and the moving story of his life were written down soon after his death by several of his own disciples; there is a good translation into English by Evans-Wentz, and an outstanding one into French by professor Bacot.

The monastic tradition of the Ka-gyü school was founded by Gampopa, a pupil of Milarepa born in 1079. His classical work *The Ornament of Precious Liberation* is still a leading manual in this school and has been translated into English by Dr Herbert Guenther.

Following Gampopa's teaching, separate schools developed under three of his disciples and one of them, Karmapa, founded the Karma-ka-gyü school and established the abbey of Tsurphu near Lhasa which continued to be the principal monastery of the order. Karmapa's first incarnation Karma Pakshi (1203–1282), an eminent teacher, was invited to China by the Emperor Kublai Khan, and the second incarnation became the spiritual teacher of Kublai's successor. He was followed in this function by all the incarnations up to the tenth, who refused to go to China saying he would rather give his blessing to a dog's skull than to the emperor; he evidently disliked court life and did not wish to be connected with it even occasionally! The fifth Karmapa is especially known as the teacher of the Ming emperor Yung-lo and his influence on the spiritual and cultural thought of China was very great.

At the end of the fourteenth century Trung-mase Rinpoche, the son of the king of Me-nyag in East Tibet left his father's palace to seek spiritual guidance. He travelled from place to place and came to the monastery of Tzurphu: there he met the fifth Karmapa Teshin-shepa who became his *guru* and under whom he remained in retreat for ten years, in conditions of the utmost austerity. Karmapa then told him that the time had come for him to go out to found a monastery and to begin teaching himself.

He travelled round Tibet to find somewhere to establish it and when he came to the valley of Yöshung he had the feeling that this was the place his teacher had predicted. He walked round the village with his begging bowl reciting the *sutra* (sacred treatise) *Aryamanjushrinamasamgita* i.e. 'the Perfect Song of the Name of Holy Manjushri' and felt that his search had come to an end when a woman came out of her doorway to put food in his bowl at the very moment that he had reached the words '*chökyi-gyaltzen-legpardzug*', which means 'plant well the banner of the victory of Dharma'. This seemed to be such an auspicious sign that he immediately decided to build his monastery on that spot. This was the beginning of Surmang; and when its monks recite this *sutra*, they still pause at these words and repeat them a second time.

At first Trung-mase built a small hut made with reeds: it was very primitive, with many corners. Disciples flocked to him, and some of them suggested that the monastery should now be given an imposing name, but he said that he was proud of his hut and since it was so irregular in shape it should be called Surmang, which means 'many cornered'.

More and more disciples joined the monastery, of whom eleven were especially notable: three of these remained with their *guru* in the hut while the eight others, who were spiritually advanced teachers (*togden*), carried their doctrine round the country. Trungpa Künga-gyaltzen was one of these: he was looked upon as an incarnation of Maitreya Bodhisattva, destined to be the Buddha of the next World Cycle, also of Dombhipa a great Buddhist *siddha* (adept) and of Milarepa.

As his *guru* had also done, Künga-gyaltzen looked for a place for

his monastery, and at one of the villages on his travels he was told
the story of Dombhipa, who when he came there was holding a cup
of *amrita* (symbolically the elixir of immortality) in his hand which
he threw into space saying, 'Wherever this cup falls will be the place
for my reincarnation'. It fell on a hill in the valley which has since
been called Düdtsi-til (Hill of *Amrita*).

This story interested Künga-gyaltzen, and when thinking about it
one night he had a dream in which his *guru* said, 'You are an incarnation of Dombhipa, and this is the place for your monastery.' He
was deeply moved, and the next day he felt that he must also throw
a cup. He said, 'If I am an incarnation of Dombhipa, may my cup
fall in the right place.' He was five miles from the village but with
the power of his word, the cup fell on the roof of Adro Shelu-bum,
a large landowner's castle on the hill of Düdtsi-til. It made a ringing
sound and at the same moment there was an earthquake. When he
was told about Künga-gyaltzen's miraculous powers Adro Shelu-
bum realized that he must be a disciple of Trung-mase, invited him
to his palace, and was so deeply impressed by him that he became
his devotee. He offered part of his home to his new *guru* to be used
as a monastery, and undertook to feed the monks. As Trungpa
Künga-gyaltzen intended to continue his own life of travelling and
camping with his disciples, he did not want to establish a large
monastery; he therefore thankfully accepted Adro Shelu-bum's
offer and used it as a house of retreat for his monks. His camps
became known as the *Surmang garchentengpa* (the great camps of
Surmang); many disciples joined them, and this mode of life was
followed by his next three incarnations who were abbots of Düdtsi-
til.

In the meantime Trung-mase in his hut monastery had gathered
a great many disciples around him. It became over-crowded, and
Adro Shelu-bum gave him a second gift. This time it was the entire
castle of Namgyal-tse which was much larger than Düdtsi-til and
had a spacious assembly hall; much land was included in the endow-
ment, together with rocky mountains where there were several
caves suitable for meditation. Trung-mase transferred his hut
monastery to Namgyal-tse, but retained the name of Surmang for
the entire group.

As death approached he said that he would not re-incarnate, as
his teaching was both his incarnation and his portrait. Garwang,
one of the eight notable *togdens* of the hut monastery, followed him

as abbot. Surmang now included Namgyal-tse, Düdtsi-til, and several small monasteries, each of which had its own abbot.

The fourth incarnation, Trungpa Künga-namgyal did not follow the camping way of life of his three predecessors, and a descendant of Adro Shelu-bum gave him the entire castle of Düdtsi-til for a separate monastery. Brought up by the disciples of his predecessor and also by the lamas of Namgyal-tse, he became a renowned teacher throughout East Tibet, and was widely known for his ability to continue for a long period in meditation without any bodily movement. Because of his reputation, Düdtsi-til though a smaller monastery and with fewer monks than Namgyal-tse, was considered to be the more important.

However, Trungpa Künga-namgyal wished to devote his life to meditation, and for six years he remained as a hermit in a cave about a mile from Düdtsi-til; then, having reached a high degree of spiritual insight he returned to his monastery. After a year or two he felt that he must travel to give his teaching outside. Asking his brother to take charge of Düdtsi-til he left without any attendant and only a white yak to carry his books and baggage. It was a horn-less breed of yak used for riding and easy to control by a single man by means of a ring in its nose. Trungpa Künga-namgyal made a tour of the holy places, traditionally one hundred and eight in number; these included caves where renowned *gurus* had meditated, ruined cities where one could contemplate the impermanence of life and past battlefields and graveyards.

Towards the end of his life he no longer needed to travel, for after he returned to his monastery disciples flocked to him, and he became the teacher of the whole Karma-ka-gyü school. He then wrote some sixteen treatises on various spiritual themes and founded further monasteries.

Following in such footsteps, the fifth Trungpa Tulku was generally recognized as an important abbot. He was honoured by the Chinese Emperor early in the seventeenth century and received the official rank of *Hutukhtu*, the Mongolian equivalent for a great teacher, with its particular seals, hat and robe; the charter confering the title was written on yellow silk. He became the supreme abbot of all the Surmang monasteries and his authority also extended over the whole province.

At that time Düdtsi-til was extremely flourishing: the third Tulku Chetsang Rinpoche, himself a great artist, had superintended

34

most of the decoration and had painted many of the *tankas* (pictorial scrolls mounted on silk). The walls of the assembly hall were frescoed from floor to ceiling in red and gold with scenes from the life of Gotama Buddha and above them were depicted one thousand Buddhas of the past, present and future, of whom Gotama was the fourth, while Maitreya will be the fifth to guide us towards Enlightenment.

Unfortunately the unusual beauty and wealth of Surmang was a cause of jealousy and the monasteries were attacked (in 1643) by the fanatical followers of Gusri Khan, a Mongol chief whose personal devotion to the then Dalai Lama and to the Gelugpa Order of monks of which he is the head expressed itself in the incongruous form of destroying houses belonging to earlier monastic foundations; such exhibitions of sectarian bigotry have been rare in Buddhist history. This time the seventh Trungpa Tulku was captured together with the artist the fifth Tulku Chetsang and the abbot of Namgyal-tse who was a noted philosopher. Though cast into prison, each continued doing the things he considered to be of most importance: Trungpa meditated and recited on his rosary the *mantra* '*Om mani padme hum*' one hundred million times: Tulku Chetsang painted *tankas* and the abbot revised his doctrinal treatises.

During their incarceration there was a prolonged drought in Tibet; many prayers were offered up but no rain fell. Finally, Trungpa Tulku was approached in prison. He handed the messenger the rosary he had used for the hundred million recitations and told him to dip it in a certain spring. When this was done a cloud rose from the spring and came down in rain over all the country. After this the three prisoners were released; Tulku Chetsang needed three mules to transport the *tankas* he had completed.

The eighth Trungpa Tulku formed a very close friendship with Gyalwa Karmapa the supreme abbot of the Order, with its two centres of Tzurphu in Central Tibet and of Karma Monastery in East Tibet. The latter was noted for its superb architecture and the artistry of its interior, as I saw for myself when I visited it in 1953. The centre of the Gabri school of artists was at Karma Geru near the monastery, and the eighth Trungpa Tulku was one of its leading exponents; he himself painted many *tankas* for Surmang and specialized in illuminated manuscripts. He was also the founder of its great libraries.

35

CHAPTER THREE

DÜDTSI-TIL AND NAMGYAL-TSE

PERHAPS a brief description of the whole monastic domain over which I had to preside will help to illustrate the background of my life.

When Andro Shelu-bum gave his two castles to Surmang, his gifts included many acres of land, so that the property extended some fifty miles in each direction. It lay at a high altitude on the border between the cultivated land and that inhabited by high-landers. The chief commercial products of the district were salt and timber from the excellent firs which grew near the Tzichu and the Kechu rivers to the south of Surmang. Barley and a little wheat were the only grain crops, vegetables being limited to spinach, turnips and a small kind of leek; besides, there was good pasturage for domestic animals such as yaks and sheep, for the slopes of the mountains were covered with short grass. Willows grew by the streams on the lower ground and in drier places another type of short willow was to be found. Higher up, tamarisk shrubs were plentiful, and above these scented junipers grew. In the short summer months the whole place was ablaze with wild flowers.

Adro Shelu-bum's castle on the Hill of Amrita had been protected by a separate fort; both buildings were incorporated into the monastery of Düdtsi-til. The fort was a large building and was used for many purposes. Both the assembly hall and the main library were situated there: some of its rooms served for storing food, others, as a treasure house for the monastery's valuables. The supreme abbot's residence was also above the assembly hall. In my time Düdtsi-til had some three hundred monks: of these one hundred and seventy were *bhikshus* (fully ordained monks), the remainder being *shramaneras* (novices) and young *upsaka* students who had already taken the vow of celibacy. Their quarters in two and three storied buildings stretched down the slope of the mountain

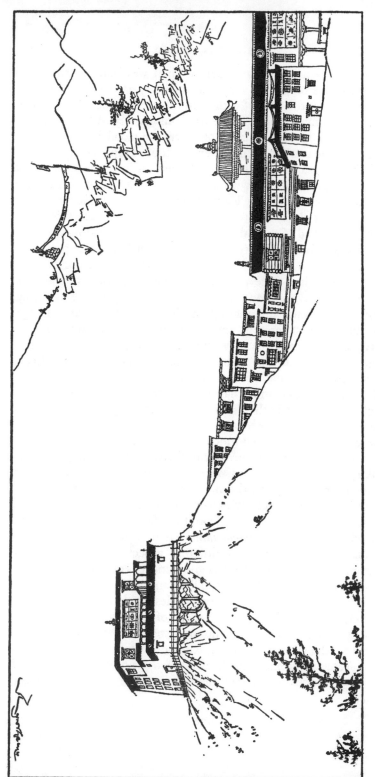

2 *Düdtsi-til Monastery*

to the river. Another large assembly hall was built on the lower ground; it was divided in two, the smaller part being for younger monks between the ages of eight and fourteen, while the main part was for the communal use of the whole monastery. A throne for the *gekö*, a senior monk in charge of discipline stood in a prominent position at the entrance from where he could keep an eye on everyone. The monks used to sit cross-legged on low benches covered with rugs and cushions, with their tables in front of them; their rows faced the central aisle leading to the abbot's throne on its high dais, while his two chief attendants sat close by on each side of the steps. At this end of the hall there were three more thrones; one on the right was for his deputy should the abbot himself be prevented from officiating. Of the other two, the one was for a senior monk in charge of the time-table for the assemblies and the other for the precentor-monk who conducted the music and led the chanting. Behind the thrones dominating the hall were three large images depicting the past, present and future Buddhas; these were some twelve feet high, gold plated with an aquamarine glittering on their foreheads to indicate the 'third eye' of universal knowledge; each was seated on a throne decorated with precious and semi-precious stones. A second assembly hall built higher up the slope was used for philosophical and other advanced studies and particularly for the 'summer retreats' (*varshka*).

Düdtsi-til again suffered much damage when it was attacked in a political border dispute during the lifetime of the tenth Trungpa Tulku; the old wall frescoes were in fact all destroyed. They were eventually replaced with the help of eminent artists of the Gabri school from Karma Geru who were employed to cover the walls as before with pictures of scenes from the life of Gotama Buddha and also with various *Buddha-mandalas*, that is to say groupings of celestial figures representing different aspects of Enlightenment. Banners hung from the balconies and hundreds of butter lamps gave light to these lovely halls. The pillars and spreading capitals were lacquered a vermillion red on which designs had been painted in different colours. Several thousands of the ancient *tankas* had fortunately been saved when the monastery was attacked; many of these were the work of Chetsang Rinpoche while in prison with the fifth Trungpa Tulku, others had been painted by the eighth Trungpa, whose illuminated manuscripts were kept in the fort library.

drawn by Sherab Palden Beru

3   *Amitayur, Buddha of Limitless Life*

Tara
(*Saviour*)

Vijaya
(*Victorious One*)

One old house, built by the fifth Trungpa Tulku on the mountain slope was kept for the very severe retreat which every monk had to observe for the period of one year twice in his lifetime. It was called the *gönkhang* (house of the Guardian Divinities).

The kitchen and food stores were in the east wing of the main assembly hall, and cooking was done on a huge stove made of stone and clay into which the fuel, consisting of dried yak dung and wood, could be shovelled through holes at its sides. The stove was so large that a cooking pot some nine feet in diameter, made of an alloy of copper and iron, fitted over the first opening, and there were other lesser openings. The large pot was used for making both tea and soup; the former was made by boiling some brick-tea in water, after which the liquid was poured into pipe-shaped barrels and churned up with salt and butter using a long-handled pestle. When ready to serve the tea was poured into a number of wooden pails with metal decorations and carried round to the monks who could ladle it into their own bowls and if they liked, mix it with roasted barley (*tsampa*). A big tank of water drawn from the nearby river was always kept in the kitchen.

The extensive store-rooms above the kitchen were divided into sections for such treasures as *tankas*, shrine objects, banners, costumes for religious dances etc., indeed all the things required for performing various traditional rites: the *gekö* was responsible for this department and both his and his subordinates' rooms were in the same wing. The sanitation of the monastery was by large cesspits the contents of which were periodically cleaned out and used to manure the fields; scrupulous cleanliness was observed everywhere. Such was Düdtsi-til when I the eleventh Trungpa Tulku was enthroned supreme abbot of Surmang.

Namgyal-tse lay some forty-five miles or three days' journey from Düdtsi-til and was the larger monastery of the two. Adro Shelu-bum's castle and its fort stood by themselves on a small hill about a mile and a half from the village; the river, fed from the surrounding mountains, flowed past its base. Trung-mase built a small house for his own use at the bottom of the hill. The monastery soon became overcrowded, and after Trung-mase's death, a building was begun on the mountain to the north east, where there was already a cave which was used as a meditation shrine. The new building was subsequently kept for spiritual retreats. Garwang Rinpoche, the following abbot, and his successors did not use the small house, but chose part of the fort for their residence, and rooms were later reserved there for the supreme abbot.

So many monks joined Namgyal-tse that three different sections were formed for specific work and teaching. In the lifetime of the fifth Trungpa Tulku a very large assembly hall was built on the lower ground below the hill. This belonged to the whole monastic community: it had very original embroidered hangings festooning its walls, with pictures inset in the spaces. The hall was rather like that of Karma Monastery, having a high chamber at its further end for the images of the past, present, and future Buddhas. These were made of clay and painted gold, while about forty images of saints of the Ka-gyü line were placed at the back of the hall.

A second assembly hall was built on a higher slope of the mountain for the monks of the Dechen-tse *tratsang* (college); it held some four hundred and fifty monks and was intended particularly for those who were interested in the intellectual approach; to start with, it had its own abbot. Another monastic building was erected on the lower part of the slope; it became the Ling-pa *tratsang*, and its three hundred and fifty monks specialized on the administrative side of Surmang. The Lama *tratsang*, with three hundred inmates, stood in a field on the level ground; among other things, it dealt with Namgyal-tse administration, but a wider responsibility fell on some of its senior members, for they had to deal with matters in the district outside Surmang proper. Each *tratsang* had its own hall, library, kitchen and offices. The monks' dwelling-houses were disposed in tiers on the slopes of the mountain, from Dechen-tse *tratsang* at the top down to the large assembly hall. Above it stood the press building in which we printed our scriptures: the *gönkhang* stood near by; Tulku Tendzin Rinpoche, who was an incarnation of one of the eight *togdens* of Trung-mase's time, had sculptured some wonderful images for it early in the present century; these were made of clay and consecrated herbs, and depicted symbolically the guardians of the teaching. The whole building had a tremendous atmosphere of spiritual presence.

Later, in the lifetime of the tenth Trungpa Tulku, the abbots of Surmang built the first seminary on the lower part of the slope.

When I was its supreme abbot, Namgyal-tse held six hundred *bhikshus*, three hundred *shramaneras* and one hundred novices; five incarnate lamas were included in this company.

CHAPTER FOUR

MY CHILDHOOD AT DÜDTSI-TIL

WHEN I was three years old, the heads of my mother's village invited her to take me to visit them. I can remember the journey very clearly. This was the first time that I had ridden a horse; it was a white one and had belonged to the tenth Trungpa Rinpoche, and when I was told that it had been his, I refused to change it for any other mount: I was put in a little chair saddle. We passed high mountains on the way, and one day we met a herd of about five hundred wild asses (*kyang*) which trotted around us and this fascinated me. My parents had always loved their own part of the country and its wild animals, so it was a great joy to my mother to get back to her home, and I too thoroughly enjoyed the change.

During the months that we stayed in our family home all our relations were exceedingly kind; they brought me cream and all sorts of gifts. However, I was never allowed to play with the children, but only to watch them at their games. They found curiously shaped stones in a particular gully and these made wonderful toys; I longed to take some back to the monastery, but this too was forbidden.

At the end of our visit, my mother took me back to Düdtsi-til, though my father remained behind; no-one told me why and I was very puzzled; then one day, a monk told me that he was not my father but my stepfather and this comforted me a lot.

All these years I had a very happy time, my mother was with me and I was not expected to do any lessons; sometimes, I was even allowed to play with other children, the sons of the relatives of respected monks.

One day I saw a man, probably a Moslem, being thrashed; he had killed a wild animal on the monastery's protected ground. His hands had been tied behind his back and the monk was accusing him of all sorts of crimes while he belaboured him with a heavy stick. I felt great pity and asked another monk about it; he replied that this was the way to uphold the law. I said: 'Shall I have to do this when I am grown up and have charge of the monastery?' His answer to this was: 'You will be able to do as you like.' 'Well,' I said, 'I will never use punishment like that.'

The tenth Trungpa Tulku's rooms in the fort at Düdtsi-til had been extremely simple and austere; their only decoration were the *tankas* hung on the silk covered walls. However, after his death my secretary and bursar wanted to change things. They employed some sixteen artists and wood-carvers of the Gabri school to re-design my residence. While this was being done, I had great fun watching the work, especially the artists painting, and the son of one of them and I used to steal their paints and make pictures ourselves, to our own great delight: I have loved painting ever since.

When the work was finished there were cupboards all round the walls; their doors were beautifully painted with ornamental designs of flowers, birds, etc., and the general colouring was gold on a red background. The tops of the cupboards formed a shelf for the many gifts of bowls and offerings which were brought to me. Behind it there were recesses framed in deeply carved and lacquered wood to hold old and valuable images of Buddhas, Bodhisattvas and eminent Spiritual Masters. Above these was a second row of niches to house images of smaller size. The walls joined the ceiling with a deep gold painted carved cornice. The wooden ceiling was coloured. The furniture consisted of several long settees with deep piled up mattresses which, in our country, take the place of chairs. My bed was like a long box filled with cushions, so made that in the day time I could sit on it and work at a long table beside it. One side of the room, over the cupboards, was exclusively used for my books; these scriptures were written or printed on separate oblong pages held together between two boards, and tied up with a ribbon; at one end the title of the book was written on a white brocade flap, and the books were arranged so that the title faced outwards.

My bedroom served both for sleeping and for private study and meditation; it opened into a sitting room where meals were served and formal visits received. My raised throne was beside the door and a row of seats ran lengthwise down each side of the room; those nearest the throne had thick cushions for the more important guests but their size gradually diminished until the end of the rows, when they became merely rugs on the floor.

Since I was now five years old, it was decided that it was time for me to begin my studies. It was a great shock to hear that a special teacher was coming to Düdtsi-til to give me lessons. One of the monks told me that he had a scar on his forehead, and I anxiously watched everyone who came for fear that it might be he. One day Asang Lama arrived; though I saw that he had a scar, I said to myself 'this can't be my new teacher', for I had expected him to be a very severe monk, but this man looked so gentle. He held his rosary in his hand and was smiling and talking to my senior secretary.

We began our lessons on the following day in my residence above the assembly hall. It happened to be the first day of the winter and snow was falling. Always before, when the monks came to sweep the snow off the flat roof, we children would play among them throwing snowballs at each other; on that day I could hear my little friends shouting at their play outside, whilst I had to remain indoors to do lessons. Asang Lama was very kind; he gave me a clay panel made in relief depicting Amitabha the Buddha of Infinite Light which delighted me, and he told me how glad he was to be able to be my teacher, for he had been a devotee of the tenth Trungpa Tulku. He began with teaching me the Tibetan alphabet and was surprised that I picked it up in one lesson. I also had to learn to recite a *mantra* or formula of Manjusri, the Bodhisattva of Wisdom. We went on with both reading and writing lessons; this was unusual, for in Tibet reading is usually taught first and writing comes afterwards.

At this time my mother's visits became less frequent; to begin with she only came to see me every other day, then every third, after which her visits became more and more spaced out, until after a fortnight without seeing her, she came to tell me that she was going back to Dekyil; I missed her as only a small boy can.

The life at Düdtsi-til was found to be too full of distractions, so it was arranged to send me to Dorje Kyungdzong, the retreat centre established by the tenth Trungpa Tulku. It was in a remote spot and had been built over the cave where the fourth Trungpa had spent six years in meditation. The centre stood on a ledge of high rock and was approached by a long zig-zag flight of steps. The front of the building was supported by pillars grounded in the rock below; its windows looked over a wonderul spread of mountains with the river

4 *Dorje Kyungdzong, the retreat centre of Düdtsi-til*

winding through the valley, and at one place one could see the junction of two valleys; the smoke of Düdtsi-til could also be seen in the distance. There was a large cave under the one in which the fourth Trungpa used to meditate; it was sufficiently big to be used as a byre for over seventy cattle which supplied the needs of the centre; these animals were cared for by the cook's family, who had their house in the cave.

About thirty monks were at the centre; they stayed there for a period of four years to meditate in complete retreat, being neither allowed to pay visits nor to receive them. Their meditation method was based on the teaching of the great Indian adept Naropa which Trung-mase laid down for the Ka-gyü school. An experienced teacher gave the retreatants guidance. Though the thirty monks were expected to stay for four years, there was some accommodation for others intending to spend three to four months only in the place; they had to conform to the same rules of discipline as those in long retreat.

My own time-table was as follows: I rose with my tutor at five for the first morning devotions, then we were given breakfast, after which my reading lesson went on till midday; this was followed by a meal and half an hour's rest. Then I was given a writing lesson for half an hour, and again reading until the evening.

There is not much variety in the staple foodstuffs of Tibet, but much ingenuity was used in the different ways of cooking; vegetables were scarce and in this cold climate really nourishing food such as meat and milk products was a necessity. Our breakfast consisted of especially made strong tea mixed with butter and salt and dry powdered tsampa with cheese and butter rubbed into it. At mid-morning we were given bowls of thick soup made with meat, thickened with barley, rice, oats, noodles or sometimes with vegetables. The big midday meal had *tsampa* dough with large portions of fried or boiled meat; sometimes it was just dried, and for a change we had dumplings filled with meat. An afternoon collation was served with curd (like *yoghourt*) and Tibetan biscuits, and at all times there was tea to drink. The last evening refreshment consisted of bowls of soup. On special afternoons we went for walks and then, in the evening, we practised chanting. I loved going out with Asang Lama; he used to tell me stories about the life of the Buddha and at other times about the tenth Trungpa Tulku. I was fascinated also to find so many wild flowers on the hills as well as sweet scented

His Holiness Tendzin-gyamtso, the XIVth Dalai Lama

Rigpi-dorge, the XVIth Gyalwa Karmapa

Lacquered pillar with spreading capital

Tsurphu monastery

(*Photo : Paul Popper, Ltd.*)

2

juniper bushes. There were all sorts of birds and animals, and the blackbirds especially were so tame that their songs could be heard all round the centre and they would come for food to the window-sills. Occasionally some of the retreatants, and particularly my tutor's friends, would come to our room to talk; I enjoyed this, for it gave me a little break from my lessons, while in the summer a group picnic was also sometimes arranged, very welcome after so much hard work.

This life continued until I was seven, when I was taken back to Düdtsi-til where all our monks were assembled, as the Venerable Genchung Lama had been invited to give a *kalung* (ritual authoriza-tion) for all the scriptures forming the Kangyür; these are the sayings of the Buddha, translated from Sanskrit and filling one hundred and eight volumes. This *kalung* gives authority to study, practise and explain their meaning and confers upon those who attend the rite the blessing of their truth. Though Genchung Lama managed to read some three volumes each day, it took him three months to complete the whole, during which time my lessons were interrupted. It was all a great experience for me, since this was the first time that I had been at a gathering which lasted for so long. Throughout that time my tutor gave me lessons in the evenings by the light of butter lamps, for though I could work at my writing during the ritual recitation, I could not do any reading.

At this stage the regent abbots of both monasteries and my secretary were not satisfied with my tutor. They thought he was a little too indulgent and spent too much time telling me stories, to the neglect of more serious studies. He was indeed almost a father to me, and we knew that if we parted we should both miss each other a great deal; however, he was over-tired and needed a rest. At the end of the ritual reading another teacher was found, and Asang Lama had to leave me. I found this parting almost harder to bear than when my mother went away.

My new tutor, Apho-karma by name, had previously taught the younger monks at the monastery, so he had had a great deal of experience, but he was more temperamental than Asang Lama. I felt unhappy in never knowing what was expected of me. My time-table was changed, and the studies now became more difficult; the paint-ing lessons, which Asang Lama had encouraged, were stopped, and writing lessons were made shorter; more time was given to reading and much more memorizing had to be done in the evenings by lamp light, with the lesson having to be repeated correctly the following morning.

We returned to Dorje Kyungdzong, but the retreatants who came to talk to Apho-karma were very different from Asang Lama's friends, and we no longer had our little jokes. There were, however, longer periods for walks and frequent picnics, but my tutor was always very serious and solemn, though he too occasionally told me stories. He was not interested in animals and flowers, and I had neither playmates nor playthings. I discovered, however, that the fireworks for the New Year celebrations were filled with gunpowder, my informant being one of the younger monks who used to clean our rooms. I persuaded him to get some of the gunpowder for me, and I concocted some sort of rockets with rolled paper and managed not to be discovered. These were so successful that I wanted to make a better firework that would go off with a bang. I was in my room working at this, when Apho-karma came in and smelt the gunpowder. He did not punish me at the time, but he never ceased to remind me of how naughty I had been.

I never received corporal punishment after Asang Lama left when I was seven years old. When he had thought that it was necessary to admonish me, it was always done with great ceremony. After a foreword such as 'It is like moulding an image; it has to be hammered into shape', he would prostrate himself three times before me, and then administer the chastisement on the appropriate part.

About this time I had some strange dreams: though even in pictures I had never seen the things that are made in the West, I dreamt I was riding in a mechanized truck somewhat like a small lorry, and a few days' later in another dream I saw aeroplanes parked in a field. Also about that time, in my sleep, I was walking through a shop which was full of boots, shoes, saddles and straps with buckles, but these were not like Tibetan ones and instead of being made of leather they appeared to be of sticky dried blood. Later I realized that they were all the shapes and kinds that are used in western lands. I told Apho-karma about these dreams and he merely said 'Oh it's just nonsense.'

When I was eight I had to learn how to perform various rites, how to intone and how to use drums, bells and various other instruments. I had to improve my reading, and I was taught the practice and history of Buddhism and about the life of the Buddha. I could visualize him among his monks in their saffron robes, for one day I had had a vivid moment of recollection. When I read about the death of his mother, seven days after his birth, I seemed to share his feeling of loss. I read the life of Milarepa many times over till I knew it by heart, and also the lives of other great saints. Guru Padmasambhava's story was my favourite, for I loved to read about the way he brought Buddhism to Tibet, established the first monasteries and taught the doctrine, and above all about his great loving kindness to all our people and the moving message he left with us when he was returning to Lankapuri, an island south west of Mt Meru; after giving the Tibetans his blessing he added: 'The people may forget me, but I shall not forget them; my eternal compassion is always with them.'

My tutor and the senior lamas found me very enthusiastic and interested in my studies, always asking a lot of questions. They thought that it would be a good time for me to learn the rules for a novice (*sramanera*), and I began my first instruction in metaphysical doctrines, though at the time it was not known that I was to be ordained.

According to Buddhist scriptures, a boy of eight can be ordained as a novice (*sramanera*), and when the news came that the renowned teacher Jamgön Kongtrül of Pepung was going to Tsurphu Monastery to give his disciple the Gyalwa Karmapa some further spiritual instruction while at the same time visiting his mother at Lhasa, Rölpa-dorje and my secretary decided to ask him to ordain me, since his route would take him near Surmang. Jamgön Kongtrül accepted the suggestion saying 'Thus I can serve and offer help to the incarnation of my own teacher.'

He was warmly welcomed at Düdtsi-til. I remember him as a small man, neat and precise in all he did, with a dry sense of humour. This was the first time that he had visited Surmang since the death of the tenth Trungpa Tulku, and he told me a great deal about him; when he saw things that had belonged to his beloved *guru* he was much moved, and because I was his incarnation, he was particularly friendly to me.

My ordination took place at the full moon. Four *bhikshus* had to take part in the rite; one was Rölpa-dorje Rinpoche and the three others were senior Lamas. I had to make profession of the monastic rules for a *shramanera* (novice) of the Sarvastivadin Order, to which most northern Buddhists, that is to say Tibetans, Chinese and

Japanese belong; whereas Southern Buddhists of Ceylon, Burma and Thailand belong to the Theravada Order. After the ceremony, Jamgön Kongtrül preached me a sermon; he said 'From today you enter the community of the *Sangha*', after which he explained to me the meaning of the life of my predecessor and how he had always kept the rule. He said that my ordination was a very important step in my life, and added, that I was the youngest novice that he had ever ordained. After giving me some further teaching and advice, he continued his journey.

I was now much less afraid of Apho-karma, who had become more understanding, and I looked forward to our walks together.

At eight years old a child is very sensitive, and it is the time to inculcate ideas which must last him his lifetime, so at the end of this year I went into retreat for a simple form of meditation. This was upon the *nyendrup* of Manjusri, the Bodhisattva of Wisdom: that is to say, I was instructed to visualize him with his various symbolical attributes and to contemplate his transcendental Wisdom, to repeat his *mantras* or sonorous embodiments, and to recite the verses which preceded and followed them. I took a vow that I would live in solitude for three months away from all contacts other than my tutor and my cook attendant; no-one might come to see me. My diet was strictly vegetarian, and I was not allowed to go outside the retreat centre. This continued until the New Year.

As my story unfolds it will be seen how the whole line of the teaching was carried to me directly from *guru* to disciple. The great Jamgön Kongtrül taught the tenth Trungpa Tulku who in turn became the *guru* of his own incarnations Jamgön Kongtrül of Pepung and Jamgön Kongtrül of Sechen. The latter, as my spiritual father, was my instructor in meditation, and Jamgön Kongtrül of Pepung was my ordainer and also gave me a great deal of teaching. Though the great Jamgön Kongtrül did in fact have five incarnations, the other three do not come into my story.

I was nine when Jamgön Kongtrül of Sechen was invited to Düdtsi-til to give a *wangkur* (empowerment rite) on the teaching of the Treasury of Spiritual Instructions (*Damngag-dzö*). This was contained in thirteen volumes, and was a selection of the sacred writings of renowned *gurus* of all the various Tibetan schools which had been collected by his predecessor.

So many monks from outside monasteries kept coming, that

Jamgön Kongtrül found Düdtsi-til too crowded and disturbing, and it was decided to move to Dorje Kyungdzong. The rites began on the day of the full moon; first with offerings at the shrine, followed by chanting and ending with a communal meal. However, since Jamgön Kongtrül was so renowned as a meditation teacher, hundreds of people came to hear him as well as to receive his blessing, and in some cases to put their private troubles before him. They established themselves in the open and in near-by caves, and soon the conditions became as involved and difficult as they had been at Düdtsi-til. Jamgön Kongtrül could get no rest and in consequence fell ill. He was forced to move to a small house a short distance from the retreat centre, and Rölpa-dorje took over the work whilst he was resting. Later, when his health improved, he only undertook to give individual meditation teaching; I remained one of his pupils.

When I first saw him, I was enormously impressed; he was so different from any other teacher that I had met. He was a big jolly man, friendly to all without distinction of rank, very generous and with a great sense of humour combined with deep understanding; he was always sympathetic to the troubles of others. Though he was not well at the time, to be near him was to experience unbelievable peace and joyousness. He used to say that now that we had met again he was my teacher as, the time before, my predecessor had been his. He so clearly remembered all that the tenth Trungpa Tulku had taught him, and all his kindness to him from his earliest childhood. He said how happy he was to give back to me that which he had received from his own *guru*, or as they say in Tibet 'to return the owner's possessions'.

I found later that every word he spoke had significance. I went to him every morning, and one day he told me that he saw me as a grown up man looking like my last incarnation.

He would say, 'Nowadays people are changing and all the world is in darkness and surrounded by suffering. My generation has been fortunate in living in a country which has been so happy; I hope suffering will not come to you. You must indeed come to Sechen to receive the full cup of spiritual milk (*pumpa-gangjö-oma*); young people like you are our hope for the future; you are like a flower in bud which must be properly looked after so that it may bloom both in our monasteries and in the homes of our people. You are very sensitive, and all of us must help you; I in particular have the privilege of cultivating you with the spiritual water of teaching and practice.'

One morning he sent for me; as I entered the room the first rays of the sun fell upon me, and he remarked that this was a very significant sign. After this, the teaching he gave me was so profound that I felt he was giving me back the spirituality he himself had received from the tenth Trungpa Rinpoche. He was overjoyed when he realized that I could absorb his teaching without any barrier between us. He told me that from now on I must continue to meditate, but must keep things to myself, and not speak about them to other people. A little later he explained that since I was still a child and would not be able to sustain concentration for a long period, I must appoint a special time for meditation and keep to it regularly. He emphasized that I must come to receive various teachings from him and particularly instruction in devotion, compassion, and the way of behaviour in everyday life. He also said that without knowing the other side of the mountain one could not risk taking to a mountain pass. I should have knowledge of both absolute and relative truths, and should realize why it is necessary for one to know more about suffering and impermanence before renouncing the world; he added that there was great meaning when the Lord Buddha turned the wheel of the Doctrine, showing the three stages of the path.

Soon after this Jamgön Kongtrül Rinpoche said he wished to leave; he explained that though he was sorry that he could not continue the *wangkur*, his purpose for being at Surmang had been fulfilled. All, and I in particular, were very sad that he could not remain with us; his visit had meant so much. He was always so full of the joy of living and was a delightful story teller, telling tales of different *gurus* and lamas, but his jokes always could be interpretated as having a second and deeper meaning, so that even while he entertained he taught. I well remember one of the stories he told us.

'Once,' he said, 'there was a great teacher called Petrül Rinpoche. He did not belong to any monastery, but travelled everywhere about the country, without any attendants or baggage. One day he went to visit a certain hermit who had been living alone in a hut for many years: in fact he had become quite famous and many people came to see him there. Some came for advice and some to test how advanced he was in spiritual knowledge. Petrül Rinpoche entered the hut unknown and unannounced.

' "Where have you come from," said the hermit "and where are you going?"

' "I came from behind my back and am going in the direction I am facing."

'The hermit was taken aback, but he asked,

' "Where were you born?"

' "On earth" was the reply.

' "Which school do you follow?"

' "The Buddha."

'The hermit was now feeling rather put out, and seeing that his visitor was wearing a white lambskin hat, he asked him,

' "If you are a monk, why are you wearing that hat?"

' "Now I see your sort," said Petrül Rinpoche, "look here. If I wear a red hat the Gelugpas will be looking down their noses, and if I wear a yellow one, the others will be at me. So I have a white one; it saves trouble." He was referring jocularly to the fact that the Gelug Order of monks wear a yellow hat and all the remaining Orders a red one. This was a little joke about inter-monastic rivalries!

'The hermit did not understand what he was saying, so Petrül Rinpoche began asking him why on earth he had come to live in such a remote and wild part of the country. He knew the answer to that one, and explained that he had been there for twenty years meditating. "At the moment," he said, "I am meditating on the perfection of Patience."

' "That's a good one," said his visitor, and leaned forward as if confiding something to him: "a couple of frauds like us could never manage anything like that."

'The hermit rose from his seat—

' "You're the liar," he said, "what made you come here? Why couldn't you leave a poor hermit like me to practise meditation in peace?"

' "And now," said Petrül Rinpoche, "where is your Perfection of Patience?" '

When Jamgön Kongtrül Rinpoche left us we all felt that something very lovely was missing; he had given the whole place such a wonderful atmosphere. We continued to receive the teaching of the 'Treasury of Spiritual Instruction' under Rölpa-dorje Rinpoche, and when it was finished I went back to my lessons with Apho-karma.

In Tibet, the greatest respect has always been felt for spiritually endowed lamas, who act as priests or teachers without being monks. Such people would have promised to keep to the *Upasaka* discipline and practise the fundamental rules of Virtue as well as to observe the *Bodhisattva's* vow of compassion with the aim of leading all sentient beings to Enlightenment; finally, they would undertake to obey the sacred word of the *Vajrayana* by dedicating themselves to the Supreme Knowledge.

Dingo Chentse Rinpoche was one of these married lamas, a man advanced in spiritual knowledge. He had been an important disciple of the tenth Trungpa Tulku and was a reincarnation of a famous author and teacher called Chentze Rinpoche, who was born in 1817. Because of his profound learning, the monks of Düdtsi-til invited him to give the *wangkur* (initiation) of *Tzochen-düpa* on *Anuyana* which contains advanced *Vajrayana* teaching. The empowerment rite lasted for a month and when it was over, Dingo Chentse undertook to give me special instruction. I felt drawn to him as if he had been my father; and thus I often addressed him without any shyness or doubt. He welcomed me as the incarnation of his own *guru*, and since I was still only a child of ten he brought me toys and sweets. He was very tall and dignified and never seemed in a hurry. Whatever he did was perfection of its kind, even the way he walked into the hall showed this quality; all he said was expressed to perfection, in fact, he surpassed anyone I had ever met; his writings were equally remarkable, and added to this he was a poet and had a gift for telling delightful stories.

All the previous year I had had a great deal to do, meeting lamas from other monasteries and taking part in many rites, so my lessons had been rather neglected, though my general knowledge and understanding had increased. Dingo Chentze gave me private teaching on *Atiyana* (*Ati* means 'the Ultimate') and handed on to me much that he himself had received from the tenth Trungpa Tulku and from *gurus* of other schools. He left after several months, which was so great a sorrow and shock to me that for a few days I could neither study nor eat. I felt this parting more severely than when my early tutor Asang Lama had had to leave me, and to fill the blank I set to work harder than before.

Soon after this Apho-karma took me back to the retreat centre of Dorje Kyungdzong as he had decided that it was now time to change my subjects of study. He wished me to give short sermons to the monks and laymen there; among them was the king of Lhathog's son whose father had been instrumental in procuring the tenth Trungpa Tulku's release from his imprisonment during some local troubles.

By the year 1949 conditions in East Tibet were becoming increasingly confused. In China there had been fighting between the Nationalists and Communists resulting in the victory of the latter. However, news travels slowly in Tibet and the Tibetans in Nyishu-tza-nga province, who supported the Nationalists, were still on their way to help their allies, taking with them about a thousand horses and much food, wool, cloth and skins. When they reached Siling they found the Communists in possession and were forced to hand everything over to them. The Communists took this opportunity to make large scale propaganda; they filmed the Tibetans in the act of handing over these things as if this was a voluntary gift; a large banquet was arranged which was also filmed in such a way as to show the friendly feeling existing between Communists and Tibetans.

Three months later we heard that three Communist officials had arrived in Jyekundo the principal trading centre of our province. They had been put in charge of the town as well as the whole district of Nyishu-tza-nga which includes Surmang. Since they were unarmed and did not interfere much at the start, both parties remained seemingly on friendly terms, though the Tibetans were still distrustful. Two months later the senior Communist official started to offer suggestions. He would say 'The offerings at your shrines are a waste of food; you should eat more plentifully and spend what you have, rather than hoard. In future you will not have such freedom. You must realize this.'

It was later discovered that this man was actually in the Nationalist secret service, as was his brother in China, but when he heard that the latter had been caught, he himself escaped to India.

About this time, my mother left her husband at Dekyil and came to live near Düdtsi-til. She helped a sister of the tenth Trungpa Rinpoche with the dairy work; she could not come inside the monastery but I was able to go out to see her, and she brought me milk, cream and curds about once a fortnight. A year or so later her husband died and she never went back to her village.

Since I was now eleven years old I had to spend my time on more advanced work. I was called back to Düdtsi-til to take the Bodhisattva vow although I had already taken it informally at the time of the *wangkur*: the vow is as follows:-

'In the presence of all the Buddhas and Bodhisattvas and of my teacher Rölpa-dorje, I vow to proceed towards Enlightenment. I accept all creatures as my father and mother with infinite compassion. Henceforth for their benefit I will practise the transcendental virtues (*paramitas*) of liberality, discipline, patience, diligence, meditative concentration, wisdom (*prajñā*), skilful means (*upaya*), spiritual power, aspiration, gnosis (*jnana*). Let my master accept me as a future Buddha, but as remaining a Bodhisattva without entering Nirvana so long as a single blade of grass remains unenlightened.'

Instead of returning to Dorje Kyungdzong, Apho-karma took me to Dechen-Chöling, Rölpa-dorje's retreat centre, for I was now to study directly under him. His appearance was unusual, for he was quite bald with a trimly pointed beard. He was very strict on keeping all rules and insisted about the need for scholastic accuracy; at rites he officiated with the greatest competence, and he had exceptional knowledge about the art of chanting. But with all this strictness, he was very gentle and understanding and always seemed to be happy in his retreat surrounded by bird and animal life; much of his time he spent in writing.

The centre for retreats stood on the slope of a mountain looking over the valley below and the mountains beyond it. Willows and scented juniper were dotted about the grass-covered hillside. The retreat was at a high altitude, and nearly every morning the mists would wreath the slopes obscuring the valley below; Tulku Rölpa-dorje sometimes called it the Garden of the Mists. I very much enjoyed this change, and so did Apho-karma who had himself studied under the regent abbot.

Rölpa-dorje lived by himself in a beautiful cave with the front walled in to form a cell; he had painted the inside a soft orange colour, and had stuck small pictures cut out of books or small woodprints on some of the surfaces, and had hewed cupboards in the walls; at one side there was a shrine of sculptured stone. Among his ornaments was a collection of small religious pieces which he would allow me to play with. The cave was complete with its own little kitchen, for Rölpa-dorje preferred to look after himself. Stone steps led steeply down from the cave to the retreat centre which was some way down.

Usually, only four monks lived in the centre for their four-year period of retreat, but there were houses nearby from which some fifteen other monks could attend the course, while at the back of the mountain, in another small valley, a nunnery had been established, mainly used as a retreat centre for some forty nuns, but also serving a number of lay disciples.

At Dechen-Chöling Apho-karma put me to more advanced general studies and also gave me some lessons in the art of poetry; Rölpa-dorje took over my instruction in primary Buddhist metaphysics. He thought that I should now begin *Ngöndro*, (the 'Prelude') as an introduction for further understanding of *Vajrayana*. This preparation for spiritual development includes:

(1) 100,000 full prostrations.
(2) 100,000 recitations of the Triple Refuge.
(3) 100,000 recitations of the Vajra Sattva *mantra*.
(4) 100,000 symbolic offerings.
(5) finally 100,000 recitations of the *mantra* of Guru Yoga, or 'Union with the Teacher'.

At the same time five subjects must be contemplated.

(1) The rare privilege given to one to receive spiritual teaching in this life.
(2) The impermanence attaching to life and to everything else.
(3) The cause and effect of *karma*.
(4) The understanding of suffering.
(5) The necessity for devotion.

I was deeply affected by all this; living in this place, studying these teachings and constantly meditating, I began to develop greater depths of understanding, as a preparation for the way of life that lay ahead of me.

One day while I was engrossed in this teaching, and actually in the act of meditation and prostration, my secretary Chandzö Karjen suddenly appeared to tell us that Chinese troops were approaching our monastery. We had heard months before that there were a number of troops in Jyekundo, though until now they had not been seen beyond the town. Chandzö Karjen had had a message that they were in occupation at Namgyal-tse, but owing to its being three days' journey from Düdtsi-til this news had not been confirmed, nor did he know if the monastery was still standing or not; he had come at once to warn us. This sudden movement of troops might mean that the Chinese were about to use force in order to occupy the whole of Tibet. Since we were already under Chinese control, this new move seemed suspicious; could it mean that they intended to destroy all the monasteries and towns and to capture the important people in every district? We held a consultation; a second messenger arrived to tell us that on the route the Communists had followed no villages or monasteries had been disturbed as the army had only marched through. He brought with him a large poster which the Communists were distributing all over the district. Under the signature of the Commander-in-Chief, it said that the Red army was coming to help the Tibetans; they would do no damage, and would respect the feudal system and the religion of the people.

We decided that though the Communists were apparently not intending to harm us, it would be wise to safeguard the treasures of our monastery by storing them in a more secure place. If it became necessary we could escape ourselves, for transport was ready at hand; after this, my secretary went back to Düdtsi-til. For a couple of days all seemed quiet; only the herdsmen had seen the Chinese troops as a string of lights silently passing the village in single file in the darkness. In the morning when Apho-karma went out to collect firewood, he could see the camp fires all around in the valley. He waited until I had finished my meditation and was having breakfast and then told me what he had seen; when the sun came out we could distinguish the glint on the soldiers' packs as the long file went further afield. Any visitors who came to see us told us how the Chinese had always paid for anything that they had requisitioned, and that the troops looked in very poor condition and seemed to be short of food, but also to have plenty of silver money. They continued to pass through day after day on their way to Chamdo, and though they met with some resistance from the troops under a gallant officer called Muja Depön near Lathog, they brushed it aside. Surmang had been asked to provide them with guides, but managed to evade doing so. It was all very worrying.

CHAPTER FIVE

IN THE STEPS OF THE TENTH TRUNGPA

EVER since Jamgön Kongtrül of Sechen had visited Düdtsi-til, when I was nine years old, his presence had been foremost in my mind. He had planted a spiritual seed; I wanted to go to him for extended teaching, and while I was at Rölpa-dorje's centre I had felt more strongly than ever that the time had now come for me to go to my *guru*.

At the end of the year I returned to Düdtsi-til with Apho-karma, the lamas seemed satisfied with my studies and as I was nearly twelve, they encouraged me to be more independent over deciding what I wanted to do. I spoke to Apho-karma about my wish to go to Jamgön Kongtrül, for I knew that the monastic committee was thinking that I should go on the traditional tour to meet people in the district. However, he gave me no direction, and only said that the decision for what I would do must come from myself.

I was invited to the retreat centre of Dorje Kyungdzong for the New Year. It was a very quiet and spiritual atmosphere, but I felt a little disturbed thinking about the decision I would so soon have to make. The venerable Karma-tendzin was the superior (*drupön*) there; he had been a devoted disciple of my predecessor and had known me for many years, as had most of the senior monks at the centre. I asked him to advise me, but he impressed upon me that I was now old enough to think for myself. Just then, the venerable Togden Tsepten was on a visit to the centre, who had not only received teaching from the tenth Trungpa Tulku, but had been his constant companion and server and was with him at his death; so I put my problem before him, and his answer was to tell me in great detail much of the life story of my predecessor.

THE STORY OF THE TENTH TRUNGPA TULKU RINPOCHE

The tenth Trungpa Tulku had been given a very strict training

59

from boyhood to prepare him for the duties of supreme abbot of Surmang. At nineteen he attained his majority, being considered ready to take full responsibility for the government of the abbey although he would still be under guidance to some extent. He realized that in order to develop his own spirituality, being thereby enabled to lead others, he must have further training in meditation, which he saw was more important than administering his monastery.

He felt a compelling urge to receive teaching from Jamgön Kongtrül Rinpoche, for when he was quite young he had heard the name of this great *guru* mentioned and had been suddenly stirred by a recollection that he had been in a spiritual relationship with him in a former life. The monastic committee, however, had other plans for him; they wanted him first to work for Surmang, it being customary in Tibet that when an abbot reached manhood, he should tour the district and give his blessing to the people; during such a tour he would be invited to preach and to perform rites; he would receive many gifts, and the fame and wealth of his monastery would be increased. Though the tenth Trungpa neither liked nor approved of this procedure, he nevertheless felt obliged to follow the wishes of his senior advisors, so he set off on the tour accompanied by his bursar, whilst his secretary remained in charge of Düdtsi-til.

The tour was very successful and brought in many donations for Surmang. This greatly encouraged the bursar, for since the death of the ninth incarnate abbot twenty years had passed, during which the monastery had received very few offerings, it needed material help. So Trungpa Tulku was persuaded to go on another tour the next year; this should have lasted for three months, but about half way through he felt he could no longer delay going to see his *guru*.

From babyhood he had been told about Jamgön Kongtrül; how he had been brought up by the abbot of Pepung Monastery as his spiritual son. As he grew older he had wanted to obtain wider instruction and had travelled for many years, visiting over one hundred *gurus* of all the schools of Buddhism to be found in Tibet. On his return to Pepung visitors came from all parts of the country to receive instruction from him, for which purpose he established a centre near the monastery where he himself composed over eighty volumes of scholarly and spiritual precepts. Before the abbot of Pepung died, he appointed Jamgön Kongtrül to be the spiritual leader of the line of the Karma-ka-gyü school.

At the time when Trungpa Tulku made the last moment decision to go to his *guru*, he and his monks were encamped beside a river and he knew if he could but get away and cross it, then Pepung Monastery lay some ten days' journey further on. He made a plan and confided part of it to his special friend Yange: he told him that he would give the monks a great treat, a picnic by the river bank; they were to have a plentiful supply of food and tea, and the customary discipline of not talking after proscribed hours would be relaxed. That evening Yange was to prepare a bag of roast barley flour (*tsampa*) and leave it with his horse, which must be ready saddled, behind some nearby bushes. At this, Yange was much alarmed, for he realized that he was planning to escape.

The monks thoroughly enjoyed the picnic, especially the relaxation of the rule of silence, and they chatted on till the small hours of the morning, when drowsiness overtook them. Seeing this, Trungpa Tulku stole away, mounted his horse and put it at the river which was in spate as the snow was thawing. He was ready to drown rather than miss the opportunity of training under the *guru* who meant so much to him. The horse managed to breast the current and on reaching the farther side the abbot decided to continue on foot, since riding implies a desire for power and for material possessions, so he tore off a piece of his robe and tied it to his horse's back, as the customary sign that it had been ceremonially freed by a lama and must not be ill treated by whoever caught it. He then set the horse free and walked on. The horse recrossed the river and returned to the camp, but the flapping of the piece of robe made it restive, and approaching one of the tents it rubbed against it to get rid of this annoyance and in doing so knocked down the tent. This awoke the sleepers who, seeing the horse, thought it must have broken from its tether. However, when they saw that it was saddled and that the saddle was the one used by their abbot, they were extremely disturbed and went to Trungpa Tulku's tent. It was empty, and some of his clothes were arranged to look like a sleeping figure in the bed. Rushing out, they woke up the entire camp. All the monks examined the horse and found that it was wet; they also recognized the robe, and were forced to the conclusion that their abbot had left them and crossed the river.

Since Trungpa Tulku was quite unused to walking, they thought that he would soon be in difficulties and that they must look for him, so they split up in four groups to search up and down both banks of the river. The group who were going in the southerly direction on the further bank found a saddle rug which had belonged to the abbot, but beyond this there were no more traces. As a matter of fact, Trungpa Tulku had purposely dropped it there to mislead them.

Travelling northward, he was all but overwhelmed by a sense of utter desolation; never before had he been all alone, having always been surrounded by monks to attend and guard him. He walked fast until he was exhausted and then lay down to sleep. The sound of the rushing river and of dogs barking in a distant village seemed to him like a death knell; this was such a complete change from his very ordered life.

He was now on the same road that he had taken with his party on their outward journey; then he had talked and questioned many of the local people about the general lie of the land and what track led to Pepung Monastery, and now as soon as dawn broke he walked on and arrived early in the morning at the house of a wealthy land-owner whom he had visited on the way through. The husband opened the door at his knock, but failed to recognize the visitor; however, since he was in monk's robes he invited him to come in. When his wife appeared she gave a cry of surprise, for she imme-diately realized who it was, and her surprise was all the greater at seeing him alone. Trungpa Tulku asked them to shelter him and made them promise not to tell anyone of his whereabouts, since the reason for his being there was a great spiritual need. They were very frightened, but felt obliged to obey their abbot, so they gave him food and hid him in a large store cupboard, where he remained all that day, and when some of the searching monks came to the house to ask if he had been seen, the landowner and his wife kept to their promise.

In the evening Trungpa Tulku said that he must move on. His hosts were extremely upset that he should go on foot and unatten-ded. They begged him to tell them what had occurred and wanted to know if there had been any misunderstanding between him and his bursar. They suggested, if this had been the case, that perhaps they could arrange for the matter to be cleared up, for their family was in a position to use its influence. Trungpa Rinpoche told them that he did not wish this, and with the greatest reluctance they let him leave, knowing that, as their abbot, it was his place to command and theirs to obey.

As he was making his way beside the river, he heard horses close

Samye, the first monastic institution in Tibet

Infant Taisito of Pepung

4　Jamgön Kongtrül of Sechen

Third incarnation of Jamgön Kongtrül of Pepung

Khenpo Gangshar

behind him, so he hid in some bushes on the bank and the riders passed by. They proved to be the bursar with a mounted party; after a short interval he was able to resume his walk and in the early morning reached another house where he was known. But by now the bursar had alerted the whole neighbourhood, so the family was informed of the situation; nevertheless, they took him in and offered to look after him, again hiding him in a store cupboard. As for the bursar, when he could find no further footmarks, he told the monks to search every house in the district. He was dissatisfied with the answers to his enquiries from the family with whom Trungpa Tulku was sheltering and ordered the monks to look in every nook and corner which they did; they found him in the cupboard where he was still hiding.

The bursar embraced him with tears in his eyes and asked why he was causing them so much anxiety. He replied that he had private reasons with which no-one might interfere. They argued all day, but ehe abbot gave no indication of his plans, though he refused to return to Surmang. Whereupon the bursar sent back for instructions from Namgyal-tse and Düdtsi-til from which, however, no reply could be expected for ten days or so.

When the message was received at Surmang, a meeting was called of all the heads of the monasteries and the representatives of the laity to discuss the matter; all agreed that their abbot must be requested to return. On receiving this reply the bursar endeavoured to persuade Trungpa Tulku to follow the wishes of his people, but from being a very gentle and docile man, he now seemed to have become very strong willed and obstinate. Another messenger was sent to Surmang to tell them that in spite of their requests the abbot would not change his mind.

After a second meeting had been called it was decided that if Trungpa Tulku could not be persuaded to come back, he should be allowed to go his own way, but with some monks and horses to serve him. When the messenger returned with this ultimatum, Trungpa Tulku was really upset, and even more so when a party of monks with horses arrived shortly afterwards. He protested against all this fuss, saying that he was a simple man whose object in running away had been to escape from this complicated way of living.

His bursar and monks never ceased to argue with him, but instead of replying he preached to them on the vanity of leading a wordly life. A deadlock was reached when he said that to go with attendants and horses would ruin all that he wished to do. There is a Tibetan saying: 'To kill a fish and give it to a starving dog has no virtue.' The Buddha left his kingdom, fasted and endured hardships in order to win Enlightenment, and many saints and Bodhisattvas had sacrificed their lives to follow the path of *Dharma*.

Finally, the bursar, who was an old man, broke down and wept. He told Trungpa that he must take at least two monks to look after him, while the baggage could be carried on a mule. This advicly coming from so senior a monk who was also his uncle, he reluctane,- agreed to accept and they started on their journey; the bursar insist ted on accompanying the party. Travelling on foot was very tiring, but to everyone's surprise Trungpa seemed to acquire new strength and when the others were worn out, it was he who looked after them. The elderly bursar became ill with exhaustion, in spite of which, he said he really felt much happier, for the more he pondered on the teaching about the difference between the material and the spiritual way of life, the more he realized how right Trungpa Tulku was to follow this path.

After ten days they reached Pepung Monastery, which was the second in importance of the Karma-ka-gyü school. Trungpa Tulku was already well known to many of the monks, but since he did not wish to be recognized they went on at once to Jamgön Kongtrül's residence some three miles beyond.

Jamgön Kongtrül himself had had a premonition the day before, saying that he was expecting an important guest and that the guest room must be made ready. The monks thought he was referring to some royal personage with his attendants, or possibly to some great lama, and they eagerly watched for his arrival; however, no-one appeared until late in the afternoon when four simple pilgrims with a single mule walked towards them and asked for accommodation. The monks told the travellers that, since an important visitor was already expected, the guest house adjoining Jamgön Kongtrül's residence was not free, therefore the travellers must find a lodging wherever they could.

The following morning Jamgön Kongtrül asked the monks if they had put his guests in the guest house; surprised, they replied that no-one had turned up. The *guru* insisted that the expected guests had arrived and told them to make further enquiries. The four pilgrims were traced and Trungpa Tulku was recognized. The monks immediately took them to Jamgön Kontrül and were astonished when the great teacher showed no sign of surprise at the manner in which the party had travelled. After the interview Trungpa Tulku had a long private talk with his *guru*, who arranged for him to occupy a house with his companions some fifteen minutes walk away, where an old monk would see to their wants. Trungpa Tulku immediately settled down to his studies, with his *guru* instructing him in meditation while the Master of Studies (*khenpo*) superintended his academic work.

For a year he was left alone, when his secretary and some monks came to see him bringing gifts and money. The secretary had a private talk with Jamgön Kontrül and asked him to encourage their abbot to return to Surmang on completion of his studies; his *guru* agreed that he must go back some day, but not immediately, for he and also his attendant monks were making such progress that it would be wrong to disturb them; he added that the elderly bursar could now return to his monastery.

After the visitors had left, Trungpa Tulku gave away all the gifts they had brought, leaving himself and the two monks with hardly anything to eat, so that they were obliged to go round with their begging bowls. The two monks were naturally very upset over this, for while the bursar had been with them there had always been enough for their requirements and they could not understand this new phase. Trungpa Tulku, however, insisted that austerity was the right course and the only way to follow the Buddha's example, as well as that of Milarepa. They must therefore beg until they had received the bare necessities of food to last out the winter. Moreover they had very little butter for their lamps; incense however was cheap and when blown upon produced a faint glow by which Trungpa Rinpoche was able to light up a few lines at a time of the book he was studying.

Now that the monks of Pepung and the people in the district knew of Trungpa Tulku's presence, they kept coming to visit him which he found very disturbing to his meditations.

After three years Surmang expected their abbot to return, and again sent a party of monks to fetch him. This time Düldzin, the senior secretary's nephew, came with them. They found the two monks who were with Trungpa Tulku very disturbed in mind; the austere way of living that had been imposed upon them was affecting their health. However, Trungpa wished to stay on at Pepung until his studies were completed, so it was decided that they should return to Surmang with the party and that Düldzin, at his own request, should remain to look after Trungpa. However, this arrangement did not prove altogether a success, for he gave Trungpa Tulku a lot of trouble. The two men had very different approaches to life: the abbot was a strict vegetarian and wanted everything to be as simple as possible, whereas Düldzin expected to have meat and disliked such plain living. Later Trungpa Tulku realized that these difficulties had been a lesson to him and that lamas had often to experience this sort of trouble and must learn to control their own impatience and accept the fact that their attendants could not be expected to live at their own high level of austerity.

At the end of a further three years Jamgön Kongtrül considered that Trungpa Rinpoche had made such progress that he could be trusted to act as a teacher himself and to carry on the message of *Dharma* to others. Trungpa, for his part, felt that if he was to carry on this work he required still more experience; he should travel to seek further instruction, as his *guru* had done, and live a life given up to meditation. However, Jamgön Kongtrül pointed out that he must compromise between taking such a path and his monasteries' need for him to return to them. He said, 'It must be according to your destiny; conformably with the will of your past nine incarnations your duty lies in governing your monasteries. This is your work and you must return to it. If you take full charge you can rule them in the way you feel to be right. You must establish five meditation centres, the first in your own monastery and the other four in neighbouring ones. This will be a beginning; in this way your teaching will not be confined to your own monks, but you will be able to spread it more widely.'

Trungpa Tulku followed his *guru's* directions; the parting was a sad moment for them both, and after a farewell party he began his return journey on foot. Back at Surmang, he immediately set to work to establish a meditation centre and to put the affairs of his monasteries in order. While he was thus engaged news came that Jamgön Kongtrül had died; however, in spite of this deep sorrow he carried on with his work of establishing the four other meditation centres all of which continued to flourish until the Communists took possession of Tibet in my lifetime.

As Jamgön Kongtrül's entrusted successor, the tenth Trungpa Tulku later became the *guru* of both Jamgön Kongtrül of Sechen and

Jamgön Kongtrül of Pepung. At Surmang, he gained more and more followers and such was the example of the simplicity of his life that he was regarded as a second Milarepa.

When he was about fifty years old there was a border dispute between the Chinese and Tibetan governments and in the course of the fighting much damage was done to both Namgyal-tse and Düdtsi-til. Trungpa Tulku himself was taken prisoner; worn out by forced marches on an empty stomach and already weakened by his austere vegetarian diet, he became ill. His devotee the king of Lhathog succeeded in obtaining his release and managed to persuade him to take better care of himself, by travelling sometimes on horseback instead of always going on foot. When he returned to Surmang there was much work ahead for him; the monasteries had to be rebuilt and at the same time he had to continue his teaching. In spite of the fact that he was growing old and was in poor health he only allowed himself three to four hours for sleep and gave his strength unstintingly to the work of rebuilding the monasteries. He always maintained that if one followed the true path financial help would be given when it was really needed. He accepted the destruction of the monasteries as a lesson in non-attachment which had always held a foremost place in the Buddha's teaching. The lamas considered that their Supreme Abbot's residence should be furnished with every comfort, but he himself insisted on complete simplicity.

Soon, Trungpa Tulku realized that he was approaching the end of his life: one day he had a dream that he was a young child and that his mother was wearing the style of head-dress peculiar to north eastern Tibet: when a new robe was being made for him he told his secretary that it should be a small one; on the secretary asking why, he turned it away as a joke. Trungpa used to say that he felt sorry for his horse, for soon he would no longer be able to walk and would cause it more trouble; the secretary was disturbed at this remark, for he thought that this meant that his abbot was really losing his health.

In 1938 while on tour Trungpa suddenly said that he must get back to his monastery; however he found it impossible to change his plans as he had received so many invitations from various devotees. When one of the king of Lhathog's ministers asked him to visit him he accepted, though this meant a long journey; the lama added that he might have to ask him to be one of the most important hosts of his lifetime. He arrived on the day of the full moon in a very happy mood, but did what was for him an unusual thing; on arriving at the house he took off his socks and his over-robe and, turning to his monks, told them to prepare for a very special rite. A meal was served, but he did not feel inclined to eat and having said grace, he told them to put the food before the shrine. Then he lay down saying, 'This is the end of action'. These were his last words: lifting himself up he took the meditation posture, closed his eyes and entered *samadhi*.

His monks thought he was in a coma, and one doctor among them examined him, drawing some of his blood and burning herbs to revive him, but with no result. The monks stood by him all the time reciting *sutras* and *mantras*: he looked as if he was still alive and remained in the same meditation posture until midnight when there was a flash of light and the body fell over.

The eye of Gnosis

CHAPTER SIX

I GO TO MY GURU

I LEFT Dorje Kyungdzong with my predecessor's story uppermost in my mind. I knew I must now discuss future plans with my secretary and bursar. When I brought the matter forward, they gave me my choice, but said that traditionally the tour round the district should be carried out; however, I had the right to do as I wished, so again I was thrown back on myself. It was much easier for me to talk to my tutor; I explained to him that what I really wanted to do was to receive further teaching under Jamgön Kongtrül of Sechen. I wanted to make a complete break from the studies I had hitherto followed and to do something quite different; I added, once one sets out on a tour there are continual invitations from all sides, which protract it indefinitely; but since the monastic committee has been so kind and has given me such wonderful opportunities for studying, I would not like to say no to them.

At this time, I received two invitations, one from the distant monastery of Drölma Lhakhang, in Chamdo province; the other from the king of Lhathog; this latter would in any case be included in the traditional tour. My lamas were delighted at this chance of encouraging me to travel and make wider contacts. The representative from Drölma Lhakhang was worrying lest I should not agree to go, for the whole district wanted to see their abbot and the disappointment would be very great if this visit was refused. This made it very difficult for me, for if I accepted I would also have to go on a lengthy tour, and if I did not go, these people would be upset. My own wish was to proceed straight to my *guru*; the only thing to do was to tell the monastic committee plainly that I must be free to go to Sechen before the end of the year. I said that I was very anxious not to go against their wishes, so we would have to make a compromise; finally it was arranged that the tour should take place, including a visit to the principality of Lhathog, for this was not so

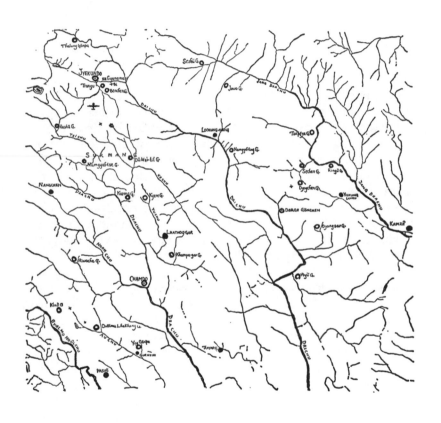

far away. I would not, however, visit Drölma Lhakhang; a disciple of the tenth Trungpa Tulku would have to go instead. Before setting out I asked my secretary to promise that on my return I could go to Sechen; he should also make all arrangements at Surmang for my intended absence.

Our travelling party was organized with a good deal of pomp. There were thirty monks on horseback and eighty mules to carry the baggage. I was still only twelve and, being so young, I was not expected to preach long sermons; mostly I had to perform rites, read the scriptures aloud and impart blessings. We started from the highlands and travelled down to the cultivated land; I was able to see how all these different people lived as we passed through many changes of scenery. Of course I did not see the villagers quite as they were in their every day lives, for wherever we went all was in festival, everyone was excited and looking forward to the special religious services, so that we had little time for rest. I missed the routine of my early life, but found it all very exciting.

When we visited Lhathog, the king had to follow the established tradition by asking us to perform the religious rites according to ancient custom. We were lodged in one of the palaces, from where we could look down on a school that the Chinese had recently established. A Communist flag hung at the gate, and when it was lowered in the evenings the children had to sing the Communist national anthem. Lessons were given in both Chinese and Tibetan, including much indoctrination about the benefits China was bringing to Tibet. Singing and dancing were encouraged and I felt that it was a sign of the times that the monastery drum was used to teach the children to march. Being young myself I was keenly interested, though this distortion worried me; a religious instrument should not have been used for a secular purpose, nor for mere amusement. A detachment of Chinese officials sent from their main headquarters at Chamdo lived in the king's palace together with a Tibetan interpreter, while various teachers had been brought to Lhathog to organize the school, which was one of many that the Chinese were setting up in all the chief places in Tibet. The local people's reactions were very unfavourable. In the town the Communists had stuck posters or painted slogans everywhere, even on the walls of the monastery; they consisted of phrases like 'We come to help you' and 'The liberation army is always at the people's service.'

The tour took about three months and I longed to get back to

Surmang so as to be able to start on the visit to my *guru*. I realized that had I been older and able to give spiritual guidance to my people, it would have been necessary to go on such a tour; but being only twelve I could not feel it was important to have all this grandeur; and though the tour still followed the traditional pattern, it seemed to have lost much of its inner meaning. These feelings may partly have been due to my youth.

On my return I stopped for a few days at Namgyal-tse to say goodbye. I had reason to be grateful to the monks at Düdtsi-til who had made all arrangements for my journey to Sechen. Two cows were ready to provide us with milk, and twenty mules which would be loaded with the baggage. Several of the novices, especially those interested in advanced studies, wanted to come to study at the same time, but only my tutor and two monks were allowed to come with me. My secretary, Chandzö Karjen, was so anxious for my well-being that he chose to come to see for himself how I settled in. Some of the monks were not very pleased that my lessons in religious ritual had had to be curtailed in favour of intensive studies in meditation and metaphysics; but for me, the joy and excitement of receiving instruction from my own *guru* was overwhelming. I had wanted to take the simple path of my predecessor and do the journey on foot, but my tutor and secretary thought I was too young for this and must be looked after; so we went on horseback and slept in tents at night. It took ten days to reach Sechen; the whole journey was most enjoyable, for the scenery was superb and each village seemed different, the local inhabitants wore the distinctive clothing and followed the customs of their particular locality.

We arrived at Jamgön Kongtrül's retreat house on my thirteenth birthday. My monks had expected a large and well appointed building, but it was very simple and unpretentious. His old mother lived with him and also one Khenpo Gangshar, together with his own mother; the two women did the cooking and looked after the cows. Jamgön Kongtrül's old tutor acted as secretary and attendant, and Khenpo Gangshar's young nephew was there to run messages etc. Everyone spent much of his time in meditation.

Khenpo Gangshar had been brought up from his earliest childhood by Jamgön Kongtrül who had considered him as his spiritual son and had educated him with the greatest care, for his father had been killed and his mother on becoming a nun had asked Jamgön Kongtrül to look after the boy. Gangshar had always been extremely studious and would apply himself day and night with hardly a break. He had memorized hundreds of texts and received the degree of Master of Studies (*khenpo*) at a very early age.

Since we arrived on the day of the full moon, my *guru* was fasting and all was in silence; when one of my monks went forward no-one spoke to him, but a note was sent asking us to come in. My *guru* showed great joy on seeing me and even before I had taken off my outer robe he came out of the door to present a scarf, beckoning me to enter without words. I told him about our journey, and when I mentioned the two cows he looked pleased, for he had wanted me to make a long stay, and since my monastery had thought fit to send the animals with me, this showed that they also expected me to do the same. I asked my *guru* to explain to the secretary Chandzö Karjen that a prolonged stay was advisable; I said that if this suggestion was made on the very first day it would carry more weight. The following day, when he could talk, my *guru* spoke to the secretary and Apho-karma; they both replied, 'The incarnation of your *guru* is in your hands: hitherto we have done our best to educate him, but now this task is yours'. Chandzö Karjen then returned to Surmang.

Jamgön Kongtrül Rinpoche decided that I should spent my first month studying academic subjects as well as meditation under Khenpo Gangshar. We were to start with the *Aryaratnatraya-anu-smriti sutra* (Recollection of the Buddha, his teaching and his disciples'). Learning this by heart meant very hard work from morning till midnight. He himself was prepared to give the initiation (*wang-kur*) on 'The Treasury of the Mine of Precious Teachings' (*Rinchen-terdzöd*), by the great Jamgön Kongtrül who made this vast collection of doctrines at a time when some of these teachings were nearly forgotten; he had searched for them throughout Tibet. The *Rinchen-terdzöd* is of the utmost importance, for it contains all the most profound doctrines that he himself had received from the tenth Trungpa Tulku.

Jamgön Kongtrül began his own preparations for the rite at four in the morning and we pupils had to be in the hall from five until eight in the evening. The *wangkur* started with morning devotions, and special offerings were made on the tenth and the twenty-fifth day of the month. During the six months of the rite there were only three breaks when our *guru* was unwell. Hundreds of monks and some abbots of neighbouring monasteries attended the course which was restricted to those who had already done the introductory practice; they camped around in tents. This was a very moving gathering, for all were aware that they belonged to the family of the *Dharma*. During the whole of the rites Apho-karma kept a very strict eye on me, for I was placed with several other *tulkus* (incarnate Lamas) who, being young, were apt to be a little frivolous, and though I was actually the youngest I was expected to behave; however, a kindly Nepalese monk who had been in India and had seen modern mechanical inventions, noticing my youth, gave me my first toy, a little engine which he had made himself; a string wound round its front wheel set it in motion in the same way as a top.

The *Rinchen-terdzöd* finished with the enthronement *wangkur* at which a disciple is chosen and given special authority to carry on his *guru's* teaching. Jamgön Kongtrül Rinpoche conferred on me this honour; I was enthroned, and he put his own robes on me, handing me his ritual bell and *dorje* (thunderbolt sceptre) with many other symbolical objects including his books. I felt very shy, as there were many lamas there of much greater learning than I who, I thought, would be far more suitable; however, my tutor and the monks were pleased to decide otherwise on that day.

When the gathering was over my *guru* advised me to join the seminary under Khenpo Gangshar, saying that he himself would give me meditation instruction every fortnight.

There was accommodation for about one hundred students in the seminary which stood on the banks of the river some four miles distant from Jamgön Kongtrül's residence; each student had his own cubicle where he slept and studied; these were in long rows connected by a covered passage and their windows looked out on a stretch of grass between the lines. Stoves were placed in the corridor beside each cubicle for us to do our own cooking, this being done for us only on festival days. The kitchen staff supplied us with tea and hot water and distributed the required fuel; if this was insufficient we would collect wood for ourselves. Breakfast was finished before five, when a gong was rung for us to begin our home work, and at eight a second bell was sounded for us to attend the *khenpo's* lecture. Before giving this he would answer any questions from the students who might want to have the previous day's work clarified. After this our names were shaken up in a bowl, and the one whose name was drawn had to reread the scriptures of the day before and to put forward his own commentary. Then the *khenpo* began the lesson of the day with careful explanations. This was followed by group tuition, and my tutor, one of the *kyorpöns* (tutors) who had been especially chosen for this office would decide if I should join the group or go to my cubicle to receive private tuition from him. I started with Maitreya's works on Transcendental Wisdom (*Prajnaparamita*) which is one of the main themes of the *Mahāyāna*, the school of the Greater Vehicle (Dr Conze has made some excellent English translations of these under the name of 'Perfection of Wisdom'); the basic trends of the Lesser Vehicle I had already studied in my own monastery.

The teaching staff at the seminary consisted of *Khenpo* Gangshar Rinpoche as the principal with five *kyorpöns* as tutors under him: the term *kyorpön* is equivalent to that of a *geshe* in the Gelug and Sakya schools, something like the English 'Doctor of Divinity'. There were also several junior *kyorpöns*. The discipline and behaviour of the students were looked after by a senior lama called the *Gekö*.

Sechen was founded towards the end of the sixteenth century and was one of the leading monasteries of the Mindröling tradition of the *Nyingma*, the first monastic Order to be established in Tibet. It was famed for the profoundness of the doctrines taught there and also for its very strict discipline. When I was there, there were eight incarnate lamas besides the two abbots, with some three hundred *bhikshus* and two hundred novices in the monastery. The buildings more or less filled the valley, with the main assembly hall in the centre. The walls of the hall were festooned with open-work embroideries and had frescoes depicting historical events; numerous shrine rooms opened out from it, and one of them contained an extensive library; in another room there were very ancient images of the eight 'spiritual sons' (*Bodhisattvas*) of the Buddha. There was a more modern image of Manjusri the Patron of Wisdom, which was heavily gilt and decorated with precious stones; besides these there was a figure of Rindzin Gyurme Dorje, one of the founders of the Nyingma school, made out of consecrated herbs and clay; it was a very rare and ancient piece of work. The whole place had an atmosphere of remarkable vitality.

My first impression was the peace and calm of the place, for the monks lived under very strict discipline though all were very happy. The drums and other musical instruments were particularly soft toned; the monks were not allowed to raise their voices and had to sit very still while meditating. Those who carried out the rites had to be accurate in every detail and all the chanting had to be done from memory, as no books were allowed. The ritual was slightly different from that practised in other schools, but I found that it had great dignity in its perfection. There were two abbots at Sechen; Tulku Ramjam Rinpoche was a great personality both spiritually and because of his wide vision in regard to practical affairs; I owe much to his teaching. He had a striking appearance because of his very large moustache, not common among our people. The second abbot, Tulku Gyaltsap Rinpoche, who was the incarnation of one of the tenth Trungpa Tulku's *gurus*, was an outstandingly saintly man and a gifted writer; he was small of stature and radiated friendliness to all who came near him; there was a deep understanding between us and his residence was like a second home to me.

By now I was fourteen and completely happy and satisfied with the work; I looked forward to the summer vacation when we would have more leisure and I would have more opportunities to be with my *guru*. At the beginning of the vacation I was staying at one of the hermitages where I could walk in the woods and practise meditation in serene solitude. Although it is natural for boys to play and want to climb trees, under my *guru's* instruction I had to control such impulses; but here everything was such as to satisfy me with the path I had chosen.

On the last day, whilst I was walking, meditating and enjoying the beauty of nature, a thunderstorm burst overhead. This sudden transition from peace to conflict symbolized what lay ahead of me, for running back to the hermitage I found that a monk had arrived from my own monastery to ask if it would be possible for me to return to Surmang as one of the senior lamas, the third next to the regent abbot, had died. Apho-karma made the most of this fact, as the responsibility of being left in sole charge of me was getting too much for him and this made him very nervous; he considered that I was overworking and thought that I might have a breakdown, so he wanted an excuse to take me away. He could not have explained all this in a letter, and he now decided without consulting Jamgön Kongtrül Rinpoche that I should return to Surmang. When the matter was put before my *guru* he was rather upset, but since my tutor was so insistent he found it impossible to argue with him and finally agreed that I should return to my monastery. To me he said

'You have received many teachings; you can now teach and practise them yourself, but later on you must come back and complete your training.' A farewell party was arranged, attended by the two abbots of Sechen and some of the senior lamas.

The following day when I went to say goodbye to my *guru* he told me that, though I must now leave, he had had a dream the night before and had seen a half moon rising in the sky; everyone was saying 'This is a full moon': 'this means,' he said, 'that you are the moon, but not yet really full, for your studies are not complete.' He gave me further advice on meditation and said sadly that he must not leave his room to say goodbye because his place was still within. I made a promise to myself that I would come back, and broken-hearted left that wonderful place.

The flower of Compassion

CHAPTER SEVEN

DEATH, DUTIES AND A VISION

As we rode down the valley I looked back at my *guru's* white retreat in the midst of firs on the hill-side and at the seminary I loved. I watched the river flowing between it and the monastery with its golden roof shining in the sunshine and I could not turn my eyes away until all were out of sight. Apho-karma was in great spirits, talking about our own monastery and the prospect of meeting his friends again, but my two monks and I were very sad, for we longed to be still at Sechen.

On the journey we had a lot of trouble with the horses and mules and most of our little party were also unwell. When we crossed the river Dri-chu, which here is some four hundred feet wide, it was in spate, and our boat made of yak's hide nearly capsized, while one of our horses was drowned.

The monks at Surmang were very surprised to see us, for though they had sent me the message, they had thought it unlikely that I would return before completion of my studies. When I arrived, they concluded that I must really have finished and expressed their delight. My tutor kept quiet, and I had to tell them that I had not completed my work. This worried them considerably and the regent abbots and secretaries felt that Apho-karma had made a mistake, particularly since the senior lama was already dead and the cremation had taken place with full rites, so that there was now no need for me to be there.

I had not long been back when a message was received asking me to partake in the funeral rites for Trale-kyamgön Rinpoche, the abbot of the neighbouring monastery of Trangu who had just died. He had written in his will that he wished for this, since he had been a great friend of my predecessor. Trangu lay some five miles south of Jyekundo. On our way we passed through the Pelthang airport which was being built by a number of Tibetans under Chinese engineers. It was a beautiful day with the sun shining over the broad valley, but its calm was disturbed by the roar of planes overhead; these were bringing all kinds of supplies, but since the runway was not completed the planes could not land and the packages were parachuted down.

Jamgön Kongtrül of Pepung, who was to officiate at the rites, and I arrived simultaneously at Trangu. We performed the ceremonies together for about two weeks. Everyone noticed that a change had come over Jamgön Kongtrül; he did not seem to be in good health.

I was obliged to return to Surmang, and before I left he said to me 'One is already dead, and one is going to die, this is the law of impermanence,' he was sure this would be our last meeting. He gave me his blessing by touching foreheads; this is the traditional way of imparting blessings between lamas of equal standing; then he said that this was to be regarded as a different kind of blessing, being the *wangkur* of the *chakra* (spiritual centre) of the head which represents the union of 'the hundred Buddha Families' (*Tampa riggya*). He laid stress on this being our last meeting; I asked him to promise that we should meet again, he said 'Yes, in one way or another.'

I returned to Surmang by way of the valley of Bi where in the seventh century King Songtsen-gampo sent his ministers to receive and welcome the Chinese princess he was to marry. Here we saw the Buddhist *sutras* which the ministers had carved on the rocks while waiting for her arrival; some of these are in archaic Tibetan and others in Sanskrit, which goes to prove that King Songtsen-gampo was a Buddhist before he met the princess, in fact he had already sent his minister Sambhota of Thön to India to collect texts; it was the latter who first designed the Tibetan alphabet for the purpose of translating the Indian Scriptures into our language.

While the princess was resting in the valley she saw these texts and added a huge image of Vairochana Buddha of over twenty feet in height which was carved in relief on the rock, with 'the eight spiritual Sons of Buddha' (*Bodhisattvas*) beside it together with some ancient Sanskrit inscriptions. We held a short service before the image of Vairochana Buddha and went on to Surmang.

I had been back some three weeks when a messenger came from Trangu to tell us that Jamgön Kongtrül had died; he brought an invitation to Rölpa-dorje, Garwang Rinpoche and myself to officiate at the funeral rites. The messenger knew nothing of what had

79

actually happened and simply said that Jamgön Kongtrül had died very suddenly. After the first shock I remembered how he had said goodbye to me. His death was a very great loss to the whole Ka-gyü school; my predecessor had been his *guru* and he had been the teacher of Gyalwa Karmapa, no-one seemed more needed, by the whole Order, in the present perplexing times. All Surmang was distressed by the news of his death and a great number of monks expressed the wish to attend the funeral.

We left hurriedly the following day and travelled day and night to Trangu Monastery where we found everyone deeply saddened by the fact that their own abbot had died a few weeks before, and now by this second death. Jamgön Kongtrül's closest companions among the monks seemed more serene and told us what had happened. He had suddenly been taken ill and suffered great pain; it was thought that he had eaten some sort of unwholesome food. After he had been moved to the abbot's house of retreat the pain lessened, but his general condition became weaker. After three days he sent for his oldest attendant to write down his will which would be important for his followers, but he did not want anyone to know about it in case they showed too much emotion. He said that his rebirth would be near Lhasa among his relations, which would give comfort to his mother, and he gave an indication of the names of the parents and the time when he would come back. He wanted his body to be cremated and that Trungpa Tulku should take part in officiating, adding that everyone must realize that death is one of the aspects of impermanence; he only continued to take medicine to please the monks. One day he asked his attendant to look up the calendar and find an auspicious date. When the day came he awoke in the morning saying that he was feeling much stronger. He had his coverlet removed and sat up in the Adamantine (*Vajra*) posture; his breathing stopped, though his body remained as if meditating for some twenty-four hours after.

After the funeral ceremonies his possessions were distributed among those who had attended him; I was given his robe, some books, and his amulet case, also his little terrier; the dog remained with me for some three years and I became very attached to it. It used to follow me when I was riding, but one day it went off hunting on its own and got trapped in a marmot's burrow.

Shortly after my return to Namgyal-tse, I was invited to visit

Drölma Lhakhang. Accompanied by my bursar we started on the journey; this was our first sight of the new highway recently built by the Communists between China and Lhasa; it gave us a strange shock, this straight dark line cutting through our mountains, built by a foreign power. It was so broad and it ran right through fields and across the spreading landscape like a deep trench. As we halted beside it, a Chinese lorry came along like a great monster with guns sticking out at the top, and a long trail of dust following it. As the lorry drew nearer, the noise that it made echoed through the peaceful valley and we were aware of acrid petrol fumes. The Tibetans living nearby had grown accustomed to such sights, but our horses were terror stricken, as we were ourselves. The Chinese always drove straight ahead and stopped for no-one; other travellers on the road were pushed aside, often with accidents to their horses and themselves. Looking back at night we watched the continual flow of the lighted lorries; we could not understand the head-lamps, and when we saw the red ones in the rear we thought the vehicles were on fire.

Drölma Lhakhang lies about six days journey from Chamdo, in the Pashö district. It is on the high plateau of Tzawa-gang and is surrounded by rocky hills with many lakes, a chilly region. One of the principal industries among these highlanders (*drogpas*) is that of weaving very fine cloth, for which purpose the people keep great flocks of sheep as well as the usual yaks; being compelled to move frequently to fresh pasturage, the herdsmen usually live in tents.

As we approached Drölma Lhakhang, the monastery prepared to make us welcome. First we were given curds and milk by a family of farmers who had been devotees of my predecessor; after which a lama from Drölma Lhakhang, who was waiting with them, offered me a ceremonial scarf as he made prostration. We then rode on until we met the young abbot Akong Tulku at the head of a procession to escort us to the monastery. They dismounted and also presented white scarves; one of my senior monks followed the traditional ceremonial of returning the scarves and hanging them round the necks of the givers. As we rode to the monastery, we were overtaken by a sudden thunder-storm with vivid lightning and hail. The Drölma Lhakhang monks and those from neighbouring monasteries with their abbots lined the approach to the monastery, where an orchestra on the roof played us in. Akong Tulku led me into the hall, holding an incense stick in his hand; then, after he had made obeisance before me three times we exchanged scarves. This was followed by my exchanging scarves in the same way with the abbots of the other monasteries. Every monk then came to offer me a scarf and to receive my blessing; to the senior lamas I gave it touching their foreheads with mine; to the other monks, I placed my hand on their heads. A monk stood beside me to hand each one a sacred 'protection cord' as they came for my blessing. When all had returned to their places tea and rice was served to the whole Surmang party. My tea was poured into a jade cup on a gold and silver stand; the rice was served me in a beautiful bowl, also of jade, and white china cups and dishes were provided for my monks. It was all very formal; Akong Tulku was quiet and reserved, merely smiling all the time. We found that we were both of the selfsame age.

Drölma Lhakhang started as a hermitage about two hundred years ago and gradually grew into a monastery. There had been a succession of Ka–gyüpa mystics there, and it had always been a centre of hospitality to spiritual teachers, while many hermits lived in its vicinity. The whole monastery had an atmosphere of serenity and spirituality, wherein it differed from some others I have seen which seemed to be more institutional.

At the time of my visit it held about one hundred and fifty monks. The building stood on a strip of land beneath a range of hills, at the junction of the river Kulha Shungchu and the Tsawa Auchu. Behind, on the further side of the hill, lay a whitewashed hermitage; its front wall supported on red pillars seemed to grow out of the rock. It had been built over one of the caves where the great *guru* Padmasambhava meditated after he had established Buddhism in Tibet. It appears that this hill had been known to very early men, for near the hermitage we found some primitive and curious rock paintings. They portrayed men on small horses done in red ochre and were protected by a surface that looked like talc. There was also an indication that very early Buddhists had lived near the site of the monastery, for at the end of the strip of land where it was built there was a single upstanding rock, and in one of its crevices sheltered from the wind and weather there was a sculpture in relief of the *dakini* (female divinity) Vajrayogini.

Across the river in front of the monastery rose the very high mountain called Kulha-ngang-ya which the people of the ancient Bön religion regarded as a powerful god and as one of the guardians of Tibet: his consort lived in the turquoise coloured lake below. Mt Kulha also figures in the story of Gesar of Ling, a famous hero who lived in the thirteenth century, the King Arthur of Tibet who also defended the faith against the unbelievers. The top of the mountain is always under snow and is known as the crystal tent of Kulha. Just before reaching the top one comes to a large cave, the floor of which is a sheet of solid ice; Akong Tulku, who had climbed up to it, told me that under the ice he had seen huge bones some of which appeared to be human, but were so large that they could not have belonged to any recent man.

Four nunneries had been established at the four corners of the mountain, being associated with the monastery of Drölma Lhakhang, whose monks could only enter them on particular ceremonial occasions. The nuns led more austere lives than the monks; they spent much time in meditation and did a great deal for the lay population when sick or in trouble. I was very impressed by the spirituality of these women. The nunnery at the west corner of Mt Kulha looked out over the turquoise lake. Near the nunnery at the north corner there was a hermitage which was exclusively used for seven week periods of meditation on *bardo*, the state experienced at the moment of death and just afterwards.

After I had been at Drölma Lhakhang for a few days, I was asked to give the rite of empowerment (*wangkur*) on the Treasury of the Mine of Precious Teaching (*Rinchen-terdzöd*), which I had received from Jamgön Kongtrül of Sechen; an immense task, as it lasts for six months. I needed a few days before accepting the invitation, for though I had received permission from my *guru* to impart this teaching, I was still only fourteen, and my tutor and Karma-norsang, who was my chief advisor, said that I must be quite sure whether or not I could really give the complete *wangkur*, as any failure would be serious. More and more people were arriving at Drölma Lhakhang, hoping to attend the *wangkur*, so I had to make a decision. I spent several days in devotional meditation in order to know what I should do; finally I asked Karma-norsang to inform the monastery that I was prepared to undertake the task.

Arrangements were immediately put in hand to prepare for the *wangkur*. It took a fortnight or so to make all the *tormas*, that is to say conical cakes decorated with discs of sculptured butter that call for great artistry; each shape and pattern has its own symbolism. I appointed a monk to make a list of all those who wished to attend, asking them if they were prepared really to put into practice the teaching they would receive.

To begin with Karma-norsang gave a ritual recitation of the *kalung* (which means 'authorization') on the sixty volumes of the *Rinchen Terdzöd* and I followed to give the *wangkur* (empowerment rite).

The following time table shows how the days were arranged.

2.30 a.m. Karma-norsang gave the *kalung*.

4.30 a.m. I prepared my teaching of the *wangkur*.

6.45 a.m. Breakfast for all.

8 a.m. I gave the *wangkur*.

10 a.m. Karma-norsang gave the *kalung*, and during this time I prepared my teaching.

11 a.m. I gave the *wangkur*.

12 noon Midday meal for all.

1.10 p.m. Karma-norsang gave the *kalung*, while I prepared my teaching.

3 p.m. I gave the *wangkur*.

5 p.m. Karma-norsang gave the *kalung*, while I prepared my teaching.

6 p.m. I gave the *wangkur*.

8 p.m. Finish.

8.30 p.m. Evening devotions.

It was hard work for everyone; however, all went well. My tutor and monks said they were proud of the achievement of one so young. They told me that I must now start seriously on my work as a *guru*, but I myself felt that I was not yet sufficiently qualified: I had many misgivings and needed my own *guru* to elucidate a number of points; moreover, I knew that one must not have too great a conceit of oneself—here was another danger. I explained my position clearly to Akong Tulku and the senior lamas, saying that even if I had been able to give the *wangkur* and to perform the traditional rites, I was not sufficiently mature to give lectures or personal teaching on meditation; however, I promised that I would do all I could to qualify myself in the future.

After that, we travelled further afield visiting other monasteries. The abbot of Yag asked me if at a later date I would give the *wangkur* of the 'Treasury of the mine of Precious Teaching' again. Turning homewards, we again stopped at Drölma Lhakhang; the secretary and senior lamas there wanted me to undertake to be Akong Tulku's *guru*, but I told them that he must go and study at Sechen, for I was certain that my own knowledge was still too incomplete and that he should be taught by Jamgön Kongtrül Rinpoche: after all, Akong and I were boys of the same age.

Winter was now coming on and on the day of our departure snow fell in enormous flakes; as there were no trees the whole place was under a sheet of white and it was bitterly cold. There is even a proverb about that part of Tibet: 'the coldness of this land will stop tea from pouring', but in spite of the weather all the monks accompanied us part of the way as a token of goodbye. They were all so friendly that this was one of the most memorable farewells I had ever experienced. Akong Tulku and I had become great friends and he was sad at our parting, but I told him we would meet again very soon at my *guru's* monastery. I said 'It is inconsistent that I who have not finished my own studies and am not fully qualified to teach should be asked to be your *guru*; you must go to Jamgön Kongtrül.' Akong Rinpoche and his monks escorted us for three miles as far as the lake and then we separated.

The people around had heard about me whilst I was at Drölma Lhakhang and I received many invitations to visit their local monasteries on my return journey; unfortunately I was not able to accept them. The only place I really wanted to make sure of visiting was the monastery of Karma, the third in importance in the Karma-kagyü school, and we made our way towards it.

The whole area around the monastery, known as Karma-geru, is famous for its art. Since early in the fifteenth century its artists have worked all over Tibet and are known as the Gabri School. All the villagers earn their living by painting. I visited the village of Pating, whose headman was considered to be the leading artist of the area; at his home I found him painting scrolls (*tankas*) and at the same time he was teaching other young artists, while his studio was crowded with pictures of all sizes, in different stages of completion. His pupils were also taught to work in clay, how to make their own brushes, to prepare their own canvasses and mix their colours. His own work was so lovely that it used to be said 'The *tankas* that Gönpo-dorje paints do not need to be blest'.

All the houses belonging to the villagers contained wonderful paintings and carvings, and their shrine rooms were in the same style as those of the monasteries. The headman's house was particularly beautiful as it held the works of many generations of his family, the early ones being the most perfect. The walls were painted with historical or mythical designs, the scrolls were all of religious subjects, and the pillars and ceilings showed decorative designs of birds and flowers which are characteristic of the Gabri school.

On the opposite side of the river the people specialized in goldsmith's and silversmith's work, particularly in smelting and casting these precious metals. All this was most interesting and, since the villagers were so skilled, I expected the monastery to be even more fascinating artistically.

The track leading to it runs beside the river which cascades through a narrow gorge bordered by high blueish rocks. At its further end an almost perpendicular rock towers above the others. High up is an outcrop of yellow stone in the form of a seated Buddha, beside which many sacred texts have been carved even though the rock is so steep that it would seem impossible for any man to have climbed up to carve them. A waterfall splashes down beside the image causing a perpetual rainbow to arch over it. Suddenly beyond this, the gorge opens out into a wide valley where the monastery of Karma was founded by Rangjung-dorje (1284-1339). It looks out over wide fields with the river flowing through them. It was of the greatest interest to me to see it, both from the historical point of view and by reason of its superb architecture, decorations and furnishings. Special masons had been brought from Central Tibet to construct its outside walls which were built out of very small stones. Its abbot had recently died and his incarnation had not yet been found, so when we arrived we were welcomed and received by the regent abbot, who personally conducted us over the monastery.

Through the entrance porch, with its staircases at each side leading up to the gallery, we entered the great hall which is said to be the second largest in Tibet. This was used for all important services, for chanting the choral office and when addressing large gatherings. The high roof over the central part of the hall rested on one hundred pillars made from solid tree-trunks some sixteen to twenty feet in circumference. These were lacquered vermillion with designs in yellow, blue and gold, and their spreading capitals were of the type peculiar to Tibetan architecture. The hall was dimly lit from windows above the gallery which rested on four hundred shorter pillars, some of them made of sandal-wood brought from India. There were various rooms opening out of the gallery some of which formed the abbot's apartment. Twelve shrine sanctuaries off the central hall were used for devotions and in one of them there were life sized sculptures of all the incarnations of Gyalwa Karmapa, the Supreme Lama of the Order; up to the eighth incarnation of the line the workmanship was perfect, but with the remaining seven it showed some deterioration. This point struck me and I felt that it might be possible for me to do something to revive Tibetan art, but Communist oppression was soon to put an end to any such dreams. One shrine room held the great library, the third largest in Tibet, containing a vast collection of manuscripts and also Sanskrit texts believed to date from the eighth century. The whole suggested that at one time the Karma-ka-gyü school had been exceedingly flourishing and that the best of Buddhist art had been preserved here.

Inside the great hall the walls were painted with wonderful scenes from the life of the Lord Buddha, and with scenes from the history of the Karma-ka-gyü school. Between the entrances to the shrine sanctuaries there were shelves along the walls on which gold and silver lamps burned perpetually. The lion throne placed in the centre of the hall was made of sandal-wood brought from a holy place in India; its back was of dark sandal-wood painted with a gold design and with a piece of gold brocade in the centre hung round with a white scarf. The throne was carved with lion designs and the brocade on its cushions had been given by the Emperor Tohan Timur when the third Karmapa was invited to China. At the end of the hall, behind the throne, three entrances led into a tremendously lofty chamber, divided in three to hold the images of the past, present and future Buddhas; these were so gigantic that the measurement across the eyes was five feet. The central image was of Shakyamuni, the present Buddha, made of moulded brass heavily gilt; all the limbs and various parts of the body had been cast separately and put together, but the head was cast in one piece with a large diamond in the centre of the forehead which, according to local stories, came from the mouth of the celestial hawk Garuda. The image had been designed by the eighth Gyalwa Karmapa (1507–1554) and he himself had carved the sandal-wood throne. The images of the past and future Buddhas were made of clay mixed with consecrated herbs; they were decorated with precious stones and each had a ruby on its forehead. A table for offerings was placed before each image.

Seen from the outside, the monastery was a grand sight with the fast flowing river below and the screen of mountains behind. It was built in three tiers; the uppermost roof over the high chamber of the three Buddha images was gilt surmounted by a golden *serto*, a crest

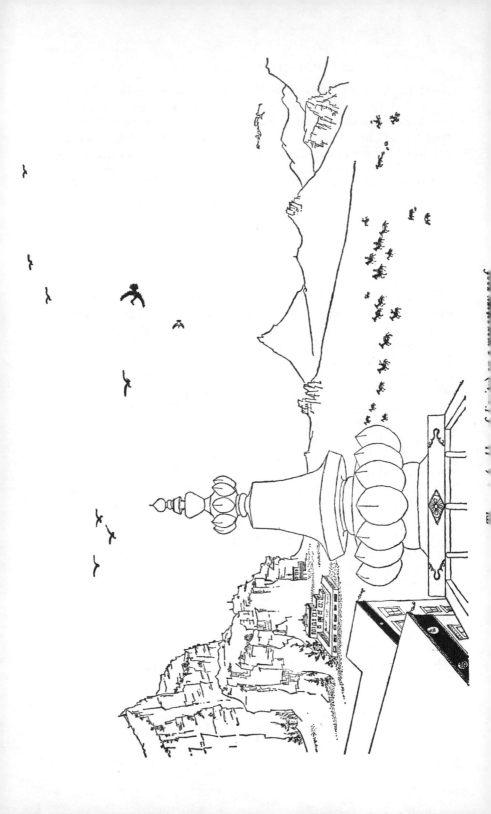

The sacred Hermitage of Limestone on a mountain roof

ornament denoting dignity, largely used in Tibet over monasteries, houses and even placed on horses' heads for riders of rank; golden chains hung with small bells ran from the *serto* to the top of the roof which also bore larger bells at each corner. The roof of the large hall spread out below, again with bells at its corners, and below it a third roof covered the gallery rooms and the cloisters outside the shrines; this also carried bells and carved wooden lions jutted out from the stone walls below them. The two lower roofs were not gilded, but above the gallery rooms there was a row of carved gilt medallions. The cloisters contained eight Buddha images and four *stupas* ten feet high, made of precious metals and placed under gilt canopies. All these had been brought from India in former times; three of the *stupas* came from Nalanda, one of the most famous Buddhist monastic universities in that country.

The Monastery of Karma was a wonderful example of the artistry of the incarnation of Gyalwa Karmapa and especially of the seventh, eighth, ninth and tenth of the line; these lamas were experts in carving, sculpture, painting and embroidery and in smelting and casting precious metals. Karma was a unique example of the beauty of the traditional art of Tibet. It was also at the time when these lamas lived that there was a rennaissance of spiritual teaching all over Tibet to which they made a valuable contribution; their writings contained important teaching to the effect that the metaphysical and the contemplative ways must be brought together.

On the hill opposite the monastery a little retreat had been built, approached by a winding path, with beside it a cluster of tamarisk bushes disposed in the form of the letter *ka* for 'Karma'.

When I left Karma monastery many invitations came which I could not accept because of the special devotions always held at Surmang during the last twelve days of each year. This was considered to be an occasion of great importance, but I had not been able to take part in it since I was eleven, having always been away at that particular time. It was the celebration of the Buddha-mandala the 'Wheel of Supreme Bliss' (*Khorlo-demchog*) and it was combined with a rite of the guardian divinity *Gönpo Chashipa* (the Four armed Protector). These rites included meditation and chanting accompanied by drums and cymbals; wind instruments joined in at the start and end of the chants. The monks had to arrange that there should be no lapse of attendance during the day or night and none of them could expect more than four hours sleep. This religious ceremony at the end of each year was intended to dispel evil and to build up new spiritual strength for the year about to begin. I had only been able to attend it three times before, and the monks rejoiced that I could be with them once more. I was so young the first time that I was only allowed to be a spectator, and then only during the day; on the other two occasions, when I had taken part in the whole rite, I had found it very long and tiring, but this year, although I was not yet fifteen, I could both understand and enjoy it.

When this rite was over, I went to spend the New Year with the hermits at Dorje Kyungdzong away from the bustle of the monastery, after which I was eagerly looking forward to being able to return to my studies at Sechen.

The Conch shell of Dharma

CHAPTER EIGHT

A MANY-SIDED TRAINING

THIS was the year 1954, and when I returned to Surmang I found that great changes had taken place everywhere. The Chinese had opened shops in all the larger towns, selling cloth, crockery, blue Chinese overalls and much else besides. In my monastery, some o the monks were wearing new robes of a slightly different style, no longer hand woven, but machine made. In the villages the women were buying modern perfumes and other exotic luxuries. My secretary had been appointed a member of the municipality under the Communists. There had been gifts of magazines such as the *People's Pictorial*, and our monks had been given posters with Communist slogans and asked to put them on the walls of the monastery; this they had very properly refused to do. Early in 1953 a Chinese official came to Jyekundo, the large trading town which the Chinese had established as the district capital. Though he had seen me before, he now wanted to ask what I thought of the Communist regime. He presented me with a roll of orange brocade and a large picture of Mao Tse-tung, and through an interpreter he described Peking, how it was the largest city in the world and what exciting things were happening there all the time. He said 'the late emperor's palace is so large it takes twenty-four hours to walk round it. I cannot explain these wonderful things, you must come and see them for yourself; the People's Government invites you.' My senior lamas were so uneasy, they advised me not to reply. These Communist officials appeared to me as quite a different sort of human being, not only in their costumes, but in their whole behaviour; their smiles had a significance different from the smiles of Tibetans: I could not understand it at all.

Even so, when I was shown a map of the world in one of the magazines, I longed to know what sort of lives other people led. Hitherto, Europeans had only travelled by the trade routes, or to

Lhasa, and they were few and far between; outside the district towns no one had ever set eyes on one. When I was with my *guru* at Sechen, I had wanted to learn other languages and had begun with the Amdo dialect which has a different pronunciation and uses words that are elsewhere obsolete; now I wanted to learn more, and hoped one day to become familiar with the European language and lettering.

However, other studies lay ahead of me; Rölpa-dorje Rinpoche and the senior lamas thought it was now time for me to learn religious ceremonial dancing. According to monastic rules, secular dancing is not permitted, but the Buddhist dancing is a spiritual exercise in awareness. The Lord Buddha is portrayed in sculpture and painting making different gestures (*mudra*), each of which has its own special significance. And so it is with our dancing; each step and each movement of the hands, arms and head has its own symbolical meaning and brings an increase of understanding both to dancers and spectators. This is seldom understood in the West where this deeply religious art is still at times miscalled 'devil dancing'. Nothing could be more ill-founded. These dances have no connection with magic and still less with sorcery, for they originally came from Buddhist India and embody the methods of different spiritual Masters.

The form that I was to learn came through Naropa, the 'spiritual grandfather' of Milarepa, and expresses the ascent from the level of a beginner to final realization. It is called the 'Great Gathering' (*Tsogchen*) and is based on the Wheel of Supreme Bliss (*Khorlo-demchog*) which is a *mandala* of the *Sambhogakaya* or 'fruition body of Buddhahood'. This dance is a speciality of Surmang.

When the main assembly hall of the *Varshka vihara* was not being used for other purposes, the religious dancing was rehearsed there, since this house lay further up the slope and at some distance from other monastery buildings so that the noise of the dancing could not be heard. The venerable Lhapten who was the *dorje-lobpön* (master of rites) was our instructor; he rejoiced in being able to hand on his great knowledge, for he was extremely expert and although about sixty-five he was still a very good dancer.

It was all a great change; in the monastery my work had all been sedentary, now it was all movement; thirty-five of us had at first to practise with the hand-drum. Afterwards, when I was in India, I found the identical instrument in old Indian paintings in a museum, and this proved to me that its use originated there. This work with the drum was, in fact, more difficult than the actual dancing, for the arm has to be held up at full stretch for over an hour at a time, then as the drum is twisted in the hand, the two weights attached to long cords rap on the vellum. To do this properly is far from easy and most tiring to start with. The drum is held in the right hand and symbolizes Compassion, while the bell in the left hand symbolizes Voidness of ultimate content. We practised in this way daily from morning till evening with only an hour's break. In the evening we had to memorize the fundamental principles of the dancing and to learn the chants that go with it.

My tutor, Apho-karma, helped me on this course; he was very knowledgeable about these things though hardly a good dancer himself, but he gave me private instruction, for he was anxious for me to excel. He expressed the thought that I should have some spare time to rest in order to offset all this physical exertion and did his best to help by giving me massage; he also began to worry about my health, since at the start I suffered a good deal through my muscles being in such poor condition; but in a month's time I grew stronger. By then we were practising other movements and I could work nearly all day long without getting tired. Naturally I was not one of the better pupils, for the other monks had started in good condition; I knew that I lagged behind them, though they and our teacher always tried to be encouraging. Still I enjoyed it very much, and the difficulties reminded me of the time when I practised prostration under Rölpa-dorje Rinpoche.

The course went on for three and a half months without interruption, for there was a great deal to learn. The dancing had three hundred and sixty different themes symbolic of the number of days in the year, and of the same number of worldly thoughts that must be transformed into the three hundred and sixty forms of Wisdom.

At the end we had a dress rehearsal and were watched by an unofficial audience. We appeared in our best robes and I had to lead the dance which was most embarrassing, for I knew that some of the others were better than I. Alas, in their kindness the audience made no comment, but this made me even more aware that I really needed criticism, and I realized how grateful I must be to my tutor for treating me objectively and never hesitating to correct me.

After three months at the Varshka Vihara I had to decide whether

93

to go back to Sechen or to stay on for further dancing lessons. I chose to go to my *guru* without delay for, as I told my secretary, it was already the beginning of summer, and if I did not leave at once, the river Dri-chu might again be in spate and difficult to cross.

As we were preparing to start we learned that His Holiness the Dalai Lama and other senior lamas had been invited to visit China. Some of my monks were very upset, fearing that the Chinese would not allow His Holiness to return to Tibet; others, however, felt that his visit might help, for he would surely make a good impression on the Communists.

Apho-karma did not want to come with me, saying that he felt old and exhausted and that at Sechen he could no longer help me for I would be under my own *guru*. I was very sad to leave him behind for he had done so much for me with his ready advice and deep understanding. Now he reminded me that I could not hide behind a tutor all my life, adding: 'On this journey you can make the experiment of relying on your own judgment, but once at Sechen, you will be under Jamgön Kongtrül; everything will be in his hands and you will not have to worry about anything.'

Many monks and friends came to bid us farewell and my table was piled with scarves offered in token of good wishes. I said goodbye to Rölpa-dorje Rinpoche, and we set off escorted by our many friends for the first stage of our journey. This time we took a different route, through the most beautiful country I had ever seen. For three days among the high mountains we did not see a single human being, though there were all sorts of animals such as foxes, musk-rats and deer, while at night we had to put a guard on our pack animals to protect them from brown bears. The whole country-side was ablaze with flowers.

On our arrival at Sechen, I found that Jamgön Kongtrül was no longer at his own residence, but was living in the seminary. We learned that the latter had been enlarged and that there were many more monks and *tulkus* present. He was not expecting me, but expressed delight at my arrival. Many old friends were still there and all told me that this time I must really complete my studies. My *guru* was giving a course of lectures on 'The Seven Treasuries', the works of Longchen-ramjam, a great teacher of the Nyingma school. He said that it was a most auspicious moment for me to join them and that the teaching would be his spiritual gift of welcome:

94

he would give me personal instruction on the previous parts that I had missed.

Visitors were continually coming for the teaching, who camped in tents all round the seminary. The atmosphere was quite different to Surmang; I found it so happy and peaceful in spite of the crowds and the noise, everyone was intent on gaining further spiritual knowledge; we all felt how the monks at Sechen had a particular charm, from those who did the menial tasks, upwards, it was like a big happy family.

Academically I had less work to do here and this gave me more time for meditation.

A fortnight later, the course was finished and the summer vacation began. As Jamgön Kongtrül was going back to his residence he advised me to travel with my monks to visit the famous Chentze Rinpoche at Dzongsar Monastery, four days' journey away in the valley of the Dri-chu. Four of the professors (*khenpos*) accompanied us and we set off southwards. On the third day we stopped at Manikengo as we had been told the story of a very saintly man who had died there the previous year. We went to the house where he had lived, and met his son and his wife who recounted the miracle that had occurred at the old man's death.

In his lifetime he had erected a group of '*Mani* stones' on which he had carved a great number of *mantras* and *sutras* and he had also set up a *chöten* (*stupa*) among them.

In his youth he had been a servant with a wealthy family, but in middle age he left his employment to receive meditational instruction in a monastery. Though he had to work for his living by day, he spent most of his nights in contemplation only allowing himself two to three hours' sleep. His compassion was so great that he always helped everyone in need, and opened his house at all times to pilgrims and the very poor. While carrying out his daily work he used to practise meditation in his own way, though his son who was a monk told him that he should carry out more formal spiritual exercises, but this he could not accept. Though he had hitherto always been in good health, three years before his death he fell ill and his family began to be very worried, yet he himself appeared to become increasingly happy. He composed and sang his own songs of praise instead of traditional Buddhist chants. As his illness became more and more serious, lamas and doctors were called in, with his son telling him that he must now remember all the teaching that he had received, at which he smiled, saying 'I have forgotten it all, and anyway there is nothing to remember; everything is illusion, yet I am confident that all is well.' Just before his death the old man said 'When I die you must not move my body for a week; this is all that I desire.'

They wrapped his dead body in old clothes and called in lamas and monks to recite and chant. The body was carried into a small room, little bigger than a cupboard and it was noted that though the old man had been tall the body appeared to have become smaller; at the same time a rainbow was seen over the house. On the sixth day on looking into the room the family saw that it had grown still smaller. A funeral service was arranged for the morning of the eighth day and men came to take the body to the cemetery; when they undid the coverings there was nothing inside except nails and hair. The villagers were astounded, for it would have been impossible for anyone to have come into the room, the door was always kept locked and the window of the little resting place was much too small.

The family reported the event to the authorities and also went to ask Chentze Rinpoche about the meaning of it. He told them that such a happening had been reported several times in the past and that the body of the saintly man has been absorbed into the Light. They showed me the nails and the hair and the small room where they had kept the body. We had heard of such things happening, but never at first hand, so we went round the village to ask for further information. Everyone had seen the rainbow and knew that the body had disappeared. This village was on the main route from China to Lhasa and the people told me that the previous year when the Chinese heard about it they were furious and said the story must not be talked about.

The following day we reached the monastery of Dzongsar which belonged to the Sakya school. The present Chentze Rinpoche had been brought up there; his *guru* had been Situ of Kathog Monastery, the disciple of the renowned teacher the great Chentze Rinpoche whose path the present Chentze had followed.

On our arrival we found there were more visitors than residents; they had come from all the different Buddhist schools of Tibet, for the seminary specialized in a great variety of teachings. We were given accommodation in the monastery and made an appointment to be received by Chentze Rinpoche on the following day. Our party went together for a formal introduction, exchanging the traditional scarves etc. after which, the lama talked to me alone. His room had been left exactly as it was in the time of the great Chentze and seemed still to exude the power of his spirituality. Chentze came down from his throne and sat on a cushion in front of me with a welcoming smile. There was a sense of peace, happiness and warmth all around him, but there was also a sense of awe, his words were so profound. He said that he was always glad to meet a disciple of Jamgön Kongtrül and particularly one who is the incarnation of the tenth Trungpa Tulku who had also been one of his own teachers; he added 'you and I are the sons of the same spiritual father'. He felt that he had no further teaching to give me since I had studied under so great a master already, but at my request he agreed to perform the empowerment rite of *Kalachakra* (the Wheel of Time) for our party and would also instruct me privately. Although I was only there for a month, I learned a great deal and a deep understanding grew between us. Chentze Rinpoche said to me 'You must look after and guide yourself, as in the future there will be no further teachers. A new era has begun in which the pure doctrine of the Lord Buddha lies in the hands of individuals; each one is separately responsible, for I do not think that we can carry on in the way we have done up till now. We can no longer rely on groups and communities. The situation is very serious, many of us are old, and perhaps it is young people like you, the new generation, who shall bear the burden.'

While we were at Dzongsar, we had a strange experience. Knowing that the monastery was the centre for a great many visitors, lamas, scholars and devotees, the Communists came with a propaganda film complete with its own batteries to give us a show. It covered their activities in Tibet from 1949 to 1953, and showed how much they had accomplished there with their so called improvements, such as roads, schools and hospitals, and how the Red Army had been warmly welcomed by the Tibetans. Since there was no public hall in which they could show the film, they made use of one of the sacred temples. Chentze Rinpoche was forced to be present, for if he were there everyone else would have to attend: this was the first time I had seen a film.

The morning of our departure was a sad one, especially with those last words from Chentze Rinpoche uppermost in my mind. I asked him to promise that we would meet again and that I would be given more time to study under him. His presence seemed to be with me for many miles of the journey.

During the interval, before the start of the new term at Sechen, I decided to spend all my time in meditation under my *guru*. Tulku Aten who was still with me as my advisor, now told me that before we left Surmang the authorities had said that I must not remain away for too long as I was needed in the monasteries, so I should finish my studies as quickly as possible. I consulted my *guru* who advised me to stay at Sechen for a little longer as I needed further instruction in meditation and Tulku Aten went back to Surmang to tell them how matters stood. I was now left with Lama Pega as my attendant and one Tsering, who like myself was anxious to have further instruction in meditation.

This was the time of year when young monks, particularly those from distant monasteries, went out with their begging bowls to collect food for the winter: those who belonged to Sechen were usually supported by local people. Since, however, many of the monks at Sechen were disciples of my previous incarnation, they looked after me and I accepted their help as it was important for me to study.

When the new term began we had to go on with our work from where we had left off; we started with the *Abhidharma*, the metaphysical portion of the old Buddhist canon, and continued with *Pratimoksha* which deals with monastic rules; we had also to study rhetoric and logic, though not so extensively as in some other schools. All the teaching was given orally, and we only made a few notes at the time for our own use.

The master encouraged me to make a comparative study of the different schools, and would explain their meeting points. He listened to my criticisms, but would say, 'It is no use just having theories, you must reflect about the meaning: you must not accept anything just because it is given as the teaching of Buddha, but always examine it for yourself. You must follow the Middle Way; if a statement is found in the scriptures, it rests with you to find out what it really means in order to have true faith. Knowledge must be tested in the same way as gold; first refined, then beaten and made smooth till it becomes the right colour and shows that it is pure gold.'

I was delighted when Akong Tulku arrived at Sechen for the New Year celebrations; we had become fast friends when I visited

Drölma Lhakhang and gave the rite of the 'Treasury of the Mine of Precious Teaching': I had then done all I could to persuade him to come to Sechen to receive instruction from Jamgön Kongtrül, and I wanted him to experience the wonderful atmosphere there. His party had had an extremely difficult journey, for the whole country was under ice and snow. Five Drölma Lhakhang monks had accompanied him, but soon returned to their monastery and only his tutor remained with him.

The Vase of the Elixir of Immortality

CHAPTER NINE

THE DALAI LAMA'S VISIT

On his return journey in 1955, after a year's visit to China, the Dalai Lama wanted to travel by way of East Tibet in order to be able to meet his people there; but unfortunately he was delayed by earthquakes that had caused damage to some of the northern roads, and he was forced to change his plans for it was only possible to visit those places that could be reached by car: so he delegated three high ranking lamas to represent him elsewhere. These were his junior tutor Trijang Rinpoche, Chung Rinpoche and Gyalwa Karmapa; the latter was to take his place at Pepung Monastery. I received a letter from Gyalwa Karmapa just before the end of the Sechen term, informing me of these plans and telling me to come to Pepung where a council was to be held to decide on the arrangements to be made to receive the Dalai Lama's message: all the abbots of the Ka-gyü school were expected to attend it. After notifying Surmang I started off with Akong Tulku, my two Surmang monks and a monk from Sechen who fortunately had a mule. Both Akong and I had already sent our horses back to our monasteries and though the abbots at Sechen offered to lend us theirs as well as some tents, I thought that we should do the journey on foot, while our baggage could be carried on the mule. Travelling proved difficult, for the spring snow was very soft and heavy; there was no wind and we suffered a good deal from snow-blindness.

When we reached Pepung we found that my bursar and Apho-karma, whom I had not seen for some time, together with many other senior lamas had already arrived. They were surprised that our party had travelled on foot.

Gyalwa Karmapa, as the representative of the Dalai Lama, was accompanied by Chinese and Tibetan officials besides having a Chinese body-guard; we had little time to change from our travel stained clothes into our brocade robes to be ready to pay our respects to him. He was very friendly and told me that he had been waiting for me. We had tea together, when he told me how relieved he was to be back in Tibet; he said that the Chinese had appeared friendly, but that life in China seemed to be rather superficial. He was interested to hear about my studies.

The following day Gyalwa Karmapa gave the Dalai Lama's message to the assembly saying:

'His Holiness deeply regrets that he has not been able to accept the invitation from the Ka-gyüpas himself. He asks people to understand the present situation in Tibet and how important it is for everyone to keep to their religious institutions. A great responsibility rests upon the leaders who must help both the monastic and the lay population. Everyone should be co-operative and remember that all are brothers.'

Then Gyalwa Karmapa went on to tell us about the visit to China. They had been treated very hospitably: the orderliness and the material advances in the country had been brought to their notice, but he said nothing about the religious and personal freedom of the people.

We could understand that the Dalai Lama and his party were not free to voice their own opinions. Between the lines, one could realize what conditions were really like in China, and what might happen in Tibet. The whole programme, as well as the Dalai Lama's itinerary, was obviously being controlled by the Communists.

The abbot of Pepung monastery, Taisitu Rinpoche, who was second in importance in the Karma-ka-gyü school, had died some years before and no re-incarnation had been found. Up till then Gyalwa Karmapa had been unable to give any indication where to look. The monastic committee now renewed the hope that the time had come for a vision and that Gyalwa Karmapa might perform the enthronement ceremony whilst he was still at Pepung. But the latter felt very uncertain about it; he had been much disturbed since his visit to China. He meditated for three days and on the fourth he had a vision. He called the regent abbot and the secretary and asked them to arrange for the enthronement at once, for he could now tell them where the incarnation had taken place. Everyone rejoiced and started immediately to make the preparations.

That same afternoon they went back to him for his final directions. He told them to go the following morning to a place where they would find the incarnation and gave them the full names of the parents, for he was in no doubt; all three must immediately be brought to Pepung. The monastery sent out invitations to attend the ceremony to the King of Derge, to lamas of neighbouring monasteries and to important laymen in the district.

The king arrived in great state with thirty-five counsellors and three hundred other people in his suite. His procession was led by a row of monk musicians, with other monks who were waving censers. The king wore a shirt of lemon coloured brocade under a gold brocade coat, with pantaloons of white silk tucked into long boots; his jewelled sword in a carved gold scabbard hung from his belt. He had a gold amulet box slung across his chest; his hat was of gold brocade with red tassels round the crown and a large diamond on the top. His four senior ministers wore the same sort of costume, but of deep yellow brocade; the other ministers were in crimson brocade; all wore rubies on their hats. The rest of the suite followed in ordinary festival clothes. All the party rode on horses bedecked with gay trappings.

The enthronement ceremony was held in the large assembly hall; the whole place, including the pillars, was decorated with gold brocade hangings as well as beautiful *tankas* depicting the life of the Buddha and the line of the Ka-gyü school. The senior lamas were in their gold brocade *töngas* (waistcoats) under maroon robes and cloaks with golden stoles at the back. Gyalwa Karmapa's throne at the right and the abbot's throne on the left, each with five cushions, were at the end of the hall, while the *tulkus* sat in rows leading up to them. Each throne had a number of cushions on it which varied according to the standing of the particular *tulku*, either four, three, two or a single one on the floor; all were covered in gold brocade: I was given four cushions. The king sat behind us on five cushions nearest to Gyalwa Karmapa's throne, with his ministers and the neighbouring laity below him. The rest of the monks were on low benches covered with rugs. Against the wall on the opposite side to the king an elaborate altar had been erected.

Gyalwa Karmapa conducted the ceremony of enthronement; scarves and gifts were piled on the table, and a *khenpo* gave a two hours' talk on the history of Buddhism, also on the history of the monastery, and expressed everyone's gratitude that the incarnation had been found. The following day a party was arranged for the king, and invitations were sent to particular lamas. For several weeks afterwards offerings were placed before the altar, including thousands of butter lamps, sacrificial cakes (*tormas*), flowers and incense. In return the king gave a dinner to the regent abbot and senior monks who, when he left, accompanied him some distance on his journey. In Tibet this is always a mark of respect.

After the enthronement, a message was received from the Dalai Lama to say when he would be arriving in Derge; he would be staying at the king's palace. Gyalwa Karmapa made this announcement to all the lamas present; there was a discussion about how to approach His Holiness and what other arrangements should be made. Particular forms, ceremonies and rules of costume had to be observed and many gifts, of which there was a prescribed list, had to be offered: a monk had to read from an illuminated script, couched in poetic form, with many flourishes begging the acceptance of the gifts by His Holiness. The first gift had to be a white scarf, followed by a gold image of the Buddha, a scripture and a model of a *stupa*, or a bell and *dorje*, as symbols of long life of the body, speech and mind; also five rolls of coloured cloth and the skins of a tiger, a leopard, a fox and an otter. The Dalai Lama would also be offered the traditional gifts of a set of robes, gold and silver coins, rolls of brocade, food, horses and cattle etc., finally another white scarf, for this is auspicious, being the symbol of purity.

On this occasion Gyalwa Karmapa would officiate at the presentation of all the gifts from Pepung as well as those from the neighbouring monasteries and from the important laity of the district; they would all be placed together in the centre of the hall in the prescribed order.

At the finish of the council meeting, Gyalwa Karmapa was invited to come for a rest at the summer residence of some of the higher ranking lamas at Pepung. These private residences were situated about half a mile from the monastery; they were charmingly built, with their own gardens and stables. The Chinese officials and bodyguard, being still with Gyalwa Karmapa, were also able to relax there; they played football in the garden and we were able to talk to them in a most friendly way and even to joke with them. Away from Communist authority, they were natural and seemed to take an interest in everything. At that time many Tibetans were on excellent terms with the Chinese, as long as the latter were out of sight of the Party members in charge.

While Gyalwa Karmapa was resting we were still able to go to have informal talks and teaching from him and I spoke to him about my idea of enlarging the seminary at Düdtsi-til; he was most encouraging in spite of the Chinese situation. All this month I spent the time usefully by meeting abbots and professors from other monasteries, while in the evenings and early mornings I worked at my own studies. Apho-karma realized that I had learned a lot during the past year and began at last to treat me as an adult.

During the time that Gyalwa Karmapa was away, the committee at Pepung had established a camp near Derge Gönchen, the capital of Derge, for we expected that His Holiness would spend a night with us. This meant a very large camp; five hundred tents were required since, besides those destined for the Dalai Lama and his party, about four hundred others were needed for all the Ka-gyü lamas who had attended the council meeting. It was necessary to obtain the approval of both Tibetan and Chinese officials for these arrangements. When Gyalwa Karmapa returned to us, we all left for the camp.

The special tent for His Holiness had a separate bedroom and sitting room and was beautifully decorated throughout. Another tent was needed for audiences and this housed the Dalai Lama's throne; there were more tents for committee and cabinet meetings and for the rest of his party. Each tent was of a different size, shape and design; most of them were lined with white silk adorned with brocade hangings and *tankas*. A gold plated *serto* (crest ornament), the emblem of dignity, rose over each tent; the tent-ropes were black with red ornaments, and the pegs took the form of gilt images of various demigods; flowers had been planted all round and the whole camp looked very welcoming.

The day before His Holiness was expected to reach the king's palace we made ready to go to meet him. First, a procession was organized to escort Gyalwa Karmapa to Derge Gönchen whose monks, belonging to the Sakya school, were to be our hosts. The procession was very colourful; eighty abbots preceded Gyalwa Karmapa and his staff, and he was followed by three hundred monks; everyone was on horseback. The senior lamas wore their maroon robes under long sleeved yellow brocade riding coats, with vermillian stoles draped across their shoulders; a cord round the waist and across one shoulder held everything in position, being clasped at the back by a gold amulet-case and joined in front with a gold tassel. They wore their summer hats of gold lacquer with round crowns and brims. The horses were gaily caparisoned and carried the ornament of the *serto* between their ears; their saddles were plated with gold while the flaps were of gold brocade.

As we approached the monastery which lay near the king's principal palace, monks with banners and musical instruments came to escort us along the road, and at the monastery we were welcomed by other musicians on the roof.

The king himself belonged to the Sakya school, so he had invited Phuntsog-photrang Rinpoche the head of that school, together with his party, to be guests at another of his residences.

The Dalai Lama was due to arrive the following day; he was to stay with the king at the chief palace. When his car was some two miles away the king with Phuntsog-photrang and Gyalwa Karmapa drove out, also in cars, to meet him. He was accompanied by his tutor, and his staff followed in two more cars. Thousands of people were lining the road which was decorated with designs in coloured sand and had a white cloth laid upon it for the cars to pass over; they had crowded in from all parts of the district to greet the Dalai Lama, but were very disappointed at seeing so little of him, since the Chinese authorities had insisted that he should travel in a closed car. The king and the two abbots escorted the Dalai Lama's party back to the palace, all going at a very slow pace with a monk walking behind the Dalai Lama's car carrying a ceremonial umbrella. The abbots of both schools stood in rows a short distance from the palace, Sakyapas on the right hand side and Ka-gyüpas on the left, but like the country crowds we could hardly see His Holiness shut up, as he was, in the closed car, nor did we see the party alight outside the palace where the king's ministers were waiting on the steps; the king himself, carrying incense sticks, then conducted the Dalai Lama into the palace to the welcoming sound of music.

Next day His Holiness gave a *wangkur* and a short talk in the great hall of the monastery. He said that our religion should come foremost in our lives to bind us together, but we should try to have a friendly attitude towards the Chinese. We sat in the first row and it was almost unbelievable and extremely moving for us to see His Holiness in our part of Tibet. Despite official pomp and ceremony, the Dalai Lama made it evident that he had come as a friend to his people, smiling his greeting as he went to his throne escorted by his solemn, formal officials. He made us feel that he really wanted to be among us in East Tibet which he had been unable to visit before. He gave me personally a wider vision, since I now understood what it meant to be the incarnation of Avalokiteshvara the Bodhisattva of Compassion, for this was apparent in the Dalai Lama's serenity and radiance, which one could feel was part of him. We were beginning to lose heart, for the Communists were becoming so powerful; it seemed as if our happy days were coming to an end: however, the presence of His Holiness gave us renewed hope that the spiritual teaching and culture of Tibet would not be entirely swept away. Yet it was sad to see him looking so thin and strained as a result of the heavy burden he had to carry.

While we were at Derge Gönchen we were taken over parts of the palace which was very interesting. It was already old when the great king of Derge, Chö-gyal Tenpa-tsering, after having conquered the surrounding province, made Derge Gönchen his capital in the eighteenth century. He used to travel incognito all round the districts to see for himself in what condition his people were living and if justice was being properly administered. We were shown the library which he had built. This had its own printing press; the wood-blocks for printing the Scriptures (the finest of their kind in Tibet) as well as the printed books themselves were stored here. This press was famous all over the country, for there were only two other such establishments in Tibet. The library was considered to be a holy place, even though work was carried on there, for its books were all connected with Buddhist teaching. Chö-gyal Tenpa-tsering, besides being a good ruler, was himself a notable scholar; he was a devotee of all the schools and his library contained a variety of important works, among them, one hundred and eight volumes of translations of the *sutras* (the *Kangyur*), a number of old and new translations of the Buddhist *tantras* and also many volumes of commentary by early Indian Buddhist scholars (the *Tengyur*), all translated from Sanskrit; the great *Taisitu* Chöki-jungne had corrected most of the proofs for the printers. The celebrated wood-carvers here were known as the Kutsi School.

The king of Derge was still very young and his mother was acting as regent. She gave us an audience and we noticed how pale and thin she looked, for she was always under the strain of dealing with the

Chinese and attending their meetings in addition to her work on state affairs. She was simply dressed in dark blue brocade and wore small gold earrings, with a reliquary round her neck and a turquoise ornament in her hair.

We also met the head of the Sakya school, Phuntsog-photrang Rinpoche who had been to China with the Dalai Lama. He told us that coming back to Tibet had seemed like a dream. He had felt before he went away that his country had reached a crisis and that the time had come for us all to consider our future more thoughtfully. While he was away he had been quite exhausted, so he said, and it was restful to be back here again, but if he seemed lazy and wished to forget the experience, we others must not imitate him; those who had not suffered the strain of this turmoil might still be able to work out clearly what should be done: it does not matter to what school one belongs, all must work together. Before we left he gave us his blessing.

When we were returning to our camp Gyalwa Karmapa asked Sang-gyenyenpa Rinpoche, an older lama, to take charge of our party, for at that time most of the Ka-gyü lamas were quite young. We were so lively and friendly among ourselves that everyone who saw us was struck by it.

Back at our camp, we finished our preparations for the Dalai Lama's visit. In the afternoon, however, to our great disappointment we received a message that His Holiness would be unable to stay the night, because the Chinese required him to return to Central Tibet; he could only spend two hours at the camp and take lunch with us. So many people had looked forward for months to this visit that the disappointment was general; it was apparent that His Holiness was prevented from doing as his people wanted, but had to obey the orders of the Communists.

The next day, he arrived in his car and the welcoming ceremony took place as planned. He blessed us by reciting the Heart Sutra of Perfection of Wisdom (*Prajnaparamita-hridaya Sutra*) and took a meal with us at the camp, after which the ceremonial offerings were duly made to him. He returned all the gifts and only kept the scroll on which the list of gifts had been written. He presented the Ka-gyü order with his own brocade robe and some rolls of hand-woven cloth and left us with the words 'my thoughts will always be with you; I am distressed at being unable to stay the night, but I am really happy to have spent these two hours with you.' Before leaving, His

107

Holiness performed the hair cutting ceremony of primary *Upasaka* for the infant *Taisitu* Lama, whom Gyalwa Karmapa had enthroned at Pepung.

While I was at the camp a messenger came from Surmang saying that a senior lama of a neighbouring monastery had died and that the monks wanted me to perform the rites. Akong Tulku and my two monks took the baggage back to Sechen, and I started on my way, travelling for the first day in company with Gyalwa Karmapa as far as Kamtho Trukha where the Chinese had installed a ferry to cross the Dri-chu. Here Gyalwa Karmapa left for Chamdo, where the Dalai Lama was expected. His last words to me were that I must first finish my studies and then improve and enlarge the seminary at Düdtsi-til. He went away at seven o'clock in the morning in rain and mist in a small car provided by the Chinese. It was all so quick that there was no opportunity to say goodbye; he had disappeared in a moment, waving a white scarf from the car. Other lama friends left at the same time in different directions, and I found myself alone with the two Surmang monks. It seemed strangely quiet and peaceful after so much bustle, and we rode on through beautiful wild valleys to our monastery some seven days' journey away.

When I reached Surmang we held a meeting for all the monks and the more important laity of the district; I told them about the Dalai Lama and I gave them his message; but like His Holiness I found myself in the same difficulty, for I could not talk openly, since there were many Chinese officials amongst us. However, having seen how restricted even the Dalai Lama had to be, I found it easier to impose the necessary restraint upon myself. Indeed, not having an official position, there was little I could do; I wanted however, to give my people as true a picture of the situation as possible, and some idea of what our future aims might be. I discussed this with my secretary, the senior lamas and the people's representatives, some of whom had been in contact with the Communists. All had the feelings of loyal Tibetans, but thought we were not in a position to do anything other than to accept the Chinese domination. At that time there was some hope that the jurisdiction of the committee which was going to be formed in Lhasa, ostensibly under the Dalai Lama, would include East Tibet. Unfortunately the Chinese had already divided up the country into separate regions, and our region was assigned to Sining which the Chinese considered to be entirely separate from Tibet proper. They said 'All Tibet belongs to us, especially the Sining district which is not even Tibet. You are part of China, and it would be entirely inappropriate to combine you with Central Tibet.' We ourselves always considered that the people who speak Tibetan and eat roasted barley (*tsampa*) as their staple food are Tibetans.

Already during the Chinese Nationalist regime of Ma-pu-fang, which preceded the Communist invasion, we had gone through much suffering. Very high taxes had been levied, but at least we had been allowed liberty of religion; now all we could do was to pray and hope that there would be unity in Tibet, under His Holiness the Dalai Lama.

When I was able to leave Surmang, I visited the monastery where the senior lama had died and we held the funeral ceremony. Returning to Düdtsi-til I called a meeting to discuss enlarging the seminary as Gyalwa Karmapa had advised. Our present one was only full in the summer and very few monks attended it in the winter. It was not even a separate establishment; I wanted it to have its own building, as this had been the intention of the tenth Trungpa Tulku. He had wanted this to be undertaken as soon as he had established the five meditation centres on which he had set his heart, saying, 'If enemies come and destroy the building, we in fact lose nothing; the worthwhileness of the deed is eternal.'

A new seminary would need more ground and many other arrangements would have to be made. I discussed these plans with my secretary and though I asked various people for donations I said I would like to contribute the monastery's share from my personal funds. People were not very enthusiastic, but because of my request they agreed to support the idea. We decided that after my next visit to Sechen, I would bring a *khenpo* back with me as a permanent head for the seminary.

Soon after this I returned to Sechen; this time Apho-karma, nine other monks and my little brother, the nine-year-old incarnate Tamchö-temphel, abbot of the small monastery of Kyere, came with me. At Sechen I was welcomed by my *guru* and many other friends, all of whom had doubted whether I would return. I found everyone in the monastery in a state of great turmoil. The reason was, so Jamgön Kongtrül told me, that they had received a letter from Chentze Rinpoche saying that he had left the Monastery of Dzongsar for good owing to the probability of the further spread of

Chinese Communism; he intended to settle permanently in India and to make pilgrimages to all the holy places; he died later in Sikkim. Everyone was very upset at his departure and Jamgön Kongtrül thought it might be wise to leave as well. The whole atmosphere of Sechen was disturbed; finally the latter decided to stay on for at least a few more years.

It gave me great comfort that I could continue my studies, for I was now better able to understand and appreciate the teaching; I realized that soon I might have no-one to teach me, so the privilege of being in contact with my *guru* was of greater importance than ever. During the summer vacation I studied with redoubled zest under my great teacher and all but completed my lessons in meditation as well as the course of philosophic studies. My *guru* told me that I should learn further from his disciple Khenpo Gangshar, one of the six senior professors at Sechen, who was not only immensely learned but was also very advanced spiritually. I thought this meant that I should invite Khenpo Gangshar to help us at the new seminary; but though the friendship between the two monasteries was very close, all this would have to be discussed with the abbots and the monastic committee of Sechen in consultation with Jamgön Kongtrül. With great kindness they finally agreed to let Khenpo Gangshar come to my monastery for an unspecified time. I wanted him to come as soon as possible and it was agreed that he would make the journey in six months' time. This meant, of course, that I could not stay at Sechen much longer. Though my own training in meditation had been completed under Jamgön Kongtrül, I still had to qualify as an instructor in this spiritual art, besides finishing my theoretical studies.

The Sechen authorities asked me to attend the summer celebration of *guru* Padmakara's birthday, and this I could not refuse since I expected it would be for the last time. The services would last for ten days under Tulku Ramjam Rinpoche, and Jamgön Kongtrül would also occasionally attend them.

The assembly hall at Sechen was very large and dimly lit. The gold on the wonderful wall paintings and hangings reflected the light of the lamps against the red lacquered pillars and, following the Mindöling tradition, a particularly fragrant incense was used, which permeated everywhere. The objects on the shrine were extremely delicate and beautifully arranged, and the carved butter ornaments for the sacrificial cakes were real works of art.

ngo Chentze Rinpoche

Chentze Rinpoche of Dzongsar

shrine room

The author (right) *with Akong Tulku*

6

Yak skin coracles on the Tsangpo River

On the tenth day of the celebration a religious dance was held: its theme was the eight aspects of *guru* Padmakara, and there were other dances connected with the 'wrathful' aspect of the *Buddhamandala*; these dances were performed by some three hundred monks. The costumes were very old and decorative and thousands of people came to watch. This was the only anniversary at which women were allowed within the precincts of the monastery and they greatly enjoyed this opportunity to visit the beautiful shrines. We ended with a *Marme-mönlam* (=prayer with lamps) and all prayed that we might be eternally united in the *Dharma*.

As I soon had to leave Sechen, my last three weeks were spent with Jamgön Kongtrül Rinpoche at his residence. He gave me his final instructions saying 'You have now learned a great deal from me, but you must still improve your knowledge. Much comes from one's own experience in teaching, reading and contemplating. A teacher must not refuse to help others; at the same time he can always learn. This is the way of the Bodhisattvas, who while they helped others, gained further enlightenment themselves. One must be wholly aware of all that one does; for in teaching, however expertly, if one's own understanding be insufficient, there is danger of simply using words regardless of their spiritual meaning; therefore you must still remember that you yourself will continue to be a pupil on the way.'

A memorable farewell dinner was given for me by the monastic committee of Sechen, for though, fundamentally, the monastery belonged to the Nyingma school, there was a close affiliation to the Ka-gyü. Jamgön Kongtrül was both a teacher and a learner of many schools and particularly of the Ka-gyü, and in this he followed the example of his previous incarnation. In such an atmosphere our vision was greatly enlarged. When I left this friendly and all-embracing society I felt a slightly narrower life was closing round me: though within my monastery, as with its neighbours, religious study and meditation were continuously practised, fewer monks came from other schools. Everything seemed to have slowed down, especially at Düdtsi-til since the death of the tenth Trungpa Tulku Rinpoche, and I was hoping to revive this spirit of expansion and development. It was a great consolation to me that Khenpo Gangshar had promised to come and help us. However, at Namgyal-tse there had been some progress; its seminary was attracting scholars from many different schools.

Akong Tulku came away with me, though he wanted to study further at Sechen. On our journey we met many monks carrying their books on the tops of their packs; their first exchange was always 'What philosophy have you studied, what courses of meditation, under what teacher, and at what monastery?' for the monasteries in that area were in a very flourishing state with constant exchange of people seeking instruction in various spiritual techniques; there were laymen also engaged on similar pilgrimages.

It was now apparent that the Communists were becoming more officious; they now checked all travellers, and we were told that they sometimes made arrests, though we were not actually molested.

On reaching Surmang I received an invitation to visit China, and the Communists also wanted me to join the Central Committee of their party. Since my secretary was already a committee member, I said it would be unnecessary for me to join as well, but should he be prevented from attending the meetings, I would take his place. Moreover as he was the more experienced man, he would be of greater use to them and he could speak on our behalf. This could not be objected to, though my monks realized that the Chinese, if their demands were not complied with, would certainly take further steps to get me in their power.

CHAPTER TEN

KHAMPAS IN REVOLT

His Holiness the Dalai Lama had visited India in November 1956 for the Buddha Jayanti celebrations held every hundred years in memory of the Buddha's Enlightenment and had returned to Lhasa the following February. While away, he had met Buddhists from all parts of the world and we now hoped that, with this publicity, he would be able to improve conditions for the rest of us, so our thoughts and devotions concentrated on this hope. Each New Year the festival of Tsog-Chen was held at Surmang, and religious dancing took place for three days from sunrise to sunset; on the fourth day this went on for twenty-four hours with hardly a break. This was the first time that I had been able to take part in it. I looked forward to doing so and practised hard, so instead of being utterly exhausted, as I had expected, I did not feel it too great a strain. I found that dancing, when combined properly with meditation, fills one with strength and joy.

Soon after the festival we sent monks and transport to Sechen to fetch Khenpo Gangshar who was to be my private tutor as well as director of the seminary. Apho-karma had already said that he wanted to retire as he was growing old and feeling very tired. He thought that he had taught me all he could, and was now more my attendant than my tutor. I asked him to remain as a member of my household and as my close adviser; he had been with me for so long and was almost a father to me. But he said that even as an adviser, the work was too much for him. He wanted to go back to meditate at the hermitage where he had once lived for three years behind bricked in doors, receiving food through a panel, so it was arranged that he should leave me. This parting was a great grief to me, but it left me freer to make my own decisions without asking for outside advice.

We were all delighted to welcome Khenpo Gangshar, who seemed happy to be with us, so we lost no time in starting the first study course under his guidance. It was indeed fortunate that he had been able to reach Düdtsi-til without mishap, for soon afterwards a great number of refugees came through from Derge, who told us that they had met severe fighting on their journey. Since Sechen lay on the further side of Derge we felt very anxious about Jamgön Kongtrül and feared that he might be entirely cut off from all further communication. This was the first serious outbreak of hostilities, and the refugees told us that the Communists were now killing many of the defenders' families; but as far as they knew the monasteries had not been touched. It was clear, however, that the outlook was becoming more threatening every day.

I had to complete my studies and this still meant very hard work; the first course at the seminary was on the *Madhyamika* (the Middle Way) and also on the sacred text of *Hevajra* by the third Gyalwa Karmapa. Besides this there was much else to claim my attention, for I had to direct Surmang, to officiate at rites, as well as to go out to the local people when they asked for help in case of illness or death, or for teaching and advice. In cases of emergency I could be called upon in the middle of the night, so I often got very little sleep.

The news from East Tibet was becoming worse every day. We now heard that the Communists had formed groups of all sorts of people, in fact, anyone that they could enlist. They had indoctrinated these men with their own ideology, and had sent them to act as spies among the villagers and to report on their activities. An order had been sent out that all arms must be handed over, and the groups went round to see that this was carried out. At the beginning the people did not refuse to give up their arms and made little remonstrance; they tried to be co-operative and peaceful. However, the Communists became more and more abusive and a number of people were imprisoned by them and this continued until the Tibetans could stand it no longer. Then for the first time they organized retaliation at Denko, Ba and Litang. Their leader at Denko, when ordered to hand over his arms to a Communist official, made pretence of doing so and then suddenly shot the official dead. This was the signal for his followers to attack the town, and many Chinese were killed or taken prisoner. The real conflict now began and the local leader became one of the leaders of the Resistance in Kham, which is the general name for East Tibet.

Refugees were leaving in ever increasing numbers, particularly from Derge, to seek shelter in Central Tibet close to the Dalai Lama. Up till now there had been little trouble around Surmang which was on the borders of Nyishu-tze-nga, though all this district was under the Communist administration of Chinghai; we had all been allowed to move about as we liked, provided that we gave no support to the people of Derge, so I was able to go on working at the seminary with about thirty other students under Khenpo Gangshar, and had more or less completed my studies in *Hinayana* (basic teaching) and *Mahayana* (wider teaching) and had also done a certain amount of work on *Vajrayana* (advanced teaching) though this needed further study.

One day I received a secret message from Jamgön Kongtrül to say that he had escaped from Sechen and was on his way to Lhasa. He would pass near Surmang and he wanted Khenpo Gangshar and myself to join him at a place on the border with as little publicity as possible and accompany him to Central Tibet. We went there and found him together with some of his senior monks and other refugees. However, by the time we reached him, his attitude had slightly changed. Instead of urging me to go with him, he said that we must make our own decision; the work that we were doing at Surmang was very valuable, and it was important to consider whether it should be continued or not. It was very difficult to know what course to follow; besides I knew that if I returned to my work at Surmang I might never see my *guru* again. We talked the matter over with the other senior lamas and came to the unanimous conclusion that we would do as Jamgön Kongtrül thought best. However, he would not take the whole responsibility; he only gave an indication that he thought Tibet could not go on as in the past and that it would be best for us to plan afresh. He said: 'The law of *karma* cannot change; each one must face his allotted destiny; each one must follow the guidance of his own inner conscience.'

The authorities at Surmang were rather perplexed since they considered that, as my *guru*, Jamgön Kongtrül should give me specific instructions. Finally, we decided to go on with our work at Surmang; if an emergency should arise, either Jamgön Kongtrül would get in touch with me or I with him. So we said goodbye, while I asked him to promise that we would meet again. He replied that we would meet in one way or another, but again said that 'the teacher is within oneself and the way is also there'. He added 'You may have to face great difficulties without a teacher; everyone must now be prepared to stand on his own feet. Khenpo Gangshar is taking my place and will help you for the time being.' We left Jamgön Kongtrül with great sorrow, and a day later he resumed his journey.

My life had evidently reached a crisis. I was faced with the knowledge that East Tibet no longer existed as a spiritual centre and everything looked very dark. More refugees were continually coming from the province of Derge. The Communists had given orders that all our villages and monasteries must be responsible for keeping order, and if we encouraged the refugees, we ourselves would be defying the Chinese government. In spite of this, since they were coming in such large groups with all their goods and cattle, it was absolutely necessary for them to have somewhere to camp; I was able to let them have some camping grounds on our land. They gave me further details about the situation in Derge. The young king's mother, in her capacity of regent during the king's minority, had been obliged to take part in the Communist committees until she was informed that she must no longer remain in the province. Then it appeared that the Communists had taken her to China and nothing further was known about her. The young king and his ministers had escaped from the palace and had formed their own Resistance group, being joined by the local militia and later by other guerillas. At first their offensive was very successful. They used to dig trenches across the roads to stop the Chinese lorries, thus enabling the Tibetans to get possession of their arms. The king's forces were supported by all the local inhabitants and together they were able to occupy most of the Chinese controlled towns in the west of Derge province. In the east, however, there was no large guerilla force, and the Communists were destroying the monasteries and taking the monks prisoners, accusing them of possessing arms though this was not true, and they also said that the monasteries would be used by the Tibetan Resistance fighters. In the central part of Derge the Communists after making friendly advances to the senior lamas, either kidnapped or shot them. Pepung was destroyed. At Dzongsar the Communists surrounded the monastery for seven days and prevented the monks from getting water, so that finally they were forced to surrender. Many senior lamas were shot and the remainder of the monks arrested.

Those senior lamas from the various monasteries who had not been immediately shot, were taken to Gönchen. There, poor country folk were brought along and force was used to make them concoct stories of the evil deeds the lamas had committed. Many Tibetans refused to comply and instead, though unarmed, they fell upon the Chinese; they managed to kill some of them and then took their own lives. One Tibetan beggar-woman when told to shoot the *khenpo* of the monastery took the pistol and shot herself instead.

My first endeavour on my return to Surmang was to carry out the last wish of the tenth Trungpa Tulku and to enlarge the seminary. It was already overcrowded since all our monks except the trainees and those specially occupied had joined it, while about one hundred and fifty monks had come from outside monasteries. The latter had already completed their earlier studies and came as what might be called in England 'post-graduates'. Khenpo Gangshar appointed four *kyorpöns* (tutors) as instructors and also gave me authority to assist in the teaching.

I at once formed a committee mostly of lay people to raise money and control the finances of the new seminary. Our first step was to increase the annual contribution from the monastic farms, which were managed by a lay bailiff. My bursar and some of the senior lamas, especially the heads of the various departments, objected strongly to our building a seminary largely to benefit monks from a distance and spending capital in this way. So I invited them to a midday meal and told them how important Jamgön Kongtrül, Gyalwa Karmapa and myself considered the seminary to be in preserving our Buddhist way of life. I added: 'Even if the Communists destroy the whole place, the seeds of knowledge in our hearts cannot be destroyed. Even if we build today and our building is torn down tomorrow, I will not regret the spending. It would be a greater regret if we hoarded and what we had hoarded was taken from us without any progress having been made in the spiritual understanding of our people. The tenth Trungpa Tulku planned to enlarge the seminary and I am only fulfilling his wishes.' Since I was his incarnation, love for me overcame the objections of all but a small minority, and work was soon started on the new building.

Our studies at the seminary in the *Varshika Vihara* at Düdtsi-til continued steadily. Khenpo Gangshar told me that I must take a teacher's course of training to enable me to be a tutor in metaphysical studies and also to give instruction in meditation. I began to teach, and he examined my pupils to see if they had really understood. Sometimes I had to teach in front of him and though I knew my subject I found this embarrassing; at the beginning I was very nervous, but later on he found less to correct and this gave me confidence.

I was now working with Khenpo Gangshar's help on the comparative study of the different schools of Buddhism and I found more than adequate material for these researches in our main library. Jamgön Kongtrül had often told me that we must make great efforts to overcome any divisions among the followers of Buddhism and how very important this was at the present time, if we hoped to protect ourselves from the destructive influences of materialism and Communism.

Although the Chinese menace seemed to be getting stronger, we went on with rebuilding our seminary. I called in silversmiths and goldsmiths and indicated the images to be made, and also arranged a meeting with the master artists, craftsmen and carpenters. The artists mostly came from the Gabri school, the gold and silversmiths from Mensar. We discussed the designs for the new frescoes and the painting of the ceiling, pillars and furniture. The particular methods of the Mensar school were used for moulding the images which were to be plated with gold.

We had to provide the workers with food and accommodation and once a fortnight every man received a present. Wages were given on completion of the work and often took the form of goods rather than cash: mostly domestic animals were given, sometimes amounting to as much as five hundred beasts, including horses, mules, yaks and *dris*. Such things as brocade, wool, furs, leather or grain were also given in payment. Supervising the builders with my secretary for at least two hours a day kept me away from work in the seminary.

By the New Year 1958 the building was finished and the golden roof of our new assembly hall erected. The monks were so proud and elated about it all that they seemed unaware of a possible Chinese menace; for myself, I could not but feel apprehensive.

The New Year celebrations with Khenpo Gangshar was a particularly wonderful occasion. We created a new ceremony for it in the assembly hall of the monastery which was attended by all the monks, and held religious debates and lectures.

Throughout 1957 at Surmang, Chinese officials had been constantly coming and going, spying out the land. Now that the Resistance party of West Derge had put guards on the border, the Communists suspected us of helping them, for both monasteries were in very strategic positions. About a month after the New Year some twenty men of the Chinese military intelligence came to Düdtsi-til. As had been done previously, we arranged for their accommodation at a nearby monastery. However, on further news coming through of the revolt in West Derge, the Communists insisted on being accommodated in Düdtsi-til. They were not pleased with the rooms we gave them and early one morning they actually came to my private residence in the old fort and billeted themselves in one of the halls. I was there alone with Khenpo Gangshar when my personal attendant rushed in almost speechless; all he could utter in his panic was 'they have invaded us', and he was hardly able to explain what had happened. Looking through the window, I saw the Chinese dismounting and unsaddling their horses; others had already taken their baggage into the courtyard. My attendant insisted that we must leave while there was still time. I did my best to calm him and told him not to show any fear. My secretary, who lived in a nearby house, then arrived. When we told him what was happening, he said it might not after all mean such complete disaster and advised us to stay where we were.

At breakfast time word came from the chief Chinese official to say that he would like to see me, so I went down. He presented me with a roll of yellow silk and a Tibetan translation of a book by Mao-Tse-tung. His interpreter said that they had come to guard the place and help us. He apologized for having intruded on my private residence, but owing to its strategic position it was essential to station troops there. He begged me to carry on with our activities and thanked me for my hospitality. As their host I gave them butter and other food-stuffs. I asked him to pay no attention to my monks who would be passing through the courtyards engaged simply on their religious duties; should they hear chanting or discussions in the night, they should not feel disturbed, for this was part of our everyday routine.

The Chinese official appeared to be smiling all the time and was very courteous. Each night the soldiers kept guard on the gate with a machine gun. I was often called upon to go down and talk to them through an interpreter. At first my secretary used to accompany me, but afterwards it seemed easier to go alone. The officers continually told me that China was the largest nation in the world and had the greatest military strength; their battleships were so enormous that horse races were held on their decks, and their aeroplanes flew with such speed that they could just scoop up any enemy soldiers. I noticed on these visits that the head official and his subordinates were Chinese, but the soldiers seemed to be Tibetans. The explanation for this was that when the Chinese took over our province they got hold of many of the Tibetan young people and took them on as servants or students; later they conscripted them into the army, although they claimed that they had joined as volunteers. I found these soldiers much more respectful and less noisy than I expected.

The party stayed quietly in the fort for about two months, but if I left to pay a distant visit, particularly in the direction of the border, I was very closely interrogated on my return.

Since for some time Khenpo Gangshar had not been feeling well and needed a change, I went with him to the holy Mt Doti Gangkar, in the caves of which Guru Padmasambhava used to meditate, and where lamas from Surmang often went for retreat. It is a very high mountain with two beautiful lakes at its foot; in one the water is green, and in the other, black. Its crest is covered in snow. The legend goes that in the Golden Age this snow never melted and shone like a diamond. In the following age it was like an onyx in which light and darkness are mixed. In the third age, however, it was to become like iron; everything would be dark and our time in Tibet would be over. When we reached the top of the mountain we found that the snow fields were melting and that great expanses of dark rock were showing.

All this made a deep impression on Khenpo Gangshar. The legend of the three ages seemed to indicate to him how urgent it was to prepare for the dark period before us; there was so much to be taught in so short a space of time. He quickly recovered his health and felt all the more inspired to continue his teaching at Surmang.

On our return, we found that the Chinese had quitted my residence. Khenpo Gangshar now decided that we should no longer give lessons exclusively to the monks who attended the seminary; the more immediate need was to teach all the people. In the autumn he held a large meeting in our assembly hall. He talked all day from seven in the morning till six at night with only a two hour break. He explained in simple terms how necessary it was to realize the times we had reached. We might no longer be allowed to perform our rituals, but this would not destroy the fundamental teaching that the Buddha had given us, nor the integrity of the Tibetan people. He quoted 'Cease to do evil, do what is good, purify your minds' that is the Buddha's teaching. We must act in the right way and be aware of ourselves. We must build our temples within ourselves. All the teachings of the Buddha, from the first, on the Truth of Suffering, to the last, on Enlightenment must be integrated and brought together in practise. Khenpo Gangshar then told them how to practise awareness and compassion. He encouraged everyone to take the vow not to kill or harm and, in order to be able to carry out this intention, to learn to control himself before acting.

After this, Khenpo Gangshar held a second meeting, this time for all the monks. He told them that they must give more help to the lay people who had no opportunity to study. The divisions between the different schools must be abandoned. They must give the fundamental training on how to take refuge in the *Buddha*, the *Dharma* and the *Sangha* and on how to develop the four "divine stations", namely loving kindness, spiritual joy, compassion and equanimity. Concerning equanimity, he stressed that human rights and non-violence were particularly important in the anxious times that we were going through. He considered that they should follow the system of the Kadampas whose teaching specializes in the means for developing loving kindness (*maitri*). The doctrine of loving kindness should be combined with that of *Mahamudra* and *Atiyana*; these two are the method of meditation on the ultimate teaching of the Buddha.

Khenpo Gangshar visited many of our hermits who had taken vows to remain in seclusion, telling them that they must experience the shock of re-entering the world and learn how to retreat within themselves. He brought them back to Düdtsi-til. Some of the monks at Namgyal-tse did not approve of this and wanted to come and debate on the subject with him, which request he gladly complied with. They put forward their case quoting from the Scriptures. Khenpo Gangshar, however, told them that theories are insufficient without practise, and asked them to stay and help the many people attending the monastery. Later, one of these lamas became his devoted disciple. People came from all parts of the district to hear the *Khenpo*. He arranged that the senior lamas and *tulkus* should mix with the community and taught that no man should consider himself to be above his fellow. He himself saw and gave practical instruction to those who asked for help. Soon, however, the audiences became so large that it was impossible for a single man to deal with them, so he divided them into groups, and arranged for some of us to give talks which he superintended. This was very good training for us and particularly helpful to me.

Although I was still rather weak in medical studies and the mathematics of cosmology which includes calculating the calendar, my general studies were now completed and it was time for me to take my degree of *kyorpön* (tutor). So for three months I withdrew from all other activities and revised my studies with the help of Khenpo Gangshar who would sometimes come in the afternoons to answer any questions I had to put.

My examination and that of two other monks took place on an auspicious day in the grounds outside the monastery which had been fenced off for public lectures, and it was attended by the neighbouring *khenpos*, *kyorpöns* and senior lamas. A central throne was placed at the end of the field on which Khenpo Gangshar sat, with four *kyorpöns* sitting in line with him. Two rows of seats ran at right angles to these, the candidates being in front so as to be ready, when their turn came, to stand before Khenpo Gangshar. The rest of the rows was filled with the attending scholar monks and *kyorpöns*. These took an active part in the examination which was in the form of a dialectical discussion: the candidate was first required to answer any question the monks shot at him, then in a return attack to put his own question to the scholars. I am told that similar practices prevailed in Christian monasteries during the Middle Ages. The examination lasted for three days; the first was the most difficult. Each day food and tea were offered to all those attending. I was given the degree of *kyorpön*, equivalent to a doctor's degree in England, and since I had already been specially trained in lecturing and teaching I also received the degree of *khenpo* (master of studies).

CHAPTER ELEVEN

LONELY VOCATION

WHILE the examination was going on more bad news came from Derge, almost every monastery had been destroyed there and the lamas had received brutal treatment. The people were more and more enraged at the attacks upon religion and a great number of peasants, both men and women, were joining together to fight the Communists. In the face of this almost universal attack the Chinese, as an act of appeasement, had released the few lamas who were still alive. We heard rumours that although Sechen Monastery had been destroyed, some of the senior lamas had not been killed.

Khenpo Gangshar waited till after the examination to tell us that since Jamgön Kongtrül was no longer at Sechen, he felt he must go back himself to see if he could help in any way. We asked him if he could not wait until the weather became warmer, for winter was now approaching; however, he thought this was an emergency which should be dealt with immediately. He said it might be possible to talk to the Communists and get them to understand the religious ideal of non-violence.

Pupils were now flocking to the seminary in such numbers that the Chinese became suspicious and wanted to know what we were up to. They knew that Khenpo Gangshar was connected with Jamgön Kongtrül and suspected that he must also not agree with the Communist regime. Ever since the Chinese had occupied the forest area near Surmang, they had been sending officials from Jyekundo to supervise the trade in timber which they had taken over in 1953 to the financial loss of the Tibetans. Now an official arrived ostensibly on the same work, but we were aware that the reason for his being with us was to spy on Khenpo Gangshar. We told our *khenpo* about it and suggested that it might be dangerous to continue our lectures. His reaction was unexpected; he said that he was delighted to have the opportunity to speak to this man about the doctrine of non-violence which would end all suffering. This he did, and also told him he would like to have further contact with Chinese officials. The spy, who was not a very high ranking person, returned to Nangchen Gar, the Chinese headquarters and one of the larger towns of the province. Soon after, Khenpo Gangshar received an official letter saying that the Communists appreciated his ideas and if he could succeed in explaining them to the Tibetan people, they would agree to all he said. They sent him a present of some rolls of silk.

After considering the matter for some days Khenpo Gangshar decided to leave Surmang to meet the officials in Jyekundo. He wanted me and some of his disciples to accompany him, and added that these were not the times for pomp and that on such a mission we should all go very humbly on foot. His pupils and the newly arrived students were very upset as they all held him in great devotion; since his arrival, a greater spirit of virtue and a wider understanding had permeated the whole monastery. Though we felt anxious for his safety we could not influence him, so the party consisting of Khenpo Gangshar, myself, and several senior lamas and lay principles left for Jyekundo. When we reached the town we met the Chinese officials and discussed the matter for about a week. Khenpo Gangshar knew that if his doctrine of non-violence was not accepted, there would be no hope of preventing terrible bloodshed. The Communist officials merely offered to report the conversation to the authorities in China; they said this doctrine only expressed the point of view of Buddhism.

While in Jyekundo Khenpo Gangshar lectured in the town to Tibetans. He was invited by the local monastery to their seminary where some of the younger students were anxious to hold a debate on his ideas. He pointed out to them that philosophical clichés did not go very far unless they were also lived. There was a discussion on loving kindness and he asked them its meaning. The young monks quoted from the scriptures, but he replied 'Quotation is no use in itself, we can all repeat scripture by heart. You must demonstrate loving kindness by your actions.'

Talking to the Tibetans in the town, he found that many of them were anxious to fight the Communists. He pointed out how very unwise it would be to attempt this, since being practically unarmed they would have no chance of success; he emphasized this both in his lectures and when giving individual instruction.

Our monks took the baggage to the ferry on the Dri-chu, and we left Jyekundo on foot to go to Gyana-mani, a village three miles away where there is a celebrated group of '*mani* stones'. The Sakya abbot Chögyal-phagpa had the foundations laid for them when he returned from a visit to China in the thirteenth century. These stones cover several acres, it took us half an hour to walk all round them. Many *mantras* and *sutras* have been carved on them besides the complete *Kagyur*, the collection of basic scriptures which in manuscript fills one hundred and eight volumes. Several temples have been built on the site, one of recent date being two storeys high. The huge 'prayer wheel' in the middle reached to the roof and was about forty feet in circumference; it needed six or seven people to turn it. Khenpo Gangshar composed some new hymns as he led us round these sacred stones, periodically stopping to give a talk on their symbolism.

We stayed two days at Gyana-mani from where the Chinese arranged for a lorry to take us to the Dri-chu. We had never travelled by motor transport before and as we got into the lorry Khenpo Gangshar noticed how excited I was at the prospect of this new experience. He turned to me and said 'You know how strong material forces are: now you are having one of your first direct encounters with them. Study what you are; don't lose yourself; if you simply get excited about the journey, you will never find out what we are really up against.'

Sechen was some seven days' journey from the ferry crossing where our baggage was waiting for us. The first four days I walked along in Khenpo Gangshar's company but did not feel strong enough to go all the way on foot, so I was allowed to ride with the baggage. We stopped at several monasteries, including Seshü, a large one attached to the Gelug Order, to which the Dalai Lama also belongs. I had always wanted to make a pilgrimage to study in the leading monasteries of the different schools and now that I had the *kyorpön* and *khenpo* degrees it would be easy to make more advanced studies of their particular lines of thought. Seshü was a monastery I had particularly wanted to visit.

Since the abbot was still a child, Khenpo Gangshar had a talk with the regent who was very interested in his teaching on non-violence as it agreed with his own scholarly point of view. He took us round the monastery, and showed us the Buddha image which had been given to Tsongkhapa, the founder of the Gelug school on his ordination; this had been made quite small so that he could always carry it with him. It had been preserved at Seshü and treated with the greatest veneration; one felt an atmosphere of holiness surrounding it. The assembly hall held three thousand monks sitting very close together, and the noise of the chanting from so great a number was tremendous. In the Gelug monasteries the study of logic plays an important part; after listening to lectures the monks congregate in the courtyard where they form debating groups according to the ages of the participants which can be from eight years upwards; we were able to observe this method. When a monk put his question to another in the group, he stood up, stamped his foot and clapped his hands to mark his points. When he succeeded, he swung his rosary from arm to arm, if defeated he swung it over his head. The monk questioned would return the attack sitting down. So the courtyard was extremely noisy and lively.

Unfortunately we could not stay for long at Seshü, and we resumed our journey in very cold weather, for the district lay at a high altitude; its farming highlanders live in tents.

When we were a day's journey from Sechen we were told that after all the monastery had not been badly damaged and that some of the lamas were then visiting a monastery close to our route. We sent them a message and they came to meet us at Phu-khung. They told us how the Communists had shut them up in one of the shrine rooms hand-cuffed in such a way that they were unable to move and had given them hardly anything to eat or drink. The Communists had made a thorough search, but found nothing, and after angry expostulations from the villagers they had released the lamas and left the monastery. The monks were allowed to stay on, though the Chinese camped all around, and the lamas had to get permission from them every time they went outside the immediate area. Other neighbouring monasteries had been completely destroyed, and the lamas were very upset by this. They did not want to leave Sechen, but feared what might still happen. They discussed all this with Khenpo Gangshar. He told them that conditions were unlikely to improve and that he could hold out little hope of his being able to persuade the Chinese to accept the Buddha's teaching of non-violence. He was afraid there would be no safety in any part of Tibet, but did not know how a whole group of monks could keep together anywhere outside.

7 *Image of Milarepa which belonged to Gampopa. A
Surmang treasure*

*e seals of the Trungpa Tulkus. The large ivory seal was offered to the fifth Trungpa by the
peror of China*

Head-dress of a Khampa woman

8

A Khampa nomad peasant

The Dalai Lama's stables at Lhasa

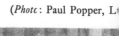

Gangshar now advised me to go back to Surmang to continue our common work, but since his pleas with the Chinese officials had not seemed very successful, I was afraid that it would be dangerous for him to remain in Derge. We had only three more days together, during which he gave me his last teachings on meditation and some other general instructions; then I had to leave. I had had to part from my *guru* Jamgön Kongtrül and now my last support, the *guru* to whom he had passed me on, was to be taken from me. I was alone.

When my monks and I returned to Surmang we found everything apparently going well at the seminary and everyone was anxious to hear what Khenpo Gangshar had been able to accomplish. During my absence the Communists had summoned my secretary to a conference. They told him that our monastery must pay fifty thousand Chinese silver dollars in taxes and that all Indian and European goods must be handed over to them and no further ones obtained; these included such things as wrist watches and also any photographs of the Dalai Lama which had been taken in India. They also said that in future I must attend the conferences in person.

It was now the end of 1958. We held our annual twelve day devotional celebration to dispel past evils and to bring us new spiritual life in the forthcoming year. It was a joyous time and I did not mind the hard work which this entailed.

I had often spent the New Year festival very quietly at our retreat centre and this year I did the same. I found the lamas there a little disturbed by the fact that they had broken their vows of remaining in seclusion as Khenpo Gangshar had enjoined. However they seemed to have advanced spiritually both through their contact with the Khenpo and other people. I explained to them that going out of their centre was not really against their vows, but part of their training, which had great meaning.

Returning to the monastery after the New Year, I spent several days discussing the situation with Rölpa-dorje Rinpoche, my regent abbot of Düdtsi-til. He seemed suddenly this year to have grown much older, and was very thoughtful. He said to me 'It seems that the Chinese are becoming more and more aggressive, and I know how brutal the Russian Communists were in Mongolia, destroying all the monasteries. Perhaps an old man like myself could escape through death; my health is no longer good, but I feel very anxious for the younger generation. If you can save yourselves, and I am thinking especially of you, the eleventh Trungpa Tulku who have received so much instruction and training, it would be worthwhile. For myself, I feel I should not leave the monastery without consulting Gyalwa Karmapa as the head of our whole monastic confraternity. As the Chinese attitude towards His Holiness the Dalai Lama and its government is still respectful, we have not lost hope that he will be able to restore order and protect the *Dharma*.'

I was now nineteen according to the European solar calendar, but by the Tibetan which dates from birth by the number of lunar months, I was considered to be twenty. Though I had been given the degree of *khenpo*, I still needed to be fully ordained as a *bhikshu*. Since I was now old enough I was able to request my regent abbot and four other *bhikshus* to ordain me; as I had already studied the canon of monastic discipline (*Vinaya*) they agreed that the ordination could take place. I was given the begging bowl which had belonged to the tenth Trungpa Tulku and the yellow robe of a *bhikshu*. I had to take two hundred and fifty vows, some of which I had already made as a novice (*shramanera*). My ordination took place at the altar in front of the image of the Buddha. This qualified me to conduct the rite of *Sojong* to restore virtue and bring purification from wrong doing which takes place on full moon and new moon days; but above all I felt a sense of maturity as a fully prepared member of the Sangha.

Rölpa-dorje Rinpoche now left on a tour to visit his devotees in and around Jyekundo and I took charge of the seminary as its *khenpo*. I still felt inexperienced beside Khenpo Zangden and the *kyorpöns* who had spent many more years than I at their studies. However, my secretary and the older disciples of my predecessor were satisfied, and I felt that I was following in the tenth Trungpa Tulku's footsteps. As I sat on Khenpo Gangshar's throne, I had a deep sense of all he had given us; more and more I felt the need of his presence and of a wider knowledge of the *Dharma*. The needs of the local people often required my presence to give teaching or to help the sick and the dying. As this meant leaving the monastery at all hours nearly every day, I realized that I must have an assistant *khenpo* who could give more individual attention to the students, and we agreed to ask Khenpo Zangden to fill this post; he also took over much of the lecturing. We were now studying 'The Ornament of Precious Liberation' (*Tharpa-rinpoche-gyan*) by Chöje Gampopa.

The sister of the tenth Trungpa Tulku, who had looked after the dairy at Düdtsi-til had died, and my mother now took charge. This made her very happy as she loved animals, but it also involved looking after the herdsmen and arranging about their wages. After a time she found this too much for her and gradually handed over the work to an assistant. When I was living in my own residence outside the monastery she was able to stay with me and do my cooking. This was a great happiness for both of us.

In the spring I received an invitation from the neighbouring province of Chamdo, some three days' journey from Surmang, to come and lecture, for many of the people there were anxious to hear more of Khenpo Gangshar Rinpoche's teachings. After a week there, a messenger came from our monastery to tell me that Rölpa-dorje was ill; immediately afterwards a second messenger arrived to say that he was dying. I at once returned to Düdtsi-til, travelling day and night without stopping. My monks were waiting for me and some forty of us went together to the place where we now knew he had died.

In fact from the start of his tour Rölpa-dorje had not felt well, and he eventually contracted severe influenza. He accepted that this was to be his last illness and chose to be taken to a village near the Sakya monastery of Thalung. When its abbot Deshung Rinpoche heard where he was, he brought him to Thalung itself, where he died a week later. Deshung Rinpoche, who is still alive in America, is a very kind as well as a learned man; he was a disciple of Ga Ngawang-legpa the mystical teacher of the Sakya School and also of the tenth Trungpa Tulku. When Rölpa-dorje was dying he stayed at his bed-side to the end asking him how his wishes could be fulfilled and if there was anything which could be done to lengthen his life. Rölpa-dorje replied that his work was finished and his duty done. For a few days he seemed to be recovering; one morning he was thought to be so much better that he could even walk. He asked the abbot to take down his will, saying that he wished to be re-born in Tsa, the birth-place of Milarepa. The abbot asked him who his future parents would be. He said he would rather leave that for Gyalwa Karmapa to discover. Deshung Rinpoche found it difficult to tell his monks this news, for they all expected his recovery; however, the senior monk of the party had to be told. Very early next morning Rölpa-dorje threw off his coverings and sat up in the *Vajra* position. He asked his monks to read his daily manual of devotions. As they finished, he had difficulty in breathing and when they held him up he said 'You don't need to help me; I can look after myself.' At that moment his earthly wishes ceased.

When our party reached Thalung the day after his death we immediately performed a short rite. I gave a talk about all he had done for us, his great kindness, and the many things he had given us, and we finished with meditation. We arranged to have his body cremated at Thalung on the fifth day after his death, for it had been his express wish that this should be done wherever he died. There was a rule that the monk who put the torch to the funeral pyre must be one who had never received teaching from the deceased. We had difficulty in finding such a person but eventually a novice who served in the kitchen was chosen. We took the ashes back with us to Surmang, being stopped on the way by many weeping devotees who wished to pay their last respects to his memory.

Our return led through Jyekundo where we were given further news of the Communists. For the last month all the Chinese officials, including the governor, had gone round the streets for two hours every morning to shovel up rubbish, dirt and even human excrement; it was considered to be good physical exercise, as well as an example to the Tibetans. I myself met the governor on the road with his shovel, cleaning up the river bank which people had used as a latrine. After we had greeted one another, our party stopped in front of the municipal building where there was a guard, and as the officials moved off, one of the guard near whom I was standing turned to me saying, 'Please give me your blessing and a sacred protective cord.' I asked him if he really meant this. 'Yes,' he said 'I have been with the Chinese ever since they entered Tibet, but more and more I feel faith in Buddhism.' I was moved; the young man could not have been out of his teens.

On our return to Surmang we held the requiem services for Rölpa-dorje and during this time I had many unforgettable talks with Garwang Rinpoche and my monks while planning various improvements for both monasteries. I little knew that this would be the last time that we would all be together at Düdtsi-til.

The monks of Kyere, a small monastery under the control of the King of Lhathog, now sent me a request to officiate at the enthronement of my young brother Tamchö-tenphel, the incarnation of their abbot. As I left Düdtsi-til, a storm was raging and fewer people than usual came to bid me goodbye, however, my mother was among those who came. I was feeling heavy-hearted at leaving my monastery; almost as if I had a premonition that I would never return. The ceremony at Kyere was a beautiful one; afterwards I was asked by the neighbouring laity to give lectures and perform rites. I then travelled further, visiting many other monasteries and villages and giving talks, mainly on the method which Khenpo Gangshar had taught. We passed several holy mountains and I was able to meditate in their caves. As we travelled, I was asked to organize retreats for many of the people in the district. These lasted sixteen or more days, during which we fasted, chanted and performed religious devotions. The fasting was severe; on the first day, no nourishment was permitted after noon, and we were only allowed to speak during a short recreation period. The following day neither food nor drink could be taken and, except for chanting, absolute silence was kept. This two day sequence continued for the length of the retreat. Those attending were lay people who adhered strictly to the Eight Precepts for the period.

The Eight Precepts are: not to destroy life, not to take that which is not given, not to tell lies, to abstain from illicit sexual intercourse and from intoxicating liquors, then not to eat food after noon, not to wear garlands or use perfume and not to sleep on a raised bed. Evidently not to take life, nor to steal or utter falsehoods, to abstain from unlawful sexual intercourse and from intoxicating liquors should be the rule of life for all Buddhists. However, if people are unable to keep to the discipline of all these, there is a simpler form that they may take, which is to make a vow to adhere strictly to one or other chosen precept for a given time, and to make an effort to adhere to the others as far as possible.

Being in the neighbourhood, I took the opportunity to visit the king of Lhathog. I found that his ministers were anxious for the king's young son to be enthroned in place of his father and they wished me to conduct the ceremony. At times, the reigning king's state of mind rendered him incapable of carrying out the responsibilities of government, hence his wish to abdicate in favour of his son. His early life had been difficult; being the youngest of four brothers, he was brought up in a monastery as he was the incarnation of a lama. However, his three brothers all died young and in order to ensure the succession he had been taken from the monastery and married to his brother's widow. This sudden change from the austerity of monastic training to the pleasures of the palace had upset his attitude towards life. This is an example of what often occurs in Tibet among incarnate lamas who have for any reason abandoned their vocation: some have died suddenly, while others seem to lose their purpose in life and become mentally deranged, or else their whole personality changes.

The ceremony of the young king's enthronement was largely secular, and as a spectacle it was very impressive. The participants wore strange traditional costumes which dated from the pre-Buddhist period.

The young king's grandfather had been a devoted disciple of the tenth Trungpa Tulku and was a very scholarly and spiritual man. He built several centres for meditation and teaching, but what made him especially famous in his day was the fact that he had collected the great library and installed a printing press. His three elder sons before their deaths had begun to build a nearby monastery for the Karma-ka-gyü school which was still under construction when I was there.

As I was about to leave Lhathog, I received an invitation from Khamtrül Rinpoche, the supreme abbot of Khampa-gar monastery, near Lhathog. He was the head of the Drugpa-ka-gyü school which had over two hundred monasteries in East Tibet. At the same time I was asked to visit Drölma-Lhakhang and Yag monasteries, both in the south west of Chamdo province. Messengers from these two places had been sent to Surmang, so there had been a delay in their reaching me. They arrived on a day when we were all in silent retreat, and this gave me a little time to consider what I should do. A system of divination called *tagpa* is used in Tibet on such occasions. A rosary is held in the hand, and after meditation and the recitation of a *mantra*, the beads are divided at random. Under the power of the particular meditation and *mantra*, and according to the number and conjunction of the separated portions of the beads, a result is indicated. I followed this method, and it appeared that I should visit Drölma Lhakhang; I knew that in these difficult times they were in great need of religious instruction and I was anxious to see my old friends who so earnestly begged me to go to them. I sent a messenger to Surmang to tell them of my plans.

I had intended to go back to Düdtsi-til to make preparations for my journey but the following day a messenger came to tell me that several Chinese officials had arrived at Surmang and wanted to count the entire number of the monks, for they disbelieved what we had told them. They were saying that I had purposely been hidden, and this was causing suspicion. The officials insisted that I should be brought to them. My secretary and all the monks felt that I must certainly return, as they did not want Surmang to be the cause of trouble in the area.

It was evident that the Communists were about to impose further restrictions and to make increasing demands upon Surmang; the monks even suspected that they might intend to arrest me. I talked the matter over with my fellow monks who were in a state of panic and, though ready to offer suggestions, they would not commit themselves to any plan: the decision rested solely with me.

Then another messenger arrived from Surmang to say that the Communists were no longer so insistent on my immediate return and that apparently they did not intend to organize their system of collective labour for another year. Nevertheless it was beginning to look as if the time might come for us to evacuate Surmang and take refuge in Central Tibet. Needing time to meditate before arriving at a decision, I went for a fortnight to a cave near Kyere with Genchung Lama, a disciple of the tenth Trungpa Tulku who came to Düdtsi-til to give teaching when I was seven years old. At night we slept in the cave, which was about ten yards deep and during the daytime we sat at the entrance where there was a small platform. At its edge, a precipice dropped sheer down to the valley. Between spells of meditating we talked together, looking out over the landscape, and in spite of many anxious forebodings this was for us both a time of strange happiness. We spoke about the thoughts that had come to us in our meditations and shared reminiscences of some of the events in our lives and of meeting our respective *gurus*. I had two rather disturbing dreams. In the first I was standing on a hill above Düdtsi-til which was hidden in a cloud of dark grey smoke except for the gilded *serto* on the roof. In the other I saw Communists in their military uniform performing a Buddhist rite in our main assembly hall. Nevertheless I decided that there would still be time for me to visit Drölma Lhakhang and return to my own monastery before it was too late. So I sent for the necessary transport and provisions for the proposed journey. Our acting bursar Yönten brought these a fortnight later, and he told me that the Communists had left Surmang, but that in the neighbouring province of West Derge they had looted and destroyed many monasteries; he added that great numbers of refugees were passing our way.

The secretary of Kyere wanted to come with us to Drölma Lhakhang, but I thought he should stay in charge of my young brother's monastery, in case an escape should be necessary. We started out on an auspicious day. According to custom, the monks of Kyere escorted us for the first few miles, and among those who saw us off were many lay devotees; we all felt deeply moved. My little brother was particularly unhappy, though he tried to keep back his tears. The correct farewell ceremony is that the escort stand in a group, while their leader waves a white scarf in a circular move-ment and gives a long whistle running down the scale. He is followed by all the group doing the same. This means 'Come back again'. The party who are leaving ride round in a circle in single file and repeat this three times.

The reader will remember that before leaving Lhathog I had received an invitation from Khampa-gar Monastery as well as the one from Drölma Lhakhang. The former now lay on our route, and we were able to pay a short visit there. I was delighted to be with Khamtrül Rinpoche again, for we had met four years before at Chentze Rinpoche's monastery. I was given a warm welcome with musicians playing on the roof. The monastery had been founded in the thirteenth century and was a leading one with some three hundred monks. All the supreme abbots had been known as great scholars and teachers. One in particular had been a renowned poet and his commentaries on the art of poetry, known as *Khamdrel* were studied in all Tibetan schools. The present incarnation (the eighth) is a scholar and an artist of the new Mendri school. I found that he was building a large seminary, all the paintings, images and decoration of which had been designed by himself. He was doing on a larger scale what I had done at Düdtsi-til and we had many inter-ests in common. Both he and his father were known for the eccentric way in which they treated their subordinates. For instance when a hall was being built they gave no indication of what the next stage was going to be, so the builders never worked to any plan, but from moment to moment as directed. When starting on a journey they did not tell their party where they were going or how long it would take. Life was never dull in their company.

Wishing to have some guidance on his future, Khamtrül Rinpoche wanted me to join in an advanced form of divination called *prasena*, which requires several days' preparation, so we left his monastery together for a nearby retreat centre where we pitched our tent in a circle of juniper and willow bushes. Khamtrül Rinpoche did not tell his monks why he was going into retreat, and they found this very strange. After devotional meditation, the *prasena* indicated that he should leave his monastery, but that his final destination should be India, not Central Tibet. It gave clear cut directions about the length of time that he should stay in Tibet, the difficulties he would encounter, and the ultimate date of his arrival in India. He wanted me to accompany him, but I felt it was essential for me to go to Drölma Lhakhang, where we were already expected.

On resuming our journey we stopped at Jigme Rinpoche's monastery, and he joined our party. He made arrangements for me and himself, with two attendants, to travel by mail lorry. The rest of the monks were to follow with the baggage. In the rear compartment of the lorry there were three Communist soldiers fully armed with rifles and a tommy gun; the driver also had a rifle. There had been spasmodic fighting with the Resistance on this road, so it was considered to be a danger zone. As we switch-backed on the very bad surface by hairpin bends over several mountain ranges both our luggage and ourselves were badly bumped about and my two attendants felt very sick. Each time we reached a crest the soldiers became very apprehensive about guerillas. On one mountain we passed a mail lorry which had broken down; its occupants had had to sleep in it and they told us of their terror when they had heard a gun in the night. Passing our fellow Tibetans on their horses we could not but think how much happier and more comfortable they were than ourselves.

At Chamdo we stayed with a Tibetan official who was the senior member of the Communist District Committee.

It was a new experience for me to sleep in a modern Chinese house with electric light, but it was only switched on for about four hours each evening. The family treated our party most hospitably. The official was a Buddhist and there was a shrine room in his house. His children had just returned from China for their summer holidays. We had the impression that they had been told not to talk about their school life; they were obviously happy to be back and had immediately changed into their Tibetan clothes and wanted Tibetan food. We thought they might ignore us since we were monks, but they were particularly friendly, coming to chat with us and even asking us to bless them. The youngest boy seemed more ardently Tibetan than the others.

The following day I walked round the town and looked at the new 'people's store'. Shopping was rather a complicated affair. First one asked if one could buy the required commodity and, if this was all right, one was given a ticket which had to be taken to another department to be stamped; finally this had to be taken to yet another department to pay the cashier who would hand over the goods. Armed soldiers were marching about the town and the Tibetans in the neighbouring villages were very uneasy.

After spending two nights at Chamdo we continued our journey in a jeep arranged for by our friend the Tibetan official. Three school boys on holiday from China came with us. They were more talkative than our host's children and told us that they had not been happy. They had found the extremes of heat and cold very disagreeable, and life at school was not at all to their liking. As we passed some of the modern machinery which the Chinese had introduced into Tibet, these boys merely said how tired they were of such things, though our party was intensely interested to see them. We stopped our jeep at Gur-kyim, a town in the area of Tzawa-gang about eight miles from Drölma-Lhakhang. Here the schoolboys got out and enthusiastically changed from their Chinese suits into Tibetan clothes. Jigme Rinpoche and I with my two attendants walked to the house of the head of the district who lived nearby. He had been ill for some time and did not appear, but his wife greeted us. She had expected a large party of monks on horseback and seeing only four of us on foot she immediately thought that there had been some disaster with the Communists and was relieved when we told her that the others were following more slowly on horseback with the baggage on mules. Since her husband's illness she had taken over his work as head of the district and this gave her so much to attend to that she said she would be unable to come to receive further instruction from me, much as she would have liked to do so. So we said goodbye and were lent horses to take us to the monastery.

It was the middle of summer and the country was looking at its best with every kind of flower in bloom, but on the day of our arrival it turned cold with rain and sleet storms. The monastery had prepared a grand ceremonial welcome which was carried out in spite of the weather. Akong Tulku led the procession holding incense sticks, followed by musicians and monks carrying banners, and a monk holding an umbrella walked behind my horse. On arrival I asked Akong Tulku to find two messengers who could be sent to Tzurphu Monastery near Lhasa, with letters to Gyalwa Karmapa, Jangöm Kongtrül of Sechen and Dingo Chentze Rinpoche who were all there together. My letters gave news of the conditions prevailing in East Tibet and of my arrival at Drölma Lhakhang. I asked Gyalwa Karmapa to counsel me how I should act; whether we should continue to maintain Surmang, or escape to Central Tibet. I wanted to know what I must say should anyone ask me to advise them, either at Drölma-Lhakhang or in any other part of East Tibet. I added 'anything you tell me I shall treat in complete confidence; I need your guidance more than ever'.

I expected it would be about three months before I could get any answers, though I told the messengers to make all possible haste.

For the next ten days I gave talks and public and private instruction to both monks and laity and asked Akong Tulku and some of the Lamas to continue the teaching after I had left. There were so many wanting to receive personal instruction that my monks had to keep order among them and arranged for them to queue up. At times the monks in charge lost patience, for which they had to be admonished. As for myself, I got no respite and even had to carry on with teaching while taking my meals.

My bursar Tsethar now arrived at Drölma-Lhakhang. He told me that the monks at Surmang were becoming anxious lest I might leave them and escape to Central Tibet. Although the Communists continued to threaten drastic changes, they had not actually carried them out and the monks had begun to take less notice of their menace. Since everyone hoped that Surmang would be able to carry on as before, they wished me to return as soon as possible, and this was also his own view. He also believed that he was responsible for what I should do. I told him that I had written to Gyalwa Karmapa asking for his advice; I personally felt that there was a very live menace from the Communists. We were continually receiving further news of the destruction of other monasteries in East Tibet and we should take this as a warning. In my talks at Drölma Lhakhang I had stressed the importance of preparing for great changes in Tibet, saying that we might be very near the time when our world, as we had known it, would come to an end. This disturbed the bursar, who continually tried to convince me that all would go on as before.

While we were at Drölma Lhakhang we received an invitation from the abbot of Yag Monastery, Yag Tulku, to visit that place and asking me to give the *wangkur* of 'The Treasury of the Mine of Precious Teaching' (*Rinchen-terdzöd*), the same that I had given at Drölma Lhakhang when I was fourteen years old. On my accepting, many abbots and lamas belonging to the different schools in the neighbourhood assembled at Yag; including the Yag monks, some three hundred were prepared to attend the initiation rite. The preparations were soon made and we began the *wangkur* with Genchung Lama giving the preliminary authorization (the *kalung*).

As I was expected back at Surmang my time was limited, so to hasten matters we began the *wangkur* at five in the morning and went on till late at night. To begin with it was hard work, but after a month I settled down to the routine, and when my attendants became over-tired I arranged for them to work in shifts. Following this programme we completed the *wangkur* in three months.

During these months many devotees came to see me bringing gifts. My bursar became responsible for these and bartered many of them for horses, yaks, *dris* and sheep so that when we returned to Surmang they could be used for the upkeep of the monastery. This distressed me; I felt that some of the gifts should be distributed among the needy and the rest should be converted into money. My bursar was obstinate: he thought my real intention might be to escape without informing Surmang, in which case money and portable possessions would be of greater use to me. Our relations did not improve.

About a month after we had begun the *wangkur* we heard a rumour that a large party of refugees had arrived at Gur-kyim, and the following day I received a confidential message from Khamtrül Rinpoche saying he wished to see me, but did not want anyone else to know about it. It was however necessary for me to tell Yag Tulku, and through him this information, though supposed to be confidential, spread like wild-fire, so that when I interrupted the *wangkur* to make a journey everyone knew where I was going.

When I met Khamtrül Rinpoche he had discarded his monk's robes, and together with his attendants was in ordinary Tibetan dress; and for the first time, I was aware of the effect on the personality of a man of no longer being clothed according to his vocation: it was only too clear that he was in disguise. He told me that he had had to leave his monastery under the pretence that he was going on a short pilgrimage; he had only informed his secretary and a few senior members of the monastic council of what he was about to do, so that the thirty monks who accompanied him knew nothing. They had already gone some distance when he told them that they had left their monastery for good. A renowned *yogin* called Chöle, who was the head of the retreat centre of his monastery, was also in the party as well as two young *tulkus* in whom there were great hopes for the future; their parents had been left behind.

Khamtrül Rinpoche again asked me to join him in using *prasena* to check whether he was taking the right course. The same answer came, namely that he must proceed without hesitation, but difficulties might arise when he crossed the frontier into India. However, if he followed the fixed timetable and did not depart from it, all would be well. Again and again he asked me to go with him, but this was impossible because of the work I had already undertaken. I told him about my own difficulties, to which he replied that I must not allow myself to be held back because of other people. We said goodbye, hoping to meet again in India. The indication that the *prasena* gave was proved to be right when, as he was about to leave Tibet, the Chinese tried to stop him; but in the end he was allowed to proceed with all his baggage. His was the only party from East Tibet which succeeded in taking baggage with them. He is now in India as a refugee.

When I returned to Yag I found that everyone thought my meeting with Khamtrül Rinpoche clearly showed that I too was planning to leave Tibet. They said, if this was so, they would like to come with me. I had to tell them that Khamtrül Rinpoche had left entirely by his own choice and though he had asked me to go with him I did not even know myself what I should do. I added 'You seem to think that I have made a definite plan to leave; this is not so, and I have no intention of trying to save myself while leaving others behind. My bursar is in a complete state of confusion and is very unhappy; I know he also thinks that at my young age I might be influenced by a restless desire for change.' We then went on with the *wangkur*.

Some weeks later Jigme Tulku, who was staying nearby, came to see me. During our journey together from Khampa-gar he had impressed me as being a very spiritual, as well as an extremely intelligent man with a practical turn of mind; he had been a devoted disciple of my predecessor. He thought that I should escape, but a large party could not fail to be noticed by the Communists and he also realized that if the people in the district once knew that I was leaving, they would in their devotion all want to come with me. He said I must understand that a *tulku* like myself who has received such deep spiritual instruction has a duty to pass it on to others, so that I might have to consider escaping, not to save my own life, but to save the spiritual teaching of which I had become the repository. I asked him to talk to my bursar and explain this to him, but he felt that it was still not the right time to do so.

While I was still waiting for replies from Gyalwa Karmapa, Chentze and Jamgön Kongtrül and we were all going on with the *wangkur*, one of my close friends, a lama from Karma Monastery, arrived at Yag. He invited me in a rather unusual manner to visit a place near Karma which lay off the beaten track and where his own very influential family could look after me. He expressed the opinion that the Communists did not intend to take over Tibet permanently, but that at present it was more dangerous to be in an area like Yag which was directly under the control of Chamdo. Surmang and its surrounding district would be much safer. He added that Surmang was expecting my return and hinted that I must not think only of myself.

A few days later another of my friends from Karma made the same suggestions in almost identical words. I realized at once that they had been put up to this by the bursar, convinced as he was that I should come back to my monastery.

As Yag was on one of the main routes to Lhasa, refugees were passing through all the time. They told terrible stories about the Communist advance, with the destruction of the monasteries and villages on the way. Many members of their families had been killed, the people had been questioned under torture and then accused of crimes which they had never committed. Lamas, monks and high officials had suffered particularly in this way. The Communists were attacking further and further westward and had already got beyond Chamdo. My monks were beginning to be concerned for the fate of Surmang. On the other hand, the Resistance forces were very active and increasingly large numbers of people were joining them every day. There was a rumour that the refugees who had already reached Lhasa and its vicinity were forming their own Resistance movement, but as yet we had no authentic news.

In spite of these anxieties, the numbers who attended the *wangkur* did not grow less. The desire to participate seemed to have increased especially among the older people; the younger ones were, however, less able to concentrate on the teaching day after day and it was not surprising that some of those attending the rites were overcome with sleep; it was therefore arranged that they should sit near their elders who would nudge them in case they began to doze. The monk in charge of discipline, the *gekö*, was on duty all the time, but his supervision was little needed, as there was good behaviour throughout.

The *wangkur* took place in the assembly hall. The teacher's throne was in the centre with the altar facing towards it but with a clear space between, where the servers could pace along. The altar, which was about twelve feet square, was disposed in three tiers on which the various symbolic objects could be arranged to form a *mandala* according to the four directions of space. A vase of pure water marks the eastern quarter with a blue scarf tied round it; this is the vase of Akshobhya Buddha the Imperturbable One, and the water symbolizes purification from the strife of wrath; the peace it brings fills the pupil with Gnosis (*jnāna*). A crown with a yellow scarf marks the south; this is the crown of Ratnasambhava Buddha, the Jewel Born; it symbolizes equanimity and the victory over selfishness. The *vajra* on the west, tied with a red scarf, symbolizes Amitabha Buddha, Boundless Light, and means discrimination, bringing compassion and freedom from desire. The bell on the north tied with a green scarf is that of Amoghasiddhi Buddha, it symbolizes the achievement of spiritual action and overcomes all envy. In the centre a bell and *vajra* are placed, tied together with a white scarf in the shape of a cross; these appertain to Vairochana Buddha, the Luminous One and symbolize the Womb of Dharma, that overcomes confusion and ignorance.

Each separate *mandala* is connected with a specific initiation. The rites were performed in order, and before each began the participants formally requested the teacher to conduct it. Each rite went through four stages; the first three corresponded to the body, speech and mind, and the fourth went beyond symbol. Usually at the end of the ritual the *wangkur* of a *Dorje-lobpön* gave the pupil authority to teach. It consisted in handing over to him a drum, conch-shell, throne and the banner of the Dharma. Some of the *wangkurs* lasted several days, others for as short a time as ten minutes.

After giving one of these longer ones I had to give eleven or twelve of the lesser *wangkurs*. Each entailed a complicated arrangement of the objects on the altar; this was the responsibility of the *chöpön* or 'server of the rites', with his assistant. Yet another elderly monk was needed to read through the forthcoming *wangkur* on the day before the rite was celebrated, so that he could instruct the *chöpön* when and how the symbolic objects were to be arranged, since each *mandala* required the objects to be placed in different positions on the two higher tiers while the offerings were laid out on the bottom tier. When the *wangkur* was given, the *chöpön* had to bring the objects from the shrine to the teacher and afterwards to return them to their places. He had to distribute water symbolizing spiritual purification, and grains of barley as a symbol of offering; it was also his duty to swing censers, so he was on his feet all day long. Our *chöpön* at Yag was an old man and he became extremely exhausted, but there was no-one to replace him. This *wangkur* on 'the Treasury of the Mine of Precious Teachings' had been long and complicated. Many of those who had attended wanted me to explain in more simple terms the significance of the spiritual teaching that they had just received. The coming of the Communists had greatly demoralized everyone; all had lost their sense of security, yet their deep faith in the religious way of life remained unshaken. The people needed a personal contact, they wished me to explain why they were so disturbed. They longed to receive more teaching provided it could be brought within their understanding. Since women were not allowed inside the monastery, I arranged for a special hall where the peasant families could come to talk to me. I tried my utmost to give help by impressing on all the necessity for regular meditation. I said they must carry out their duties and daily activities in the spirit of meditation, and if there should be no external *guru*, they must develop the teaching within themselves. I regretted deeply not being able to devote more time to them as my presence was now urgently needed at Surmang.

CHAPTER TWELVE

INTO HIDING

THE day that the *wangkur* of *Rinchen-terdzöd* ended was a momentous one and a special service was held. But it was also the day when the messengers returned with the replies to my letters asking for advice. Gyalwa Karmapa gave me no indication of what should be done. He said it was important for me to carry out what spiritual work I could under present conditions. He was glad to learn that I had been doing well in teaching others and that the *wangkur* I had just given had been so beneficial. Dingo Chentze Rinpoche replied with a poem; in it he said more or less the same thing as Gyalwa Karmapa, but added 'The darkness of the barbarians sinks deeper and deeper into the heart of the country. He who would light a torch must do so from within himself. There is no need for disturbance of mind; the worthwhile minds will win.'

The most distressing verbal news was that Jamgön Kongtrül of Sechen had been captured by the Communists. Gyalwa Karmapa and Chentze Rinpoche were trying to get him released, but I felt pessimistic myself. All three had been together at Gyalwa Karmapa's monastery of Tzurphu. Jamgön Kongtrül Rinpoche never took any thought for his own safety and, knowing this, the two others had been taking especial care of him, even to the neglect of their own work. The situation was becoming increasingly dangerous, and refugees in their hundreds were pouring in from East Tibet, many of them disciples of Jamgön Kongtrül. A particular group of some three hundred people had suffered many casualties on the way, and since they were his ardent devotees they had begged him to come to perform the funeral rites for the dead and to stay for a fortnight and give them spiritual instruction. Gyalwa Karmapa and Chentze Rinpoche tried to dissuade him, but he himself felt he had to go. He said, 'this stage in their lives is a time when they most need spiritual help and it is my duty to give it to them'.

When he had been at this refugee camp for about a week, it was attacked by the Communists. Jamgön Kongtrül told the other refugees not to bother about him. He sent the majority off round one side of a hill, while he and his attendants went the other way. He told them 'What will be, will be; one cannot escape one's *karma*'.

For the first night he was able to find shelter in a small monastery, but the following day the Communists discovered him and took him prisoner. One of his disciples, who held a senior post in Tibet, did all he could to get the lama set free, explaining that he had nothing to do with politics. When Jamgön Kongtrül was interrogated by a Chinese officer he was completely outspoken. It was natural for him to express his own spiritual attitude in his replies. The Communists may well have found his attitude difficult to understand, since it did not conform in the least to their creed, and though his sincerity may have impressed them it failed to obtain his release. During the *wangkur* at Yag I myself had had a certain presentiment of these events for I suddenly got a strong impression of his physical presence; it was almost overwhelming. Also that night I had a vivid dream in which I saw him riding bareback on a white horse carrying volumes of the scriptures and his own reliquary. He spoke to me and rode on by a steep rocky path up the mist shrouded mountain. In the distance, he seemed to drop his books which rolled down the path and fell on me.

Dingo Chentze Rinpoche had opened my letter to Jamgön Kongtrül and sent me a reply saying 'You must not depend too much on others. If all acts are performed according to the Dharma they cannot fail. Gyalwa Karmapa, Jamgön Kongtrül and I have been looking for somewhere on the borders of Tibet and India to establish a community, but so far we have been unsuccessful. Indeed, until there is freedom from the bondage of egotism, there can be no permanent refuge and no abiding place in the world.'

The messengers told me that the relationship between the Dalai Lama's government and the Chinese still appeared to be more or less cordial, but that on their route they had seen a number of military camps, some belonging to the Communists, others to the Resistance volunteers; it had been almost impossible to travel. The Resistance army had been organized by a Khampa, Gönpo-trashi, a wealthy merchant from Lhasa. When the Communists ravaged most of East Tibet including his own property, he closed his business in Lhasa and himself organized a force of guerillas, giving everything he still possessed for their expense and his example was followed by other wealthy men.

The main headquarters of the Resistance was at Tzöna. There was no secrecy about the fact, but the Communists appeared to ignore it. Our messengers who had seen these East Tibetan volunteers in their Khampa uniforms said that they showed great dignity and that they all seemed very young and enthusiastic. They added that in Lhasa itself the inhabitants always showed a marked dislike towards the Chinese.

When the letters were brought to Yag the whole monastery was anxious to know their contents, though some of the monks feared that the news would only be divulged to a chosen few. I felt there was nothing in these letters which need be kept secret. I had been given neither instruction nor advice, so I asked the more senior monks what they now considered would be the best plan for me to follow. They suggested that since my *gurus* had given no indication whether or not I should leave Tibet, they must have thought there was no immediate danger and that all was going to turn out well in the end. It was beyond them even to imagine that the Chinese could take complete control of Tibet and that they would destroy all the monasteries and change the whole Tibetan way of life. The bursar was foremost in this opinion. A few lamas however, including the abbot Yag Tulku, thought that my *gurus* meant me to choose my own path. They were very concerned at the news about Jamgön Kongtrül and considered that I needed to be very careful myself. This was all extremely difficult for me; any decision I might make would affect not only myself, but all the monasteries in the district, particularly those connected with Surmang, as well as the lay population. Everyone looked to me as their authority and were prepared to follow my lead.

Though we had now finished the *wangkur* of *Rinchen terdzöd* the preparation and celebration of the *Vajra-amrit* (elixir for spiritual health) rite was still to follow. However, we delayed these devotional exercises for three days in order to have time to discuss our immediate plans. I had more or less come to the conclusion that I should do as Surmang wished and return there, though a few of my monks agreed with Yag Tulku that I should effect an immediate escape, which would be easier to do from Yag; other monks from Surmang could follow in their own time. I arranged a meeting with our own monks at Yag and asked Yag Tulku and Jigme Rinpoche to attend it. On the first day everyone was non-committal. That evening Jigme Rinpoche came to see me saying that he thought I should not go back to Surmang, though of course the decision rested with me. He said he intended to take a strong line about it on the following day. This he did speaking with great emphasis. My bursar was convinced that he was trying to influence me to escape and that what he was saying ostensibly on my behalf was merely his own opinion. I said little myself at the time except that I believed great changes were inevitable and that the Communists would take over the whole of Tibet. The same afternoon Tsethar the bursar came to see me and let fly. He accused me of taking advice from people who did not belong to our monastery and who had no right to interfere with our affairs. He added that it was his duty to look after me. I must understand, he said, that I represented the entire Surmang group of monasteries and its devotees; all looked upon me as their head and only they had the right to serve me; with that he left. I realized that it was useless to reply.

The next morning I asked him to come and see me again. I told him that I was quite prepared to offer up my life for Surmang. I had wanted to talk to him about this for some time, but thought he failed to understand that I was not thinking about my own preservation; I added 'It is disquieting that you never consulted me personally: you should have done so before putting the matter before others. However, I see your point and am very grateful that consideration for our monastery should come first with you. There is a proverb in Tibet which says "Two beggars need not dispute about how to run a king's affairs". The decision rests with me, but I am ready for anything. If you wish you can take the responsibility.'

In order to calm him down I tried to explain all this as serenely as possible, but I also said that we could not afford to delay a decision. I told Yag Tulku and Jigme Rinpoche of this conversation and asked them not to make any opposition, however anxious they were for my personal safety. On the third morning of the meeting the bursar was a little hesitant since I had laid the responsibility on to him. He merely said that he thought the right thing for us would be to return to Surmang; however, he did not wish to take the final decision which must be mine alone. I then spoke, saying that I knew my first duty must be whatever would be best for our monastery and since all my monks were waiting for me to return there to direct affairs, there was no alternative but for me to come. Silence then fell upon the meeting, until my bursar exclaimed 'Is that all?'

We now began nine days of devotional meditation for the preparation of the *Vajra-amrit*.

In the meantime arrangements had to be made for our departure from Yag. The bursar seemed pleased that I had agreed to return to Surmang, but still showed that he did not wish to carry the whole responsibility. It will be remembered that when I was at Drölma Lhakhang I had received many gifts and that he had bartered these for flocks and herds without my permission. He now wished to take these animals with us, which meant that we would require at least twenty men to load and unload the animals besides the herdsmen, and we would have to camp on the way. The monks, after having so looked forward to this return, now began to be a little anxious for our safety, for we had just heard that Andrup Gönpo-trashi's army during their passage from Lhasa had been successful in attacking many Communist camps, and that they had reached Pashö, where they had broken into the town's arsenal. They had raised fresh forces and appeared to be going in the direction of Chamdo. This meant that there was already fighting on the route to Surmang. The bursar now suggested that we should leave the animals behind, and ourselves split into small groups wearing lay dress. I agreed, saying, 'we must not force the issue, if there is no alternative, this is our *karma*'.

We were expecting to celebrate the *Vajra-amrit* on the following day, but that night as I was going to bed I suddenly felt ill and was in such pain that I fainted. At the same time the roof beams cracked in one of the shrine rooms in which devotions were being held at Drölma Lhakhang, which was felt to presage a disaster.

It was the custom in Tibet, when a person was taken ill, for his friends to send gifts to some of the lamas in the district asking for spiritual healing through their meditations, and Tsethar did this now on my behalf. One was sent to a lama who held a senior post under the Chinese administration. He sent back word that though he was sorry to hear of my illness, the arrival of the gift was a blessing, for it enabled him to let me know through the bearer that the local Communist Committee had been discussing how they might get hold of Trungpa Tulku and were trying to discover where he was staying. He added that news had come through that a resistance group was centred around Surmang and that the fighting there was very heavy.

147

A number of people had come to Yag for the celebration of the *Vajra-amrit* and to receive its blessing. They were told about my sudden illness and Yag Tulku officiated in my place. Jigme Rinpoche, who was a doctor, was now determined that I should rest. He had never approved of my returning to Surmang, though he declared it was not his business; but now he insisted that I must rest for at least a month. Everyone realized that I was too ill to travel and that I could not stay at Yag for much longer.

My bursar consulted Yag Tulku, Jigme Rinpoche and other senior lamas. They decided that he should go back to Surmang and find out what the position there really was, and in the meantime I should go wherever I felt inclined, but in secret: when Tsethar returned, we could decide what further steps to take.

Tsethar at once made arrangements to leave Yag with all except four of our monks, taking letters from me addressed to both the monasteries of Surmang in which I said that I hoped they would understand how I always wanted to serve them and that they must not think I had any wish to stay away. I begged them not to make any unnecessary resistance against the Chinese. I fully understood how difficult things were becoming, but there was no point in using force. which would inevitably lead to their extinction. On the other hand, if things got really bad they should try to join me in the Yag district which was nearer both to India and Central Tibet and where the local people were ready to help us.

Tsethar arranged for our herds to be looked after by some friends around Drölma Lhakhang. I advised him to take money and portable articles which could be exchanged, both for his own journey and for Surmang should the need arise. He followed my advice, though he said he was quite certain there would be no emergency and that on reaching Surmang he would immediately put my residence in order in preparation for my return. I repeated how very delicate our position was with the Communists, and that we must not show any antagonism towards them.

Some of the monks and lay people escorted his party for two days. On their return, they told us that they had met some people from Surmang who had said that the Communists had already collected all the arms in the district, even meat choppers, and had posted guards at the ferry across the river and at all points of importance on the road. We knew that if my bursar were to be captured, our own position would be in jeopardy as the Chinese would then know where I might be found. I had been recuperating at Yag for a week when we heard that the Communists were stationed on all the routes between Riwoche and Chamdo, though as yet no-one knew how far their troops had penetrated beyond that area. We felt sure that they were in control of the ferry of Dongdrong Trukha, but it was uncertain from what direction they would approach us. All this was extremely disturbing.

My bursar had again assigned Yönten to carry out his duties, and since my private secretary had also left with the party for Surmang, he had been replaced by a monk from Drölma Lhakhang. One personal attendant remained with me and these three, together with a monk in charge of the horses, formed my immediate staff; all the other monks serving me belonged to Drölma Lhakhang.

We discussed our plans among ourselves. Invitations came from various people who had attended the *wangkur*; they offered to look after me and suggested that we might be concealed in the remoter parts of the country, but I was not convinced that it would be safe even there.

After a week's rest I was feeling stronger, so we were able to have a final session of devotional chanting together with a communal meal, ending with the *Marme Mönlam*, at which we prayed for a reunion of teachers and pupils and gave thanksgiving for the grace and knowledge we had received. All who were there held lamps which had been lighted from a lamp on the shrine. As the teacher, my lamp was the first to be lit, and from it the flame was passed on to all who were present. Then each person tied his white scarf to that of his neighbour and finally to mine so that the white band linked us all, and they all repeated after me a chant which resounded through the hall. The flame of the lamp symbolized the light of gnosis (*jnana*) which is individually received, but is an indivisible Unity in itself. The chain of white scarves represented the purity of those holding it to strengthen their spiritual life and persevere with the teachings they had received. I thanked all those who had been at the *wangkur*; I had learned in the teaching and they in attending. I said 'none of us know what the future may bring, and we may never be allowed to be together again in the flesh, but spiritually we are one. Our having had this opportunity to be together is the beginning of a union that will last for many lives. To bring all this into our daily lives we must continue our efforts to follow the promptings of the *guru* within ourselves. We must keep the balance between our mundane activities and our strivings for spiritual perfection. We must do our best to help all beings caught in the suffering that the world is now experiencing. We who have had this wonderful time together must now disperse. The assembly hall will soon be empty, with the shrine, the throne and the decorations all dismantled, but we must not be too distressed. With the menace from the Chinese becoming ever more severe, everything demonstrates the impermanence of earthly existence.'

We felt that my future plans must be decided upon within a week, for the Communists might discover that I was at Yag. There were many suitable hiding places in the district, but it was difficult to choose one without offending the many other kind people who had offered help. So I went into retreat at Yag and resorted once more to *tagpa* divination. The answer was that the country round Yo would be best, the local experts concurred and my friends agreed to supply me with food.

I was still considered to be in retreat, my yellow curtains were always drawn and it was not really known whether or not I was in the monastery of Yag. I asked an elderly lama whose room was next to mine to sound his bell and drum each day as if it came from my room: then I left in the middle of the night. Jigme Rinpoche and his brother came with me, also my personal attendant and one monk. Our horses and baggage had been sent on ahead to a place on the outskirts of the monastery where Jigme's brother and his servants were waiting. Yag Tulku who had accompanied us then went back. It was bitterly cold, we missed the heated wall of the monastery, and the night was so dark we could see nothing and had to trust to our horses to follow the trail.

The following morning at about seven we reached the house of the landowner to whom the valley of our projected hideout belonged. He gave us a warm welcome and we were thankful for the hot milk he offered us, for we were frozen. A fire of ox dung was immediately lit; it was smoky and gave out little heat, but it helped to restore us, after which we started off again. The landowner himself led us to our hideout which we reached in about five hours. We crossed a mountain pass which led us to a valley used for grazing cattle in the summer, but which was uninhabited during the winter months when the pass was under snow. Here the yaks used to be left to look after themselves, only the females (*dris*) being driven down to the farms for the winter. The further end of the valley was inaccessible, being cut off by a high gorge through which the river Yochu escaped into the Gyemo Ngülchu by a series of cascades and gorges. These grazing grounds were unknown to all except the local herdsmen and the landowner, and the place itself was called the Valley of Mystery.

We now had to look for the best place to set up our camp, so we slept where we were for the first night and started searching the following day. Up and down the valley there were a few primitive shelters used in the summer by herdsmen, so we picked on one of them at the far end on the banks of a frozen stream. The weather was fine and there was hard frost at night, though as yet no snow.

The landowner remained with our party to help, and we all set about putting the shelter in order. It was built up against a large rock and the walls were of loose stone. In order to put our tents inside we had to remove the roof. My tent and Jigme's, which he shared with his brother, were of white canvas, while my attendant and the monk who did the cooking had a larger one made of yak's hair, which also served as a kitchen. After three days the landowner with his own and Jigme's servants went back, leaving us with large supplies of butter and dried cheese made of boiled *dris'* milk, as well as a lot of cakes made with butter, dried curd, hard cheese and a particular kind of vegetable flour made from a kind of artichoke which had been roasted before being ground. All this was in addition to what Yag Tulku and Akong Tulku had sent with us. When our kind host left, he said he hoped he would be able to visit us occasionally and give us news of the latest political developments. He encouraged us to remain there for a long time, for he thought it would be impossible for the Chinese to find us in that remote place. He did not think that we would ever be completely cut off, as when the snow became deep he could in an emergency open up the path with yaks.

This was the first time that I had found myself isolated from the world without any visitors and almost without attendants. I was, however, ready to stay there for a long time as I had brought with me some sixty volumes of spiritual instruction.

We used to go out together to collect wood, but my attendant was rather upset that I should share in such domestic work, for he considered it his duty to do all these things for us. The birds woke us up each day and my mornings were spent in devotions and meditation. As the frost became more severe, it was almost impos-

sible for me to use my bell and drum as the metal was too cold, and
we had to wear our sheepskin coats all the time. My young attendant
was utterly self-sacrificing and only thought of my comfort, neglect-
ing his own. He always managed to keep a fire made of twigs going
in my tent both morning and evening, though it did little but warm
my face as I gazed into it. I used to eat the midday meal with Jigme
Rinpoche and his brother and we took long walks together in the
afternoons; in the evenings we used to gather together with our two
attendants in Jigme's tent which had an outlet for the smoke and
was larger than mine. Jigme was in his fifties, not tall but very tough;
he had a very practical way of looking at things with a wonderful
sense of humour. It was never dull in his company, for he was an
excellent story-teller and having travelled on pilgrimages to many
places including India, he told us lots of amusing yarns about his
experiences.

As the winter advanced, the yaks which had been left in the valley
came down in herds to the lower pastures; it began to snow very
heavily, causing avalanches and rocks to fall with a tremendous roar
which at first we thought came from Chinese guns. As the snow was
so deep we had left off expecting visitors, but one day a man
suddenly appeared. It was an old servant of Jigme on horseback with
two yaks laden with food-stuffs. The snow had reached up to his
stirrups, but the man said that he had not felt the cold as intensely as
when he had had to travel in the biting wind. He brought us some
butter and milk, which were all the more acceptable as we had long
been without fresh food. He had no political news to report, but told
us that Jigme's sister was very ill. He also said people were beginning
to doubt whether I was still at Yag.

He brought me a letter from one of my friends, a *tulku* who had
gone to Yag to ask for my advice; he wanted to know what his
monastery should do in regard to the Communists. Yag Tulku had
told him that I could not be disturbed as I was still in retreat, but I
would write to him later. I was able to reply telling him that the
situation was becoming very serious and that if his monks were
thinking of escaping, it might be best not to delay too long. Both
from a religious and a practical point of view it was very important
not to cause any open antagonism with the Chinese which would
only hasten disaster.

Jigme and I were feeling a little lonely and we longed for more
company; since the servant was returning, I sent a letter to Akong

Tulku to suggest his coming to join us. On receipt of it
diately made preparations to come, and was with us in tim
in our devotions preceding the New Year.

A local landowner sent several horsemen to bring us Ne ....
offerings of food and gifts from Drölma Lhakhang and Yag monasteries. These were so lavish that we had almost more food than we
could eat. The horsemen gave us some rather vague news about the
Resistance forces which were fighting quite successfully in several
parts of Tibet.

About three weeks later my bursar arrived with another monk.
He had failed to reach Surmang, and the news he brought was
extremely distressing. He told us that when he left Drölma Lhakhang he was able to cross by the ferry over the Dzachu because the
Communists had withdrawn their guards after collecting all arms in
the district and making lists of all the local families and their
possessions. They had been planning to establish a military camp
near the ferry, but owing to an attack in the neighbourhood from the
Resistance they had for the time being been obliged to leave the
place. So Tsethar was able to proceed and had great hopes of reaching Surmang, but on his way towards Lhathog he met travellers who
told him that Surmang had been attacked about a month previously
and Namgyal-tse had been destroyed; only very few monks had
been able to escape. Düdtsi-til had suffered less; the senior secretary
and a number of the monks had been able to get away and they had
made for the district of Lhathog which appeared to be safer. On
making further enquiries Tsethar was told that they had found
shelter in the monastery of Kyere. On his arrival there he found the
party, and also my mother and two sisters who were in a house near
the monastery with my young brother the abbot. In tents all around
there were a number of villagers from the neighbourhood of Surmang: the Communists had told these people that they could not
remain in their own homes as they would be in danger from the
guerillas; they must therefore go to Jyekundo under Chinese escort,
but would be able to return later when the situation became more
settled.

Tsethar was told that a few months previously the Chinese had
arranged a very large and important meeting to be held in Jyekundo, sending invitations to all the influential lamas and heads of
the district. This was a customary procedure, but this time there was
a difference, for the invitations were more in the form of an order;

since to decline would only worsen the situation, the majority
agreed to come. At the meeting, the Chinese explained that they
were there to guard the Tibetans from possible danger; to empha-
size this point the hall was surrounded by Communist troops. Each
day the Chinese asserted with greater vehemence their sole right to
authority, and eventually they tried to force the Tibetan representatives to accept Communism. All the Tibetans present understood
that if they did not agree their lives would be in danger, and Rashü
Behu the head of the Rashü district, decided to escape. He walked
out of the hall to where his bodyguard of five men were waiting with
his horse, and they made off at a tremendous pace. The Chinese
pursued them but did not catch up with the fugitives until their
horses broke down, compelling the party of six to alight. A terrible
fight ensued in which, after killing five or six Chinese, Rashü Behu
himself was killed.

After this the Chinese became much more aggressive in their
attitude: the body of Rashü Behu was brought back and displayed
in the hall and a week later all the Tibetans who attended the meeting were arrested.

The Chinese now called meetings in the twenty-five districts
under Jyekundo to impress upon the people that they must change
to the Communist way of life. They were told that if they did not
comply with these orders the lives of their representatives who had
attended the meeting would be forfeit. This was more than the
people were able to stand: they protested that their representatives
could not answer for each one of them. When the Chinese demanded
that everyone hand over his arms, the Tibetans rose in open revolt
and armed resistance was organized in all the districts, each of which
had its own centre of Chinese administration.

The small Communist office in Namgyal-tse just outside the
monastery was the first to be destroyed and similar attacks were
made throughout the twenty-five districts of the province. They
were successful in all the smaller centres. The resistance fighters
eventually reached Jyekundo and occupied the large monastery
overlooking the town, which was still in Chinese hands, thus cutting
off all communications with it. They had also tried to cut the
Chinese road between Jyekundo and China but at each attempt it
was immediately repaired by the Chinese. Many of the towns on this
road were taken by the Tibetans and very severe fighting took place
in Trindu, where the Communists in order to protect themselves had

mined the roads. But the Resistance troops drove cattle in front of them to explode the mines and over a thousand Chinese in the town were killed. These successes continued for about one and a half months. The Communists, however, then received reinforcements and their overwhelming numbers forced the Resistance party back.

Though the Chinese in Nangchen expected their compatriots to arrive soon, they were in a state of siege and had run out of food and water. In their desperation they resorted to strategy. They sent two Chinese who knew Tibetan out of the town disguised as lamas who, as they gave people to understand, had been forced to leave their hermitage. These men approached the resistance troops and pretended that they were still under a strict vow of silence; to avoid having to talk they went on fingering their rosaries, their lips appearing to be repeating *mantras*. They both looked so genuine that the resistance men believed they could be relied upon. The junior of the two indicated in dumb show that Chinese reinforcements were less than a mile away. At this the besiegers left their trenches in order to combat the oncoming Communists. The two lamas suddenly disappeared, and the Chinese in the town were able to make a successful sortie for food and water; when the Resistance troops returned to their trenches, having seen nothing of the Communists, they realized that they had been tricked. Fresh Communist troops arrived five days later and routed the besiegers.

The situation was now becoming very serious for the Tibetans; nearly all those living in monasteries or towns, particularly the able bodied, were made prisoners. The Communists now in command were completely ruthless; the whole order of behaviour was changed. Those who had been established in the administration before the invasion and had had friendly relations with the Tibetans, now had no control.

The Communist army was arriving in thousands and using automatic weapons hitherto unknown in Tibet. From their headquarters in Jyekundo and Nangchen they were sending their troops in all directions capturing the inhabitants and destroying the monasteries and the homes of the peasants. Some of the Resistance took shelter in Namgyal-tse Monastery. It was attacked by Communist troops from Nangchen and the fight went on for nearly two days, leaving most of the Tibetans dead in the monastery, as well as several hundred Communist soldiers. The whole place was looted, and the buildings destroyed. Dorlha, who had formerly been senior in the

Jyekundo administration, was in command of the insurgent party; he fought with extreme bravery and then managed to escape. A few monks were able to get away and some of them discarded their robes and joined the Resistance, others were killed and the majority captured. Garwang Rinpoche, the abbot of Namgyal-tse, had disappeared after attending the meeting at Jyekundo.

By now there was not a single monastery left to carry out its religious functions, between Düdtsi-til and China. All the districts were full of the wounded and the dying. Chinese troops were everywhere, while the people who had escaped were now starving. Women and children left in the villages were in no better plight. Many mishaps befell those who tried to escape; there were diseases and accidents, small children fell from their horses, and everywhere there was shortage of food.

As for Düdtsi-til it did not escape the common fate. It was attacked from the north: Chinese troops broke into the library and threw out all the valuable books, tearing off their covers; the good Tibetan paper was either just strewn around or else was given as fodder to their horses. Those treasures of the shrines which were made of precious metals, such as images and lamps, were broken up and the metal was sent off to China. The precious painted scrolls were taken down and used as trays on which to serve the soldiers' meals of meat and rice. Everything of value in the monastery was removed; they even broke into the tomb of the tenth Trungpa Tulku and left the embalmed body exposed.

Those monks who were able to escape had no other alternatuve but to abandon their monastery without attempting resistance. The elderly lama who directed meditation at the retreat centre was, however, taken prisoner with some ten other monks. They were confined in the *gönkhang*, the temple of the Tutelary Deities. This was the oldest part of Düdtsi-til and dated from the sixteenth century, since when it had always been used for special spiritual activities. It was half chapel, half dwelling house. The elderly lama told his fellow prisoners, 'Since this building has been set aside for meditation, it should still be so used, and this experience should make us realize its true purpose. We must accept that what has happened is all part of our training in life. Indeed, this is our opportunity to understand the nature of the world and to attain a deeper level. Though we are shut up here as prisoners, our devotions should be the same as if we were freely gathered together in the assembly hall.' He went on in this way, and gradually, as this deeper spiritual teaching was put before them, his companions recovered their calm.

The prisoners were scantily fed on a small daily portion of roasted barley (*tsampa*) and given hot water to drink. The younger monks who had been captured were sent out to remote valleys under an armed Chinese guard who also wore Tibetan clothes; they had to search for Tibetans in hiding and tell them that they must return to their villages. Everyone was questioned about me, but the monks themselves did not know where I might be found.

The building itself was left intact, being used together with the surrounding houses as an army base. From there the Chinese attacked all the neighbouring monasteries and villages, bringing their prisoners back to Düdtsi-til. The fort which had been there in the time of Adro Shelu-bum and had become part of the monastery, was now used once more as a watch tower.

The Chinese army stayed at Düdtsi-til for about a month. They had intended to make it a permanent centre, but on receiving orders from army headquarters they evacuated the place, carrying away everything which might be of value to themselves; the prisoners they took with them. The cattle in the district had all been rounded up and sent to Jyekundo airport which was in a flat valley a few miles from the town. The journey was a cruel one for the prisoners, as their captors were ordered not to delay, so they travelled night and day, with the Tibetans on foot and the Chinese on horseback. When they reached Jyekundo, the women were sent to the airport to look after the cattle; their children were taken from them and placed in communal nurseries under strangers. All able bodied men and a few women were put on forced labour for road-making and those who were too old to work were sent to concentration camps, together with those senior people who had not been shot.

Before the armies left the district, the Communists had entered the houses of the better class Tibetans and ransacked them; they had taken the clothes of the masters and made the servants wear them, and the masters had been forced to put on the servants' clothes.

The country was full of informers: the newly arrived Communist army made use of everyone who could help them, such as Chinese officials previously established in the district and Tibetan youths who had been recruited into their army when they first invaded Tibet; a number of these boys deserted to the Resistance, but those who had remained with the Communists became useful as guides.

My secretary gave me news about what had happened in the wild and sparsely inhabited country north west of Jyekundo. The whole area, known as Changthang, is a vast plateau and exceedingly cold. Knowing that the Communists were advancing from the north east, the people of these high regions escaped to the north west and lived in large camps. The Chinese now sent troops to attack them, having sighted their camps from their aeroplanes.

When the inhabitants left their villages, they had taken most of their cattle and personal possessions with them and this had made their camps very conspicuous targets for the Communist planes. Near the Lake of Heaven (*Tengri Nor*) there was a terrible fight; the refugees had camped beside this long lake which has a rocky mountain on one side; women and children were put behind these rocks for greater safety. The Communists attacked from three sides and the fighting went on for two days at the odds of one hundred and fifty Tibetans against a thousand Communist troops. Though the situation was desperate the Tibetan men fought with such bravery that, despite many casualties, the women and children were saved.

All these things had happened whilst I was at Yag, but no-one had been able to communicate with me at the time.

The bursar also told me that my mother and my two sisters had gone to visit my young brother, the abbot of Kyere, before the serious outbreak of hostilities and had stayed on there when conditions became dangerous. My mother sent me a message saying that she was relieved to think that I was in a safer place; I must not worry about her; if I had to leave the country she would be content for she thought only of my safety.

The refugees from the area around Surmang had been alloted camping sites and grazing for their cattle by the people living near Kyere; they still thought they would be able to return to their homes and our monks also expected to go back to Düdtsi-til; all thought that the Communists' threat to return would not be carried out. My bursar said he had done his best to encourage this belief. He had gone to Düdtsi-til himself with a few monks and found all the buildings intact, so he had arranged with some poor herdsmen still living in the neighbourhood to take charge of them. At the monastery he had seen the desecrated tomb of the tenth Trungpa Tulku with the body exposed and on his return to Kyere had sent a party of monks to cremate it.

As soon as he got back to Kyere he had called a meeting of our monks; all agreed that they should return to their monastery and had written the letter which bursar Tsethar had brought with him. It said they hoped to resettle at Düdtsi-til and begged me to return to them; they asked me to think over the matter carefully, for if, during the life of the eleventh Trungpa Tulku, both monasteries ceased to function it would be a disaster. I asked the bursar how he had been able to travel through the country in its present disturbed state; he replied that he had been aware of the danger and moved cautiously. I then asked him if other communities intended to return to their monasteries; to this he answered that, as far as he knew, no-one else had such an intention. I wanted to know what were the individual opinions of my monks in regard to myself and he said that they were quite satisfied with the action I had taken to avoid danger; in fact, I had relieved them of the great responsibility of taking care of me.

It was difficult to reply to the letter, though it was obvious that decisions could not be long delayed; I used *prasena* again, which indicated that I should not go to Kyere and that I should even leave my present retreat fairly soon.

My answer to the letter was as follows: 'We should not think only of the survival of our monastery, nor of my own reputation. You must see that the whole country has been devastated. If we try to re-establish Düdtsi-til the Communists will inevitably return and the suffering will only be repeated; probably we shall all lose our lives. Where I am now, we are in the province of Central Tibet; unless a change for the worse takes place here, we are in a better position than at Surmang. My monks must consider the possibility of remaining where they are or of coming to this area; I think nothing would be more dangerous than to return to Surmang.'

I read my letter to the bursar and added 'I agreed earlier to return to Surmang, but this was in the hopes of saving our monastery. Now, if I join you, we will certainly be a target for attack from the Communists and their persecution of our people will begin all over again. They will believe that I encouraged the resistance; this will only lead to further bloodshed. I think there is little hope of re-establishing our monastery, but I will not attempt to escape myself before I have received further information from our monks at Kyere.'

The bursar had little to say in reply; incurably sanguine, he clung to the belief that everything would end well. He was obsessed with the calamity which had overtaken Surmang and failed to recognize the fact that the disaster was one involving the whole country. Though my companions were in favour of my leaving the district immediately, we decided that I should stay on where I was until an answer came back from Kyere. As for Tsethar, he went to Drölma Lhakhang with the monk in charge of the horses to make arrangements about our animals which were being cared for in the neighbourhood; he now wanted to exchange them for money and portable articles.

The weather was now improving and the valley where we were hiding was bursting into spring. Akong Tulku and I, sometimes accompanied by Jigme Rinpoche and his brother, used to take long walks along tracks that animals had made through the willow and juniper scrub. There was so much to see; birds, including the white goose, and many animals such as musk deer, brown bears, Tibetan pandas and foxes were to be seen. To hear a fox barking is considered to be a bad omen in Tibet; one full moon night after the New Year we heard one followed by the cries of jackals; the sound echoed from rock to rock and was frightening in the silence and loneliness of the valley.

The next day a messenger came to tell Jigme Rinpoche that his sister was dying; he and his brother left at once, saying that if his sister recovered he would return. A few days later he sent to tell us that his sister had died; her body had been cremated, but he would very much like me to perform the funeral rites. He said that on his return to his family's house he had realized how very cold we were in the Valley of Mystery and, since his house was a large one, he could hide me there without difficulty. He would let others know that he himself was engaged in special devotions and must remain in retreat, so no-one would know that I was there. I was of course to travel by night; he also asked Akong to come with me. My attendant monk was delighted at this invitation, though he admitted he had made much progress in meditation in the solitude of the valley. I myself felt no inclination to go; we had grown fond of the place. I had been able to work a good deal, but had not finished a book I was writing on meditation, showing its gradual development up to the final fruition.

Jigme Rinpoche had been so exceedingly kind to us that I thought we must accept his invitation for a short time; we knew that his sister had been a nun and a very saintly woman. We asked the young monk who had come with us to the valley to look after our things; the landowner had sent an old nun to attend to the yaks, so he would not be left entirely alone. As we started on our journey, I had a presentiment that we would not return to the valley that had sheltered us so well.

The snow on the pass was very deep and I had to walk behind my horse, holding on to its tail to pull me up the slope. On reaching the summit, we ran into a blizzard; the prayer flag on the cairn was all but torn away by the wind and only just showed above the deep snow. It was even more difficult going down the other side of the pass. I had to walk in front of my horse, holding on to the reins; the horse, being steadier than myself, was able to act as a brake in case I slipped. We travelled all through the day and reached the land-owner's house towards evening; there we waited till it was quite dark. He himself wanted me to return at once to the shelter of the valley, for he thought there could be no safer hiding place from the Chinese. The night became colder and colder; it was pitch dark, but our guide knew the way and, hurrying along, we reached Jigme Rinpoche's house before the dawn broke.

The warmed rooms were welcome, though our frozen hands and feet tingled painfully; the contrast between our primitive life in the valley and the comfort of Jigme's house could hardly have been greater. It was a very quiet place; since the funeral rites were in progress no visitors called, but from the windows we could see the constant stream of Communist troops and lorries going along the road on the other side of the river.

This sudden change in our surroundings did not seem to suit my health, and after we had performed our devotions for a week, Akong Tulku's bursar arrived; he consulted with Jigme Rinpoche and they decided that, since I was not well, it would be unwise for me to undertake the strenuous return journey to the Valley of Mystery. They thought that there were equally good hiding places within easier reach. In fact, there was a cave I had long wanted to visit, so I asked them if they thought it would be suitable as a hiding place; to this proposal they agreed and said they would make the necessary arrangements.

Akong Rinpoche went home to his monastery and I left with my attendant for the cave, starting off at midnight; our guide was an elderly nun from one of the Drölma Lhakhang nunneries. As we could not reach the place before daybreak we rested on the way in another large cave on the south side of Mt Kulha Ngang-ya. The road ran beside the mountain, but the cave was so high up that we had to climb beyond a moraine to get to it. It had two divisions, an upper and a lower, we put our horses in the lower one. We were not able to light fires for fear that they would give away our position, but we had plenty of dried meat and cheese with us, and our saddle rugs were useful for bedding. As soon as it became dark we resumed our journey; there were villages on the way and we passed by one of the local nunneries. Akong Tulku had arranged for some of his monks to get our cave ready, and when we reached it we found a fire already lit and food and bedding laid out.

The cave of my choice had been discovered by Lama Möntrug; his story is remarkable. He was born in the late nineteenth century in an area on the borders of Assam where the people believe in nature spirits, which they propitiate by animal sacrifices. This had distressed Möntrug from his early childhood and while still young he decided to leave his home. He pretended to be going on a hunting expedition and walked towards the Tibetan border; on his way there he came to the retreats of several Tibetan hermits. They told him about Thöga, a lama of Drölma Lhakhang, who had founded the four nunneries in that district. All he heard from the hermits encouraged him to seek out Thöga Rinpoche who became his *guru*.

After three years training under this Master he undertook a long retreat and, being accustomed to climbing, he searched the nearby mountains for a suitable cave. Mt Kulha Ngang-ya seemed a good situation so, using a pickaxe, he started to hollow out a cave in the rock. After a day's work he had got through about a yard when he came to an opening into a natural cave with a hole in the roof that could serve as a chimney. A tunnel led to a second cavern, with a natural window looking out on a steep and inaccessible part of the mountain. Lama Möntrug remained here to meditate for the rest of his life.

We found the cave wonderfully warm; for fuel, we burnt a plant called *gongmo-potho*, which grows in strange woolly clusters between the rocks; the nuns gathered it for us. A mountain stream ran nearby. This was an ideal place for working on my book, as there were no interruptions and no great hardship from the cold; the only drawback was that I had nowhere to walk so that I lacked exercise. The nun remained with my attendant, to cook and look after me: the two lived and slept in the front cave which was also our kitchen. After a week, however, I found the constant ministrations of the good nun somewhat distracting; I wanted to be left alone to meditate. When she told me about another cave some three hours' ride further on, on Mt Kyo Rinchen-pungpa, which with its surrounding villages was owned by her family, I sent word to Akong Tulku to have my horses brought to me and we moved on again.

When we reached this other mountain, we found the cave blocked. However, the owner very kindly provided a black tent, which was put up near the cave on a flat ledge high up the mountain side. This ledge was sufficiently large for me to walk about, so I could now again take exercise. There was a waterfall on one side, which at that time was frozen, and behind its icicles ran a clear passage through which I would walk out and up the rocks, with no danger of being seen from below. In the rarified air I could hear herdsmen in the distance calling to their animals. At night the cold was intense; several blankets and a well made sheepskin coat imported from the west of Tibet did not suffice to keep me warm. My attendant found his native sheepskin and felt rugs better suited to this climate.

I remained there quietly for a few weeks and was able to finish my book, which filled about one thousand sheets of Tibetan paper. The landowner's herdsmen got to suspect, however, that there was a lama in retreat somewhere on the mountain. The rumour spread quickly to the neighbouring village. All the inhabitants were very excited and thought it might possibly be me. The headman climbed up to our ledge to find out and when he saw me he used the Tibetan saying 'A golden rock has fallen on our doorstep', adding that it was fortunate for him and his fellow villagers that I had come to their neighbourhood. He was quite sure that the news of my whereabouts would go no further and that my retreat was as safe as any other hiding place; he assured me that all the villagers would look after me. He came again next day with his son and daughter-in-law bringing barrels of curd and other food supplies. He said that his wife would like to visit me on the following day; she had not been able to come with them as she had stayed at home to look after the house. The news that he brought about the present situation in the country was that the Resistance party was fighting in the area round Kongpo, where the Brahmaputra enters India. At Chamdo, the Chinese were becoming more and more oppressive; however, he thought that his part of Tibet was safe, and if I wanted to move from my present retreat, there were several equally good and remote places where I could lie concealed.

On April 11th, at dawn, we heard neighing and the monk in charge of my horses appeared. He told me that my bursar, who was still attending to the business of selling our cattle at Drölma Lhakhang, was growing increasingly worried about the situation. The Communist troops had now suddenly appeared in the vicinity, so he had sent this monk with my horses to ask what I thought should be done. The messenger had left the evening before and on his way had seen Communist troops marching towards Pashö. They were telling the people that the Chinese had already gained possession of Lhasa and that they were now about to take control of Pashö district. The troops were coming from different directions, some from Chamdo and others from Enda, north of Drölma Lhakhang. He did not know what had happened at the monastery or to Akong Tulku after he himself had left.

This news could mean one of two things; either the troops would go direct to Pashö or else they would attack each of the monasteries on the way. My *tagpa* (divination) indicated that the danger was certainly increasing but that there was no need for immediate alarm. I realized that I could neither go to Drölma Lhakhang nor to Yag, so I sent the monk back to make preparations to move our luggage. He wanted to know the exact date on which he should be ready. I told him, at the full moon, on April 23rd. This was the Earth Hog year, 1959, and I was now twenty.

After he had left, a second monk came with a message from my bursar; Drölma Lhakhang had not been disturbed, for the Chinese had gone direct to Pashö. I went down to the nearby village, where I met a business man who had come straight from Chamdo. He told me that the military had been in complete control there since the first week of April. They had put loudspeakers everywhere telling the people that the Dalai Lama had been forcibly abducted by the guerillas. They said that the Chinese had always intended to liberate the Tibetans and that they were there to bring great benefits to the people by peaceful means. They had, however, been forced to fire some guns in Lhasa when the guerillas attacked them and Norbulingkha, the Summer Palace, had been slightly damaged, but now everything was all right: they added that the Chinese had been obliged to take over the civil government because the Tibetans had broken the 'Seventeen Point Agreement' of 1949; they also declared that Tibetans must not have any contact with the foreign 'Imperialists'.

My informant told me that Tibetan officials who up till now had worked with the Chinese were being arrested and all telephones in their homes had been disconnected. Every bridge on the two Chamdo rivers was being guarded. The townspeople looked frightened and miserable and all gaiety was at an end. Everyone entering Chamdo was questioned as to his reasons for travelling. Part of the monastery was being used as a jail, though a few monks were allowed to remain in the rest of it; however, anyone visiting them was sighted through field glasses and accused of being a spy. The Communists had dug trenches on the hills round the town and it was estimated that some forty thousand troops were encamped in the vicinity. The Chinese had tried to encourage the Tibetans to return to their homes, telling them that there was nothing to fear and that everything that had taken place was to their advantage.

By April 14th the Chinese had gained complete control in Pashö. They had interned the lamas in the assembly hall of their monastery. The place was desecrated and everything of value removed. All the officials in the town had been captured and the food from the monastery and the government stores, as well as from the local shops, had been taken and sent away to Chamdo. A temporary concentration camp had been set up. The fact that resistance forces under Andrup had previously visited Pashö now made things worse for the inhabitants. On their way to the town the Chinese had captured any travellers on the road and had forced them to accompany the army, so no-one had been able to give any warning of their approach. Previously the Communists had not actually done any damage to the surrounding villages, but the people there were living in terror of spies who might give them away later.

CHAPTER THIRTEEN

MUST WE ESCAPE?

WAITING for the 23rd, I went down to the village where I stayed with several families in succession. Yag Tulku came to see me, which was a great pleasure as he had always been so helpful with his mature advice and had shown such understanding about my diffi-culties at the time when the bursar was so insistent that I should go back to Surmang. This time, however, his mind was taken up with the Chinese situation; he seemed to be more nervous than I was myself and could give me no clear guidance. I told him that I had fixed the date for my departure; it was to be on April 23rd. He wanted to come with me, but said that he would have to bring some of the senior monks with him and also a good deal of baggage. We discussed the route and I pointed out to him that we might have great difficulty in crossing the Gyemo Ngülchu river, for there was only one bridge, and at other places it was crossed by ferry. Since the Communists were in control at Pashö, they would probably have put guards all along the river. We had no knowledge of the conditions at the bridge. I tried to explain to Yag Tulku that this would not be an easy journey like the tours we used to make, this time it was going to be a life or death escape. We would have to reduce our baggage to a minimum and make ourselves as inconspicuous as possible. He still wanted to come with me, but felt he must first consult his secretary. He thought that the baggage question could be solved if he came with us on horseback with a few monks only bringing whatever was required for the journey; a small additional number of mules would suffice to carry the most valuable possessions, leaving a second party to follow consisting of the other monks with yaks to transport the remainder of the baggage. However, he doubted whether he could make all these arrangements by the 23rd. I emphasized that the party must be kept as small as possible, or there would be no chance for any of us. If many people wanted to try and escape, they must split up into smaller groups and travel separately. Whereupon Yag Tulku went back to his monastery to collect his party.

The monk horseman who had come to see me in my mountain retreat was now returning to Drölma-Lhakhang. I gave him a letter to Akong Tulku telling him that I had decided to leave on the 23rd and that, if he wanted to come with me, he must discuss the matter with his monks and come to an early and firm decision. I thought it unlikely that Drölma Lhakhang would be left in peace after what had happened in other parts of Tibet and particularly at Surmang. Should he come with me, I promised his monastery that I would do my best to look after him, but I realized that such a journey might be dangerous for both of us. My own date for departure was fixed and I had every intention of sticking to it. Yag Tulku might be coming with us and, if he decided to do so, I had told him that his baggage must be severely cut down. We should have to keep to a small party; with every additional person the danger would become greater and my own responsibility would also be increased; moreover, there was always the possibility that others might wish to join us on the way; this was how I wrote to my friend Akong.

Until the 22nd I remained in the village and then set off at night for Drölma Lhakhang which I reached at six o'clock the next morning after a roundabout journey avoiding villages, while a tremendous snowstorm was raging. Both Akong Tulku and my bursar had tried to keep our plans secret, but the news of my intended departure had leaked out and on my arrival at the monastery I found a number of monks and villagers assembled who wanted to receive my blessing and to consult me about what they themselves should do. Some of them suggested organizing local resistance. I had very little time to talk to them and none to give any individual advice, so I spoke to the crowd in the assembly hall. I told them it would be useless to attempt to fight and, since I did not even know myself where I was going, I could offer them no concrete suggestions. At the moment I was thinking of Central Tibet; however, they must realize that there was danger everywhere. I told them to remember the teaching we had shared during the *wangkur*. Before I said good-bye they all filed past me to receive a blessing, after which I left hastily for fear of further delays as more and more people were arriving.

Akong Rinpoche had decided to come with me with the approval of his monks, but my bursar had changed his mind; he could not bear to leave so many treasures behind while I, for my part, kept firmly to the decision to travel on horseback with a few mules to carry the basic necessities for the journey. It was arranged for a Lhathog woman to inform my monks at Kyere about my departure. After all this delay, our party could not even wait to have a meal, though my attendant and I had not eaten since the night before, so we set out on empty stomachs. Yönten came with us as acting bursar and the two attendants who had been with me in the Valley of Mystery were also of the party. Akong Rinpoche brought his two brothers and we were also joined by Lama Geleg, the monk who had taken the *kalung* when I gave the *wangkur* at Yag. A young novice from Drölma-Lhakhang and an older monk from the retreat centre also came with us. The older monk was a very spiritual man, prepared to face any difficulties and dangers.

We started with a tearful send-off from all the monks of the monastery. It was a desolate moment for Akong Tulku who was leaving his own monks, especially the senior ones, who had brought him up with such loving care. My bursar accompanied us as far as the nunnery which was to be our first stopping place. We had some thirty horses and fifty mules with us. The neighbouring villages had been asked to watch out and report if any Communists were in the district.

On our arrival at the north nunnery I found the nuns very calm and thoughtful over the turn in affairs. They asked me to advise them what to do, saying they understood that they must accept whatever fate might bring. Some of the nearby villagers came to see me and we all talked for about an hour. As soon as there was a pause, the nuns offered us a meal which was very welcome. After we had eaten I went up to the hermitage and found the nun who was in retreat there. She was more concerned with my well being than with her own personal danger. We had a spiritual talk and I encouraged her to consider the disturbances of this life as an element in her meditation.

Our party spent the night in the shelter of the nunnery and we talked until late in the evening. During the day all the baggage had had to be sorted and properly packed. No-one except the nuns knew that we were on our way to escape or for how long we would be staying at the nunnery; in fact, we disappeared after an early breakfast.

Not long after, we met a man who had just crossed the river by the bridge without meeting any Chinese; this was cheering news. The next night we stayed in an isolated house belonging to a celebrated doctor, who welcomed us warmly. He specialized in the use of herbal remedies and had several sheds where he kept a stock of local herbs together with other medicines imported from India. A wonderful meal was put before us, in which special spices were used to flavour dishes our host himself had invented. He was convinced that at the moment we had nothing to fear from the Communists. Next day he gave us detailed instructions about what food to eat or avoid on our journey, also telling us where the water was good, bad or medicinal.

We set out very early in the morning; some of the neighbouring villagers, however, had somehow got to know that we were in the district and came to ask for my blessing and also for advice and this delayed us somewhat. Our next stop was by a lake surrounded by five mountains, known as the Five Mothers; these had been held to be sacred by the followers of the old Bön religion. Here we had tea and then changed into ordinary Tibetan civilian clothes with European felt hats such as many people wear in Tibet. As I have mentioned before, such a change of clothes has a bad psychological effect on a monk, it gave one a sense of desolation.

Our track now led us over heights, with the land sloping down to a distant river. A message had been sent to Kino Monastery which lay some miles from the bridge, announcing our coming. On the way down we were overtaken by Akong's tutor from Drölma Lhakhang who had followed us to see that all was well with our party. A little further on we met a traveller coming from the direction of the bridge; he too reassured us saying that there were no Chinese in the vicinity. Since the monks at Kino had been forewarned, they had prepared a small procession to welcome us at the entrance to the monastery. Its abbot was a married lama who lived outside the precincts but was still in charge of the community, while the *khenpo* (master of studies) lived within the monastery and acted as deputy abbot. Being received with all the traditional monastic ceremonial, I felt a sense of personal shame at appearing in lay dress. During our three days' stay there many people from the surrounding villages came to ask for a blessing and to put their personal troubles before me. We had to be particularly careful in this place since it lay near the bridge, so that there was always the possibility of the Communists coming this way, since Pashö lay only a few miles up stream, on the river Pashu which joined the Gyelmo Ngülchu just above the bridge; this gave the place a certain strategic importance.

Kino Tulku and his wife now wanted to join our party. Unlike Yag Tulku, he was quite prepared to leave all his possessions behind. His wife came from near Drölma Lhakhang and they were both great friends of Akong Tulku. He said that since his friend was leaving and the situation with the Communists was becoming ever more menacing, he thought they should escape with us. He and his wife made immediate preparations for the journey and decided to bring with them two monk attendants, five horses and eleven mules. A man with his wife and little daughter also asked if they could join us. They had sold up their home and bought three horses in addition to the two they already possessed.

According to information received locally, if we could cross the bridge the country on the further side would be safe as it was under the administration of the Resistance. We made ready to go on and Akong's tutor returned to Drölma Lhakhang; he was in great distress over having to leave us for he realized that this was a complete separation from his beloved abbot.

We soon reached the Shab-ye bridge which we crossed without difficulty; on the further side we met a guard of the Resistance army who checked our party to ascertain that we were not carrying arms. One of my attendants was carrying a rolled up pictorial scroll over his shoulder and the guard thought it looked suspiciously like a gun! When we had been cleared we were given passports. We enquired what steps were being taken to protect the area and were told that the whole district was being guarded and they thought that the Communists would not be able to break into it. He was very optimistic and said that the Resistance were even preparing to attack. We told him that the Communists had spread a report that the guerillas forced His Holiness the Dalai Lama to leave Lhasa early in March and that he had escaped and was now in India; also that Lhasa was now entirely under Communist control, though we ourselves did not believe this to be true. The guard likewise thought that this report was merely Chinese propaganda. Most of our companions were greatly cheered and muttered among themselves that such tales as these were not to be taken too seriously.

All the party felt relief at not being in immediate danger. We stayed the night in a house in the village and Kino Tulku's monks returned to their monastery. The next day, getting up very early before sunrise, we started off to cross a high mountain range by a very steep zig-zag track; our animals had to stop frequently to regain their breath; we met some of the resistance soldiers coming down it. At the top we saw stone defence works which had been built on both sides of the road. Some of the soldiers came from the Lhathog district and among them was a doctor who knew me. He told me that he had left his home as a pilgrim and had joined the resistance army in Lhasa before the crisis. All the soldiers were tall, well set up men and looked very war-like; most of them carried rifles but a few only possessed old-fashioned muskets. The young soldiers seemed enthusiastic and proud to wear their military medals hung on yellow ribbons, inscribed with the words 'National Resistance Volunteers'; they were all singing songs and looked very cheerful. My personal attendant Karma-ngötrup, who had a simple optimistic nature, was much impressed with them; he said he felt sure that the Tibetans would get the better of the Chinese for, according to the law of *karma*, we who had never molested other countries must now surely deserve the victory.

On the further side of the mountain we stopped and spent the night in tents, and the following day we reached Lhodzong, where we met a man from Kino who was partly in charge of the resistance troops. He told me his story, how he had met the commander Andrup Gönpo-trashi, who had impressed him as being a man of outstanding character; he thought that with such a leader directing their forces, the Resistance must be successful. My informant had been a senior official with the Riwo-che administration and had been held in the greatest respect by everyone in the area. Kino Tulku wished us to consult him about our escape plans but, when we did so, he was unable to give us any useful advice; and in fact, he only expressed the opinion that it was unnecessary for us to leave the country.

Reaching Shi-tram Monastery we found the monks there quite calm and engaged on their ordinary routine, but beyond that point we began to meet with difficulties. On the main road to Lhasa there were so many resistance soldiers going in both directions, that very little grazing was available, added to which we found all provisions very expensive. We decided therefore to bypass the main road and follow a more roundabout track which brought us near the home of some of Kino Tulku's friends with whom we stayed for several days. The young abbot of Sephu who had been one of my pupils at the *wangkur* came to see us while we were there. He wanted to join our party with his mother, his tutor and several monks. I explained to the tutor that this escape was likely to be a difficult business; we did not yet know where to go, there was so much uncertainty about what had happened at Lhasa itself; therefore I advised him to think things over carefully before deciding whether to join us or not. Supposing that the monks of his monastery wished to come with him, this would make further difficulties and would endanger the whole party. When ten of us left Drölma Lhakhang it had been unanimously agreed that the party should be kept small; but already we had been joined by other people together with their baggage. The next morning the tutor came back to tell us that his abbot, who was in a great state of excitement, was determined to come with us. He had sent a message to his monks telling them that he had decided to escape but that, since I had insisted that it would be impossible to travel in a large group, they must understand that they could not come with him. When the young abbot joined us he brought about twenty more mules to add to our transport. After several more days on the road we came across Urgyan-tendzin, a young monk going on pilgrimage to Lhasa. He also asked to join us, and Kino Tulku told him that he could put his luggage on one of his own mules. We found him most helpful with loading and unloading the animals, and afterwards, at critical moments of the journey, he proved an invaluable member of our party, full of resource and courage.

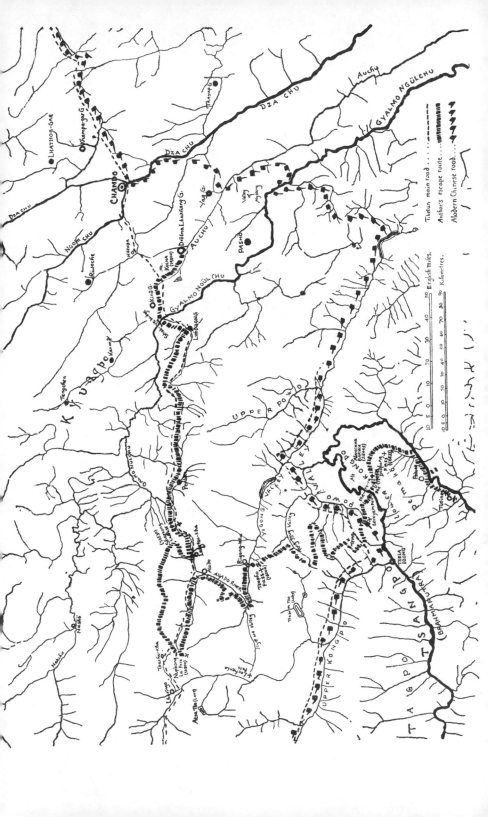

CHAPTER FOURTEEN
IT MUST BE INDIA

THESE early weeks were really enjoyable; it was spring and the flowers were beginning to bloom in the good weather. We were all feeling much more cheerful and looking forward to visiting Lhasa; we talked of the time when the resistance army would defeat the Chinese. The one thing that puzzled us was that we never met anyone on the road returning from Lhasa, all travellers were going towards it. When we made enquiries in villages we passed on the way, some told us that the Resistance were in command at Lhasa, though most people agreed that the Dalai Lama had gone to India for safety, but they thought he would soon return. We were still wearing civilian clothes, and no-one knew who we were. Some of the villagers took us for Resistance officials.

Now that we were no longer on the main road the way became more mountainous; however, we were not the only party to choose this less direct route, other groups of refugees from East Tibet were also travelling by the same way. Among them there were some people who had escaped from Nangchen, including the secretary of Ramjor Monastery in company with a few monks and eight or nine village families. The secretary asked us if we knew what had happened to Trungpa Tulku and said how sad it was that none of the lamas from the Surmang district had been able to get away: when he was told that I was Trungpa, he was overwhelmed. He gave us details of what had occurred at his own monastery, telling how the Communists had invaded it when the monks were holding a special service in the assembly hall. They had closed the entrance and had immediately shot a few of the monks, after which they arrested the others accusing them of hiding arms. The abbot came forward and tried to explain that he had always done his best to preach non-violence to his followers, but even while he was insisting that there were no arms in the monastery he was shot in the forehead

orje-tsering, district official

Yönten, a Surmang monk

The King of Derge's Cabinet

A resistance Khampa (*Photo :* Paul Popper, Ltd.)

Yaks loaded with barley and firewood (*Photo :* Paul Popper, Ltd.

by the officer in command. The monks, including the secretary, were forced to bring down their library to be destroyed, being also made to hammer to pieces the images with their own hands. Many people in the surrounding villages were also arrested and taken to Nangchen with the monk prisoners. However, an order came from the Communist headquarters that most of the troops were to proceed elsewhere, so that only a few soldiers were left to guard the prisoners some of whom were able to escape, the secretary being among them. He added that any villagers who had been left in their homes were now also trying to escape.

As we were going over another pass we met Tulku Chime of Benchen Monastery whom I already knew; we were thankful to find him alive. I asked him if he had any news of the supreme abbot of Benchen, Sang-gye-nyenpa Rinpoche, Dingo Chentze's brother, who had looked after the young *tulkus* on their return from meeting the Dalai Lama at Derge Gönchen. He had heard nothing about him, except that he had left their monastery the year before and had reached Central Tibet, where he was staying with Gyalwa Karmapa. Benchen monastery, which was near Jyekundo, had been attacked and all its treasures had been looted by the Communists; and since it was so near the airport half the building had been used to house members of the Chinese staff, while the assembly hall had been turned into a storehouse. The monks had scattered in all directions; he himself had gone to his family in the Nangchen area and they had all escaped together; most of them were now living in a large refugee camp. Such stories made my monks realize that we had no alternative but to escape.

By May 21st we reached a place near Pembar Monastery. Here it was necessary to get into contact with Pu Dündül, the commander in the Resistance who was in charge of all that area. Kino Tulku said he would go to this officer since he was personally known to him, with Yönten to accompany him. Pu Dündül gave them a passport for our party. He said that although no definite news had been received from Central Tibet, he was confident that the resistance army was doing well and he was shortly expecting Andrup Gönpo-trashi to arrive with his troops. When he discovered that the young abbot of Sephu was with us, he said that no-one from his district could be allowed to leave; everyone must remain in the area to fight. The following day the abbot's tutor went to see him and begged him to allow the boy to escape, but he would not hear of it, so we had to leave the unfortunate young abbot and his companions behind.

It now was necessary for us to regain the high road, as there was no other pass across the mountains, and we arrived at a place called Urgyan Tamda. There was a small temple in this village which was famous because it held an image of Urgyan Rinpoche otherwise known as Guru Padmasambhava, the apostle of Tibet; we held a special service there as it was the tenth day of the month according to the Tibetan calendar, which is the particular day for these devotions. We were also shown Tsongpön Norbuzangpo's saddle and a Tibetan version of the Chinese Book of Changes (*I Ching*) which had belonged to him. He was a merchant who lived in the seventh century and his name was still honoured, for he was a very spiritual man, besides having compiled the first written record of Tibet's trade with other countries.

Ahead of us lay the very high pass of Sharkong La; it was extremely steep and the weather was very stormy, so when we had got about half way up we camped for the night. Several resistance soldiers who were guarding the pass came down to us to beg for food and transport. We gave them some food but said we had no animals to spare. They seemed to be very keen on guarding the pass and were strong young men, but only equipped with old fashioned muskets.

The next morning we returned to the climb; the weather was still bad, with a strong wind blowing in our faces which made progress difficult. The baggage kept falling off the mules and we all had to help in getting the loads settled again and this caused delays. Three young men came down from the pass whom we discovered to be deserters from the resistance army on their way home. They said that the Chinese were very strong in Central Tibet and Lhasa itself might be under their control, but they had no first-hand information. They could tell us little about conditions on our route, for they had travelled mostly by night, following mountain tracks. As there were only three of them, they had managed to escape detection; they said they thought that concealment would be more difficult for a large party like ours.

When we reached the top of the pass I, Kino Tulku and Akong Tulku dismounted to give the traditional traveller's shout of victory, after which we duly added a flag to the cairn. Meanwhile, the rest of the party had gone ahead. The track on the further slope was very steep and covered with fine slate dust which made it extremely slippery, so we dismounted and this greatly delayed our reaching the next camp. When we got there tea was ready and our tents were pitched; it was pleasant to chat over a warming cup of tea. Some of our party thought that since the three soldiers had deserted, they might be feeling a little guilty and thus have been led to exaggerate about the hopelessness of the situation. They had been so vague about everything, it appeared that they really knew very little. We came to no decision about our plans, but felt a little uneasy because of the fact that no-one was travelling towards Lhasa on this main road.

It began to rain heavily, so we decided to remain encamped during the next day; early in the morning, while we were sitting in camp, some men on horseback were seen coming towards us. They were wearing dark clothes and some of them were carrying rifles. Great was our surprise when they turned out to be Yag Tulku with his devotee Dorje-tsering, the head of the district around Yag, whose wife, brother and two attendants had also accompanied him. As we drank tea Yag Tulku told us that his baggage was following on some sixty mules; he and his party had hastened on ahead to ask us to wait for it to arrive. He gave us the serious news that Pashö had been completely overrun and that conditions at Chamdo were extremely bad. He said that nothing had happened as yet at either Drölma Lhakhang or Yag. There was a strong resistance force in the Trayap district who had cut the road when the Communists were taking lorries full of loot from Pashö to Chamdo and thus they had succeeded in recovering much of the stuff.

I was delighted to see Yag Tulku again, but realized that his arrival could only mean further difficulties for us all since he had not followed my request to travel lightly; to add to my anxiety, he told me that yet another party was on its way with more baggage loaded on yaks which go very slowly. The exit from Yag had been so public that all the villagers around that place and Drölma Lhakhang had begun to panic. They thought that if all their spiritual directors were leaving there was nothing left for them but to follow; a large party had started and was now also on its way. Yag Tulku sent a message to tell those of his monks who were in charge of the baggage mules where they could find us and again he asked me to wait for their arrival. This obliged us to stay in the same camp for several days, during which time some of the local villagers came to see us thinking that we were resistance troops. They brought food as an offering to the soldiers and were surprised when we offered to pay for it.

Knowing the surrounding country they were able to tell us where we could find grazing for our many animals.

When Yag Tulku's mules arrived we decided to stay where we were for another day or two to concert our plans. Looking at the camp, it appeared enormous and I wondered how we would ever manage to escape with so many men and animals. We had to push on, and on our way down all we could see were endless ranges of mountains stretching out before us. After a couple of days we came to a place called Langtso-kha where we camped by a small lake surrounded by rocky hills. We were told that resistance troops from Central Tibet had already arrived at a nearby village, which meant additional complications for us, for at this point the valley entered a steep gorge where perpendicular rocks in places went right down to the river, so that the track could not be carried further on the same side of the water and travellers had to get across to the opposite side. For this primitive bridges had been built. Even then, there were parts of the gorge which were so steep that no path could run alongside the river; in these places the pathway had been taken over the rocks and, wherever it was blocked by impassable rock faces, platforms made of planks had been built around the obstacle, these being supported on posts fixed into the cliff below. We were not sure if these would be strong enough for heavy loads such as ours and the road all along was so narrow that it was evident that, if we happened to meet Resistance troops coming from the opposite direction, neither party would be able to pass. However, we could not stay by the lake because of the difficulty of finding grazing for our many animals, for what little there was was needed for the resistance army.

We sent some messengers ahead to enquire if further troops were to be expected; they were told that at the moment there was a lull, but more men were expected shortly, and some important leaders had already arrived. Yönten and Dorje-tsering went down to the village to buy supplies and to see the officer in command. He told them that fighting was going on in several places, but did not mention Lhasa. He also said that he was expecting more troops at any moment. He had found the bridges across the river and the platforms on the road were in very bad condition and was arranging for their repair. There was nothing for us to do except to wait where we were. Meanwhile the weather had improved; I had my books with me so I started a study group. Having finished the book on meditation, I began to work on an allegory about the kingdom of

Shambhala and its ruler who will liberate mankind at the end of the Dark Age.

Akong Tulku with his young brother and myself used to go for delightful climbs on the surrounding mountains which were covered with flowers. The local landowner proved very friendly; he frequently invited the senior members of our party to meals and allowed us to graze our animals on his land; also peasants came to see us and sold us some food. One day Karma-tendzin came through with his detachment; they were returning from Lhasa after its fall to the Chinese. We had known for a long time that he had left his home to join the Resistance. Numbers of refugees were coming back along the road together with the soldiers, and we realized that it would be impossible for us to travel against the traffic. Some of the refugees came and camped near us by the lake. They told us all sorts of rumours; some said that the Dalai Lama had come back, others, that the Chinese troops were advancing towards our area. With such crowds of people escaping, there was a growing shortage of food and grazing, and our friend the landowner and the neighbouring villagers were getting very anxious about it. In comparison with these hordes our party seemed quite small. We knew, however, that we must make plans to move elsewhere, and learned that if we retraced our steps we could follow another valley going north westwards. So we thanked the landowner for all his kindness and broke camp.

It was now early June. We travelled for about a week; each day we had to cross a high pass. One day, we passed a man who came from Lhathog, he told us that he had escaped with some nine families, with one Repön as leader. They had brought all their possessions and animals with them and had established themselves in a small valley nearby, where the country was very open with good grazing. The following day they all came to see us bringing barrels of curd, cheeses and fresh milk which we much appreciated, for on our travels we had had all too few milk products. They suggested that they might follow us, but when they realized that we ourselves did not know where we were going, they thought that they also should make no plans for the time being. I gave them my blessing and we moved on. The next day we came to Khamdo Kartop's camp; he had been one of the King of Derge's ministers, and was a follower of Jamgön Kongtrül of Sechen; he had some forty families with him. He told us how his party had fought their way westward in spite of having women and children with them. Their young men were strong and experienced; they had been successful at Kongpo and had captured some of the Communists' ammunition. Now they were in the same position as ourselves, not knowing where to make for. Khamdo Kartop had the same views as myself, he did not want to be responsible for looking after other refugee parties. He knew that there was no chance of going towards Lhasa since the main road was strictly guarded and said he thought that the resistance army still had their headquarters at Lho-kha; they had fought with great bravery in Central Tibet, but had too few men and very little ammunition. He had heard that Andrup Gönpo-trashi had gone to India and, like myself, he was sure that we must all try to get there. In any case we could not stay where we were, on the border of the territory controlled by the Resistance.

I returned to our camp to hear the news that Lama Urgyan Rinpoche was leading a party of refugees from the east in the hopes of reaching India. He was going south by a holy mountain which was a place of pilgrimage. Kino Tulku knew all about the country there and thought that it might be a good plan to go towards India by the Powo valley. We held a meeting in the camp to discuss the situation. Some thought that we should join up with Khando Kartop's party, but none of us were in favour of fighting, so this did not seem to be a very sensible move. Others suggested that we should follow Lama Urgyan. However, our party for the most part wanted to keep separate, for if we joined with other groups our numbers would become dangerously large. Since we knew that we could not stay where we were, I decided that we must continue southwards at least for a few months, and by that time we would know more about the state of affairs in Tibet; refugees were coming in from all directions and we would soon learn what was happening everywhere. I sent Dorje-tsering to inform Khando Kartop of our plans. I said that in the future we might wish to co-operate, but for the present I had decided to act on my own.

A further three monks had joined our party; they had no transport and Yag Tulku took them on to help him. Before we left, Repön, who was directing the refugee encampment, sent his son to have a further talk with me. His group thought that they should sell some of their things to buy horses and then join my party. He wanted to know what we had decided to do and if I would allow them to come with us. I told him that we were still uncertain about everything and that each day things were becoming more complicated. He replied

that even so they all intended to follow us. I advised him not to part
with his animals, or to follow us too soon, because all the routes were
over-crowded with refugees and we might not be able to get
through. However, they went on getting rid of their possessions.

Some soldiers came along who had escaped from Norbu Lingka,
the Dalai Lama's summer residence outside Lhasa; they gave us a
graphic account of what had happened there. They had witnessed
the Chinese shelling the building and seen some of their fellow
soldiers killed. No-one knew whether the Dalai Lama was still within the walls; there was, however, a suspicion that he had escaped.
They had also seen the Potala being shelled; the bombardment had
begun at a signal from a Communist gun. After the attacks on the
Norbu Lingka and the Potala there was no possibility of further
fighting, for the Chinese had taken up positions in big houses in the
town and were firing from them. It was obvious that all this had been
prepared for some months previously. These men had escaped, but
a number of resistance soldiers would not leave the place and they
had all been massacred.

Another man told me how he had left Jyekundo with a large group
of refugees. They had reached a place half way to Lhasa in the flat
country round Changthang when they were sighted by Chinese
aeroplanes and Communist patrols attacked them from all directions. The fighting was severe; among others the abbot of Jyekundo
monastery was shot and all the wounded were left to die, while the
survivors from the battle starved to death as the Communists had
taken all their food and possessions. The refugees had, however,
actually succeeded in shooting down one of the enemy planes. There
were many different groups of refugees all around that area, and the
Chinese were everywhere. My informant's particular camp had been
attacked seventeen times. On one occasion, when the group were
trying to go forward and most of the men had gone ahead to secure
a passage through the surrounding Communist troops leaving the
women and children in the camp to follow after them, a husband
and his wife had put their three young sons, aged between eleven
and eight, on their horses, and while they themselves were saddling
their own animals the boys' horses took fright and bolted. The
parents took it for granted that the horses were following others
leaving the camp, so went on themselves to the agreed camping
ground; however, on reaching it there was no sign of the children
and the mother in despair jumped into the river.

The man who spoke to me had witnessed the whole tragedy and went on to tell me how several days later when he was scouting round he had discovered the three boys sheltering from the rain, under a rock; two of their horses were nearby, the third was dead and the children were starving. The eldest boy had tried to cut out some of the dead horse's flesh, but his small knife had been useless for the task. The children asked him where was their mother. Since another attack from the enemy was expected at any moment, the man could not take the children with him; however, he managed to arrange with some nearby herdsmen to look after them. He had later met their father in Lhasa and told him how he had found the boys.

One important piece of news reached us about that time: we were told that Gyalwa Karmapa had left his monastery some weeks before the fall of Lhasa, with Dingo Chentze Rinpoche and his brother and the newly found incarnation of Jamgön Kongtrül of Pepung, who was still an infant, also the young *Taisitu* abbot of Pepung: many abbots and lamas had travelled with them. They had gone through Bhutan to India and had been able to take some of their possessions with them. This news left my monks in no further doubt that we too must face the hardships of escape. They could not, however, understand why, if Gyalwa Karmapa had arranged to escape himself, he had given no indication of his plans when I wrote to him from Drölma Lhakhang. I explained to them that none of us could advise others in such a situation; I was in the same difficulty myself when asked for my advice, since I did not even know where our own party could find refuge.

Some of the troops who were passing through told us enthralling stories; the resistance soldiers who had fought at Kongpo had been very brave, but they had been forced to retreat, for they could do nothing against the superior arms of the Chinese; their spirit was still unbroken and they were ready to carry on the fight at any time.

We now made our way across a range of mountains in a south-westerly direction and after negotiating the high pass of Nupkong La we reached the China to Lhasa main road in front of the bridge at the western end of the dangerous passage through the gorge which we had not dared to attempt before. There were many refugees going the same way. We camped in a small field from where we could see the road. I was apprehensive and scanned it carefully through field-glasses; it certainly looked impossible; however, when I saw a man with some baggage mules going across it, I thought it might be feasible. We asked some villagers for their help with our animals and started off at daybreak the following morning. Fortunately no-one was coming from the opposite direction. We found that as long as the animals were left to themselves they were all right; we were able to reach the last bridge safely about noon and stopped at the first small camping ground beyond it, for with so many refugees on the way, we thought we might have difficulty in finding another suitable place.

Nearby, we met a number of monks from Kamtrül Rinpoche's monastery of Khampa-gar, among them the same Genchung Lama who had served as *chöpön* (director of rites) for the *wangkur* at Yag; with him he had his sister who was a nun, and there were also a number of villagers in his party. The monks gave me a distressing account of how their monastery had been invaded by the Communists. They had all been imprisoned and the senior lamas shot one after another. Only a very few monks had escaped from the monastery itself, the party on the road having mostly come from the retreat centre; it was sad to see how, after so many peaceful years of monastic life, they now found themselves in this tragic position. They were, however, enormously thankful that their abbot had been able to escape to India. I was a little afraid that they would want to join us, for our party was already far too numerous; before they could suggest anything, I hinted that we had no set plans ourselves; I said we had already been forced to change plans suddenly several times. However, they decided to try to get to India from the west side of the gorge. Only the *chöpön* and his sister asked to come with us; they each had a horse and some mules for their baggage.

CHAPTER FIFTEEN

REFUGEES ON THE MOVE

WE travelled eastward along the main road to Alado where there is a junction of two rivers; we followed the southern one for a few miles and turned into a valley on its west side. It was much warmer here; the country was green and covered with trees of the holly family as well as bamboos. This valley was thronged with refugees going the same way; when we asked them where they were going to, they said that they were just following the people in front of them. With all these animals on the road there was less and less grazing available; we passed the carcasses of many beasts which had died on the road and they made the air putrid. When we camped it was difficult to find a clean spot; all possible sites were so crowded that there was hardly enough space to stretch the tent ropes. Many of the refugees wanted to consult me; they thought that a party like ours must have a plan. The only answer I could give them was that I had no clearer ideas than themselves; we were simply all going in the same direction. The lamas among the crowds continued to carry on their devotions, and the valley echoed with the sounds of their chanting, their drums and other musical instruments. The people were wonderfully cheerful, they laughed and joked and sang among themselves. We went on like this for several days. The queen of Nangchen and some of her ministers were in a large group among the refugees; she was still cheerful and welcomed me warmly as we exchanged white scarves. She was a little disturbed about the direction that we were all following and had sent several messengers to different places to make enquiries about alternative routes; none of them had returned. A steep and very high pass lay in front of us which was still under snow. It was a strange sight to watch this dark stream of people looking like a black ribbon stretched over the white landscape of the pass. I walked beside the queen and was surprised to see how tough she was; she preferred to go on foot through the snow rather than to ride. After crossing the pass we went down to a series of valleys; there was more room here for camping and we were no longer distressed by the proximity of dead animals. We followed the valleys circling between the hills; the queen decided to stay with her party in one of the smaller ones, but all the rest of us went on. When we thought that we had crossed the last pass on our route we discovered on the following day that there was an even steeper one rising ahead of us. The road leading up to it was so dangerous that one of our horses with its load fell over the precipice and we were not able to recover anything. At the top we found there was a broad plateau where we could all camp. Karma-tendzin was already there; he was recruiting all the able bodied men among the refugees for the resistance army. Lama Urgyan Rinpoche was also camping there with a party of monks; I had not met him before although I had heard a great deal about him, for he was a disciple of my predecessor and also a great friend of Gyalwa Karmapa who used often to consult him on specially perplexing questions. He was an old man and considered it his duty to give advice to a young person like myself. He told me not to go to India but to stay where I was; he thought it strange that I had such a large following. I had to explain to him who everybody was and how some of us had met at the *wangkur* which I had given at Yag. I said that we all had made up our minds to try to get to India; he was very firm that I should not go with the others, though my friends could do as they liked, and added that this was a request as well as an order. I asked him various questions about Gyalwa Karmapa and my other friends in Central Tibet. He himself could easily have gone with them, but he had not wished to do so. I wanted to know if he thought that it would ever be necessary for him to escape to India and he replied that he thought the time might come, though he was quite sure that this should not be attempted at present, for there was certain to be a lull before such a step would become imperative. He added, 'this plateau and all the valleys below it are holy places of pilgrimage. We should all join together here in meditation to gain spiritual strength so that we may carry on with our normal duties.'

Karma-tendzin, the guerilla captain, had his son with him on the plateau; he was not thinking of going to India at that time, being entirely intent upon the work of the Resistance. He could give me no suggestions about what route we should follow or even about the advisability of our attempting to escape or not. On the plateau there was an acute shortage of food, grazing and space. I pointed out to him that he was the only person who could deal with the situation and direct these vast crowds to spread themselves in different parts of the country. It was impossible for the local inhabitants round here to provide necessities for so many people. He agreed that this should be done; however, he felt that he must first get the able-bodied refugees and the local men to join the resistance forces. I told him how Pu Dündül was organizing local groups and not allowing anyone who could fight to leave his district. Throughout our travels we had found that in all the villages the men were eager to join in the fighting against the Communists.

A further influx of refugees arrived on the plateau. They had travelled quickly, having little baggage, and had passed a large party coming from Drölma Lhakhang and Yag travelling in a group with Jigme Rinpoche and my bursar who were bringing the heavy baggage loaded on yaks. This group had crossed the Shab-ye bridge and had arrived at Lhodzong where they were stopping since they were now uncertain whether or not to continue their journey in view of the fact that the situation around Drölma Lhakhang and Yag seemed to have quietened down. At the same time a messenger came from Kino Tulku's monastery to tell him that all was quiet there. My own party had again been growing restless, feeling that perhaps our flight into the unknown had been unnecessary. This led to a long discussion, since it seemed as if Lama Urgyan's advice might after all be right, in which case should we not delay trying to go to India and wait for a lull in the hostilities? In the meantime, I made enquiries from the local people about the country around and about what mountain tracks we would have to follow if we decided to continue on our way to India. They all told me that it would be impossible to travel by the valleys or to cross the mountain ranges at this time of year, for all the rivers would be in spate; which meant in effect that we would have to remain where we were. I myself was quite determined that as soon as it was possible we should carry out our plan to escape. I felt I must inform the party at Lhodzong of what we intended doing; Akong Tulku's elder brother and one of Kino Tulku's monks volunteered to take the message. In my letter I said that in any case we intended to make for India; there was no question of turning back. Lama Urgyan, however, took it for granted that we were following his advice and not immediately leaving the plateau, so he urged us to make a pilgrimage to the holy places in the nearby valley and even named a date for us to go there. We were a little doubtful whether it would be possible to cross the high mountain pass which lay in the way and I thought the wisest plan would be for only three of us, namely myself, Akong Tulku and one monk, to make the attempt under Lama Urgyan's leadership. When we joined him he asked where were the rest of our party, for he had been very excited at the prospect of conducting our whole group, animals included. I explained to him that the others had not come because we thought there might be difficulties in crossing the pass. Actually when our small party reached it the snow was so deep that we found it impossible to get through.

Most of the refugees had by now gone on to the Nyewo valley, so the plateau was no longer so crowded. We decided to move to its farther end to a level spot near a lake. Yönten went to Nyewo to get provisions, but found a scarcity there and this made us realize that we must eke out our provisions and rely for the most part on *tsampa* and wild vegetables. Karma-tendzin was also staying at this end of the plateau; he had a battery radio with him and we used to listen in to the news both from Peking and Delhi broadcast in Tibetan. The Peking programme was full of propaganda saying how wicked the uprising had been, when the Chinese had only come to Tibet to liberate its people; however, they had now settled all the disturbances and there were very few resistance troops left in Tibet. The broadcast from Delhi said that the Dalai Lama was already in Mussoorie.

It was a surprise one day when Repön's son suddenly appeared at our camp. His father had sent him on ahead to tell me that they had sold most of their possessions and animals and had bought extra arms and ammunition from fellow refugees. They had got past the gorge with its difficult piece of road, had crossed the bridge, and were now on the track leading southwards where they were waiting until the son could scout out the route ahead and see what camping grounds and grazing were available. I told him all I knew and he went back.

A number of senior lamas had now also arrived on the plateau, having travelled with various groups of refugees. Lama Urgyan thought it would be a good plan if they, together with our party, were to cross the holy mountain to a small valley beyond it, which was in the heart of the pilgrimage country. The local people had suggested to him that the pass could be crossed if they sent unloaded yaks first to tread down the snow, and they had offered to help him in this way. On studying this plan, however, I saw that the valley in question was extremely small; there would be no room for such a large party and the conditions would be so crowded that we should fare even worse than before. I did not want to offend Lama Urgyan so I told him that if the yaks cleared the way, there was no need for us all to go together, my party could follow later. I would let him know if we decided to go first to Nyewo valley. His party made three attempts with yaks, and the third time they were able to cross the pass. I would certainly have liked to have gone on pilgrimage to these holy places and also to have further talks with Lama Urgyan, but there was no further opportunity to do so. We heard later that when his party reached the valley they found it was so narrow that there was not enough room for them, moreover it was a highly dangerous place where rock falls were frequent and in fact some of their horses were killed by falling stones. Meanwhile Yönten sent some food to us from Nyewo, but stayed on there himself hoping to buy further supplies.

After the talks I had had with Lama Urgyan, I realized how important it was for me to go into retreat for a short time to renew my strength. In any case I thought that we should move nearer to Nyewo and hoped I might find a suitable place for a retreat while on the way there. Climbing down from the plateau we crossed the river below it. We now had to go up a steep zig-zag track which led across a pass in a high mountain range. It was dangerously slippery, for here all the ground was covered with a white slimy mud with no vegetation. Had an animal slipped, it would have crashed down on the people behind. The top of the pass was like a knife edge; however it was easier going down on the other side, where there were trees and undergrowth. We came to a nice little open valley which seemed a good place for a camp; a few refugees were already there at the farther end. In this quiet spot I was even able to go on with my writing; however, the peace did not last for long, for all Repön's party soon arrived on the scene. They were very considerate and put up their camp about a mile away from ours. A few refugees were passing through who told me that bursar Tsethar's party were close behind on their way to join us. Akong Tulku and I walked round the surrounding country until we found a suitable place where one could go into retreat; it was less than a mile from our camp in a wooded spot. It was agreed that visitors could come for an hour in the morning and for a couple of hours in the afternoon if they would bring me some food; I could make my own fires. I took with me my tent, a small shrine and some books. Here it was possible to relax after so much turmoil, thus gaining spiritual strength in order to face whatever lay ahead.

The first few days I heard some strange animal noises round the tent at night and felt a little uneasy; however, I soon found that these visitors were not dangerous. This part of the country was very different to my part of Tibet, it was warmer and there was a much greater variety of trees and plants and many more animals and birds. The moonlight shone through the trees forming a shadow like lace work on the tent.

One morning, Karma-ngötrup came to see me; he was breathless with excitement telling me that large brown bears had come in the night and had attacked our horses and mules. They had killed one horse and mauled several others; they were returning every night. Several days after this he found a bear's footprints just outside my tent; others of our party also came to implore me to leave my retreat but I had no fear myself and stayed on where I was. One is ever in the grip of the law of *karma*, so it is senseless to worry overmuch.

Some days later we received an alarming message from Yönten stating that the Communists were coming through the Nyewo valley; the refugees were all in a panic trying to find hiding-places. I still thought we might stay where we were for a further day, since if the Communists should come there was nothing we could do anyway. The following day another messenger arrived to say that it was a false alarm; some resistance soldiers had been mistaken for Communist troops.

We already knew that after his mother had been sent to China by the Communists the young king of Derge had organized a resistance force in East Tibet which had been joined by other local leaders. We now heard that he had been forced to escape accompanied by a number of his ministers with hundreds of refugees following, and they were now close to Lhodzong. They had fought their way from Derge and had been fortunate in suffering few casualties and little loss of baggage. The party had gained such a reputation for bravery that the mere fact of their being in the same neighbourhood gave other refugees renewed hope. However, conditions in all the area round Lhodzong were daily becoming more and more trying;

ngbo peasants threshing barley

unt Namcha Barwa (The Fiery Mountain of Heavenly Metal)

12

The main Brahmaputra Valley

refugees were crowding into every valley and the shortage of food and grazing was acute.

Nyewo was also becoming disastrously congested; in its vicinity there were few places left where other refugees could shelter, and since all the rivers were in spate at this time of year it was almost impossible to get across them to look for empty camping sites.

Though the Chinese already had possession of most of the country, the resistance forces still held the high pass at the end of the Nyewo valley; in order to get supplies they continually raided the Communist troops on the other side, in which operation they had been very successful. I was extremely uneasy, however, for if the Communists managed to take the pass they would inevitably attack us. At one moment rumours came through that they were actually approaching but fortunately there was no foundation to these reports, for after some severe fighting they failed to get through. I knew, however, that sooner or later we would have to quit this valley, though no-one could offer any suggestion where our party should make for; the final decision would have to come from me. I felt that as soon as I returned to the camp I would be caught up again in a ferment of agitation, and I still needed to be quiet in order to concentrate on the problem of how we could proceed. I therefore decided to stay in my retreat for a further two weeks, which I spent in intensive meditation. One night I had a vivid dream that I was leading a party of pilgrims to a holy place. Communist soldiers were on guard beside the road, but they appeared not to see us. We came to a river, the waters of which were tinged with blood. I had just crossed it by a bridge of logs when I heard a voice behind me saying, 'Some of the pilgrims have fallen into the stream'. I had not seen this myself, for I was resting on the further bank. This dream made a great impression on me.

Bears had again attacked our animals; the messenger who came to tell me about this was followed by a second monk with the news that my bursar had arrived at the camp ahead of the baggage party in the hopes of discussing things with me. He was in a complaining mood, grumbling that nothing was being properly organized; it shocked him to think that we could ever have allowed bears to get at our animals. He considered the place we had chosen for our camp to be completely unsuitable and said that we must go back to the baggage camp which was on the farther side of the high pass; he felt quite sure that there was no immediate danger from the Communists.

I asked about the conditions in his camp and soon discovered that they were just as bad as in ours; the place was very overcrowded and no-one knew where to go next. They had lost many of their animals through lack of grazing, besides being short of food themselves. In spite of these difficulties, Tsethar was determined that we should retrace our steps and join them and he told Yag Tulku and Kino Tulku that this must be done. When they hesitated, he said that they could do as they liked, but that his own abbot must definitely go back. We argued about it for three days, till I finally decided to reject all his proposals and informed my party that I thought our best plan would be to go forward to Nyewo, as many of the refugees who had preceded us there had by now dispersed in various directions. Yönten was having difficulty in sending food supplies over to our valley and if we went to Nyewo food would be nearer at hand. I told Tsethar that it was out of the question for us to go back to his camp. I reminded him that I had travelled over a large part of the country and had a fairly accurate picture of what was happening; I considered that our only hope lay in getting to India. He must now take active steps to sell all useless baggage and only keep the most portable things. To this he would not agree; he said that everyone else had taken all their baggage and yaks with them. However, all my younger companions were so strongly of my opinion that he finally gave way, saying he would do his best, and went back to his own camp.

Akong Tulku's brother now returned, having met the baggage party on their way to join us. He was very critical about the way we were always changing our minds as to which direction to take, whereas Tsethar's party had come straight by the main road. He said that since I still appeared to have no real plan he must now take Akong Tulku and his young brother back to join Tsethar's party; if later on I made a definite decision about the route to be followed and Tsethar's group agreed, his own group could then re-join us. The night that he was with us the bears came again and mauled his horse, which added to his opinion that our camping ground was not well chosen. I reminded him that when I planned my escape I had written to Akong Tulku stressing that he must decide for himself whether he wanted to come with me or not. When he replied that he wished to join me, I promised the people at his monastery that I would do my best to look after him. Now it must again be his own decision and if he wished to join Tsethar's group he could do so;

but the responsibility of looking after him would no longer be mine. Akong Tulku's brother was rather overwhelmed by this argument so, after the two of them had talked it over, he said he thought that perhaps he should go back to the other camp and try to persuade the people there to dispose of their extra baggage; but he also told me that in any case he would like to rejoin our party before long.

I now left my retreat and returned to the camp. We held a meeting and decided to go on to Nyewo. It was now the first week of July. Another very high mountain ridge lay before us; going up was not difficult, but the descent on the further side involved us in a drop of some nine thousand feet. We were tormented by flies and it was very hot and exhausting, so we camped as soon as we reached the bridge below the pass. When the villagers learned that I was in the party they welcomed us warmly and various families invited me to stay with them and perform devotional ceremonies. Yönten had to buy supplies without it being known that they were for us, or the people would have undercharged. Again many refugees came to be blessed and to ask for advice.

News reached us here that Lama Urgyan was finding it difficult to get supplies in his little valley and might possibly come to the valley where we were staying, so it was evident that I could no longer think of going on a pilgrimage to the local holy places.

There was also some more serious news; the Communists were moving towards the borders of all the districts still held by Resistance troops. We heard aeroplanes at night and the local people were getting frightened. Since we were all facing the same possible danger, there was a great deal of sympathy shown and I was able to get much local information about possible escape routes. It appeared that if we were able to cross the junction of the Alado and Nyewo rivers, there was a rough track across the mountains leading to part of the lower Kongpo valley. However the river had been in spate since early spring so no-one had been able to cross, nor was it known what the conditions might be like on the further side. People told me that it would be impossible to build any sort of a bridge with the river in its present state and no ferry boat could cross it. We thought, however, it might be possible for our horses to swim across, but were told that the track beside the river ran further on through a steep gorge and that since a recent earthquake this path had been impossible for baggage animals because huge rocks had fallen across it. The local villagers could not really tell us much about this route, since none of them had actually followed it. I wondered if I could possibly do it all on foot, always having been accustomed to riding, and Kino Tulku and Yag Tulku felt even more apprehensive. However they were determined to try.

News reached us that the Derge resistance leader Khamdo Kartop was thinking of coming in our direction and that the queen of Nangchen might also wish to escape by this same route; both of them were still fighting their way through. It seemed possible that we might have to organize a large joint party, rather than make the attempt with only our own small group. At all events it was essential to keep our plans to ourselves, otherwise too many refugees might want to join us, thus making the party quite unmanageable. It was all very complicated.

Rumours had it that the Communists had by this time overrun the greater part of the country and were massing troops in the north east, while more were coming in from the north west; they were in full force in the Kongpo valley and in the south.

Various families had left Jigme Rinpoche's and Tsethar's groups to come to Nyewo, and Repön's party also arrived after losing many of their yaks. They all wanted to join us. Besides these, a party of some eighty people from Dorje-tsering's area, led by one Lama Riwa arrived quite unexpectedly and attached themselves to us.

I went down to inspect the river with several men, including Urgyan-tendzin who had proved a most knowledgeable and competent person. There were no large waves, but the current was very strong. Urgyan-tendzin thought it was difficult to cross but that it might yet be managed, so we sent a letter to my bursar telling him that we intended to attempt the crossing.

A few days later I was asked to perform a funeral ceremony on the other side of the Nyewo river. We had almost finished it when news came that the Chinese were in the upper part of the Nyewo valley where the Resistance troops were fighting them. As we returned to our camp across the river we found the bridge thronged with refugees pouring through it in the opposite direction. Friends whom I met on the bridge all told me that I should be going the other way, as the south side of the water would probably be dangerous. When I got back to our camp, I found all our party beside themselves with anxiety. Some of them wanted to follow the other refugees to the north side of the bridge, and all those who had lately joined our party had already gone. My people hardly dared to trust me in case

I might have some different plan. Karma-tendzin's second-in-command was already on our side of the river; all the local people were in a state of panic, with the males arming themselves with daggers, knives or axes, in fact with any weapons they could lay hands on, for though they had no rifles, they intended to resist as best they could. Up till then we had not heard any sounds of guns or fighting. I sent a message to Karma-tendzin's lieutenant asking for the latest news of what had occurred in the Nyewo valley. He had heard nothing definite; as far as he knew no eye-witness had seen any Chinese and he himself was waiting for a further message. After waiting for a couple of hours, I decided that we must move. I spoke again to the locals who were unable to tell me anything fresh.

The Knot of Eternity

CHAPTER SIXTEEN

TRAVELLING THE HARD WAY

WE were now left with only our own party, and there were three alternative ways for us to follow. The first was for us to try to cross the turbulent Nyewo river in spite of the fact that we had very little information about the route and did not know whether any Chinese were in these parts. Moreover, should we attempt to go this way, we would have to leave our animals behind and go on foot. Another way would be to go on horseback through Kongpo keeping to our side of the Nyewo river; this might be very dangerous, for it was more than probable that Chinese troops would be in occupation of much of that area; besides, there would be an added difficulty in our having to cross the very high Lochen Pass. Thirdly we might join forces with Kartop and perhaps also with the queen of Nangchen in order to break through to the south west by fighting our way. Since a move was necessary, I decided to go first to a small valley I knew of, near the point where we would attempt to cross the torrent if we decided to do so. It had a very narrow entrance which opened onto broader land suitable for camping; the grazing was good and there were no villages in the valley, nor had any other refugees discovered it. We travelled by night, keeping on the alert all the time in case we should hear the sound of guns. A man was left in the Nyewo valley to report any further news of the Communists' approach. The following day he came to tell us that nothing had happened and that the valley was deserted. Headquarters sent me a message to say that the Chinese had come from Kongpo through Lochen Pass on their way to Nyewo, but the resistance troops had attacked them and captured one of the Chinese guns, also rifles and much ammunition. The local people who had rushed off with the refugees were now returning to their homes. They wanted our party to come back and begged that I should stay with them to perform various rites. However, I decided to leave the camp where it was and went backwards and forwards myself to perform whatever rites were needed.

The suddenness of the Communist scare seemed to me to have come as a warning that we might expect them in our area at any moment. They were definitely intent upon occupying this small pocket of country. We heard aeroplanes at night. I consulted all the senior members of our party and it was decided that we must move and that the only possible route was the one across the difficult river, which definitely meant travelling on foot down the gorge. Urgyan-tendzin said that, if I was determined to go that way, he would do his best to help in the crossing. He had previously suggested that we should procure some leather suitable for building coracles; now he immediately set to work on having one made. When it was ready we took it down to the river to make the experiment. He attached the coracle to the shore with a long rope; then got into it himself and paddled across; he found it quite easy to reach the further bank. A second coracle was put in hand. I sent some of our horses and baggage mules back to Tsethar with a message to tell Akong Tulku about our plan, suggesting that his party should follow. The rest of the animals and baggage I sent to Lama Urgyan, with a letter saying, 'The wind of *karma* is blowing in this direction; there is no indica-tion that we should do otherwise than attempt this way of escape. Events are changing so suddenly, one cannot afford to ignore the dangers. I hope you will make up your mind to carry out your plans without delay and that they will work out well with the blessing of Buddha.'

With all this public activity of building coracles and sending the animals away our plans leaked out. Repön's group and the refugees under Lama Riwa together with various other small parties returned to join us; they camped all around our valley which was really too small for them to share. All of them were determined to come with us and they expected me to assume the leadership of the whole party which now amounted to one hundred and seventy people. We still did not know whether the Communists were on the other side of the river or not. I resorted to *tagpa* (divination); it indicated that no Chinese were there. We organized some porters among the local people, so were still able to take a part of our possessions to be bartered later for necessities. I had about thirty porters to carry my own things and altogether one hundred were needed for the whole party.

We started our expedition with two coracles each holding eight people; Urgyan-tendzin had taught a second man to paddle, though he did most of the work himself. I had a great feeling of happiness that we were starting at last. We had just got under way when a messenger arrived from Karma-tendzin asking me to join forces with his group, but I replied that his offer had come too late, we had already made our plans and could not go back on them. The soldier who brought me Karma-tendzin's message had been in the fight at Lochen pass; he gave me a vivid description of it all. He was a member of some patrols on the mountain side who were hiding behind bushes overlooking the pass. They watched the Communists creep forward and place their guns in position to attack the front line of the resistance troops, who were still behind their entrenchments. The patrols waited until the attack began and then closed on the enemy from all sides. The soldier himself had jumped on a Chinese soldier just as he was about to fire a gun which the Resistance troops succeeded in capturing.

Many of the lamas and refugees in Nyewo sent kind messages when they heard that we were leaving. A man had gone ahead of us to the next village to warn the inhabitants of our approach, for visitors seldom came to this remote part of the country and we thought our large numbers might cause alarm. Everyone had to carry some of the baggage; my attendant disapproved of my doing this and wanted to add my load to his; I had to make it clear to him that each of us must do his share; Kino Tulku carried the heaviest load. We felt that we must acclimatize ourselves to this difficult way of travelling, so we made our first day a short one. The rough track ran beside the river which now plunged through a rocky gorge. It was obvious that no animal could be brought this way, for there were a lot of huge rocks on the track with deep crevices between them, spanned by fallen pine trees; men could only move in single file. At night it was difficult to find enough space to lie down and our bedding was of the simplest. The country here was much warmer and damper than the parts we had come from, with more luxuriant vegetation. The nearer we got to the village of Rigong-kha the worse the track became, till we were faced with a very high cliff coming right down to the river. I was horrified when I looked at a very sketchy zig-zag path going up this cliff. I had expected a track, but there appeared to be nothing more than a broken chain dangling at intervals, beside what appeared to be little cracks in the rock. One of the porters told me to watch the first of their men going up; he had a load on his back and never seemed to hold on to anything, but just jumped to the footholds cut in the rock; I thought I could never do it. Some of the younger men failed to get through unaided and had to hand the baggage they were carrying to one of the porters. The latter offered to carry some of the older men on their backs, but this kind offer was not accepted, it seemed too dangerous; instead they went up very slowly roped to porters in front and behind. When they got half way some were so frightened that they refused to move and the younger people had to be firm with them saying that the porters were not going to hold on to a stationary person; they must pull themselves together and carry on. All this took a very long time. I was one of the last to attempt the passage and, while waiting, I had time to study everyone's methods of tackling the awkward passage. The porters, by agreement among themselves, had selected the best men to carry me up, but I said I would prefer to walk. What rather disturbed me was that after so many people had climbed up the same shallow footholds, a lot of slippery mud was left on them; I was wearing European rubber-soled shoes which slip easily and this made it difficult to get a grip on the narrow footholds. However, I did not find it as hard as I expected.

When I reached the top of this hazardous ascent I found myself on a very narrow ledge with a sheer drop beneath it. I asked the porters 'what do I do next?' They told me that there was a long ladder from the ledge going down to a rock in the middle of the river; from this rock there was a line of bridges made of pine trunks which crossed a series of rocks to the farther bank. The porter looked very cheerful and said 'It's only a ladder; just follow me.' I was still roped to the two porters. When I got on the ladder I saw how immensely long it was; we seemed to be so high up that a man at the bottom looked like a mere dwarf. It was made of single pine trunks lashed together from end to end, with notches cut in the wood for footholds. When I climbed down the first few notches I could see the swirling green waters of the river underneath; a few more steps, and I felt I was poised in space over an expanse of water. There was a cold wind coming up from a large cave under the rock into which the river was pouring; worst of all, the ladder shook in a terrifying way with the weight of the many porters who were there trying to help me. All our party who had reached the bottom of the ladder stopped to watch me. I was told that the porters

7 *The perilous route to Rigong-kha*

had had great difficulties with some of the older men, who had been so frightened that they had nearly fainted. There was great rejoicing when I rejoined them at the bottom. When we reached the dry land we pitched camp and from here we could see the ladder and the ledge some hundred feet higher up. Next day's track proved to be no better than the last; no part of it was on the level and we had continually to climb up cliff faces more than a thousand feet high, sometimes only by footholds cut in the rock. However, after our first experience these held no terrors for us. In places we had to make up the roadway itself because, since the Chinese had come into Tibet, this route had been little used and much of it had been disturbed bys the earthquake of 1950 which had been especially severe in thi region. I was getting more acclimatized to walking and sleeping under these rough conditions.

The porter whom we had sent ahead to Rigong-kha returned with a local man to welcome us to his village. He told us that there were no Chinese in Rigong-kha, though they were further eastward in the valley; however, there were strong resistance forces in Upper Powo who believed that they could push the Communists back.

Kino Tulku had been too energetic, the very heavy loads which he had chosen to carry were beyond his strength and his eyesight became affected. We feared it was a blood clot; however, there was nowhere on the track where we could stop, so the most important thing was to get him to the village as soon as possible. From where we were we could see small farms in the distance, but there was still a long way to walk and it was all uphill. There were very few streams and we found the going very exhausting without any water to drink. When we came to a field about half-a-mile from Rigong-kha we stopped for the night and some of our party went up to the village to buy food. They found most of the villagers very friendly. Kino Tulku's eyes had been growing steadily worse and the whole camp was very worried as we thought this might affect our plans. The following day a number of the villagers came to visit us. They were very surprised at finding so large a party and could not conceal their curiosity, for they had never met people from East Tibet other than a few pilgrims; no other refugees had come this way. In this isolated village the inhabitants had never seen horses, mules or yaks, their only domestic animals being small buffaloes and pigs. Their dialect was a mixture of Kongpo and Powo and they wore the Kongpo dress, which for the men was the ordinary *chuba* (gown) made of

woollen cloth worn under a long straight garment made of goatskin
with the hair on the outside. These were belted at the waist and cut
open in the middle to slip over the head. The women's *chubas* were
also of wool; they wore caps edged with gold brocade and they all
carried a good deal of jewellery, chiefly in the form of earrings or
necklaces; their boots were embroidered in bright colours.

The climb up to the village was easy and the people there gave us
a warm welcome. We were a little afraid lest some traveller coming
from the eastern side might turn out to be a spy, but actually there
was no need for anxiety on this score. The villagers had had no
authentic news of happenings at Lhasa; some vague rumours had
reached them through the Communists in the lower part of the
valley: when we assured them that the Communists had taken
control in Lhasa and that the Dalai Lama had escaped to India, they
still would not believe it. Traders coming to Rigong-kha brought the
news that though the resistance forces had fought very bravely in the
Tong-gyug valley and had at first held the bridge, the Communists
had finally gained possession of it. Now, all the area as far as
Chamdo was in Communist hands; they had re-built the road from
Chengtu in Szechuan to Chamdo and their troops were everywhere.
In all the districts they had started to form rigorous indoctrination
groups. It was now certain that they would penetrate before long
into the Tong-gyug valley, barring our further route along it, so we
were obliged to revise all our ideas on the subject of the best route
to follow. Up till then we had been hoping to follow the Yigong river
to where it joins the Brahmaputra, almost at the point where that
great river turns down towards India. There was nothing to be done
but to find another way. We asked the villagers if they knew of any
other route by which we could cross the military highway the
Chinese had constructed, but though they supposed that there
might be some tracks across the mountain ranges, they really had no
idea how we could get through to Lower Kongpo. Some people
suggested that we might join forces with the Potö resistance group,
but they were some distance away and in any case we were not bent
on fighting.

There was a small temple in Rigong-kha and the villagers asked
the lama in charge of it to invite me to stay with him so that I could
perform certain rites on their behalf; they also wanted me to preach
there. People from several small villages in surrounding valleys came
in order to ask for a blessing and some of them suggested that we

could still hide in various remote places in the vicinity where there would be little chance of the Chinese finding us. Since no other refugees had come to Rigong-kha, there had been no inroads on their food supplies and all the villagers were very generous in giving us hospitality after our arduous journey.

Meanwhile, we were preparing for further travels, giving our heavy goods such as rugs in exchange for food, particularly such items as *tsampa*, dried meat, butter, cheeses and pork fat. Our porters had been sent back to Nyewo as soon as we reached Rigong-kha; they had been ever so helpful and, though not long with us, we had got to know them very well. We gave them a number of presents such as jewellery, cloth etc. as we had little money; but they were so modest that we had difficulty in persuading them to accept even that much. As we parted they wished us a good journey and expressed the hope that we might escape the Communists.

We stayed at Rigong-kha for about a fortnight; it was now the end of August and we decided to move to the small valley of Tso-phu, lying due south. There are two high passes at the upper part of this valley, one leading south east and the other south west. We had not decided which to take; however, we thought this valley would be on our way and it was not very safe to remain at Rigong-kha for much longer. First we had to re-cross the river. The group of refugees under Lama Riwa decided to stay on at Rigong-kha saying they would join us later. The rest of us, who included Repön's group and some other refugees, went down to the river, taking some men from the village to act as porters. The torrent was so turbulent that it had been impossible to build a bridge across it. Instead, a thick hemp rope had been fixed to the rocks on either bank. A pulley on it was attached to a belt to hold the passenger; a long rope affixed to this was held between the men on the opposite banks. The weight of the passenger carried him into the middle of the river, and the men on the further side hauled him up the rest of the way.

Even while we were crossing the river we were told that some Communists were coming this way. In case they appeared suddenly we were resolved to cut the rope.

Kino Tulku's eyes had improved under treatment, but now his legs began to trouble him so that he was only able to walk very slowly. He believed his illness to be incurable. His wife, however, was determined that we should all keep together; she was beside herself with anxiety; it was difficult for me to know what to do.

However, after the scare that the Chinese were behind us, Kino Tulku himself decided that we were not to stay behind on his account, saying that he would go to a small village in a nearby valley where he could rest—a sorrowful parting for us all. We were still keeping in touch with our friends in Rigong-kha who sent us supplies and gave us the latest news. I sent a messenger to the village to ask them if they knew of anyone with a knowledge of Lower Kongpo who would be prepared to come to India with us and act as guide. They promised to find someone; they had several people in mind and thought it would not take more than a week to send a man. I sent a similar message to Kino Tulku in case there was anyone in his village, but no-one appeared, so we started to go further down the valley. We had yet to decide which of the two passes we should take. A lama came to see us from Rigong-kha; he told us that he had brought his party from Nyewo following our lead. The conditions there had grown worse, more and more refugees were crowding into the area and there was a very serious food shortage, also a good deal of illness. Everyone was saying that Trungpa Tulku's party had shown the way of escape and many people were starting to follow, though others had decided against this course, on hearing what a difficult track we had had to traverse on foot. The people at Nyewo had not understood what direction I would take after Rigong-kha; they thought we would be going further along the Yigong valley. The lama told me that he had met some groups already going that way. I said, 'they must be mad since it is known that the Communists are now in that area'. He replied that it was all right, for the Communists had now withdrawn, so he had heard; he added that the eighty refugees under Lama Riwo, who had intended coming with us, had changed their minds and were going with other refugees by the Yigong valley.

It was now early September, and the weather was breaking up with frequent storms. It was likely that there would be a lot of snow on the passes and the road might be blocked. It took us some four or five days to reach the far end of the valley, from where we could really study the terrain, and we now concluded that the Tso-phu pass which went in a south easterly direction was the one which we should take. It appeared fairly easy, though rain was falling continuously which would mean a lot of soft snow higher up. I sent an advance party to investigate; they were only able to get about a quarter of the way and were then driven back by severe storms.

They had found that the fresh snow on the pass was very deep, but thought that if the weather improved, even for three or four days, a crossing would be practicable. No news had come through concerning a possible guide for us. A local man offered to find one within a week saying that, should he fail, he would come back to discuss the situation with us; he added 'if I don't come, you may take it that I am dead'. The weather now cleared suddenly, but still no sign of a guide or of the local man; we concluded that he must really have died.

There was nothing we could do except wait as patiently as possible. Yag Tulku and I with a few monks decided to go into retreat. I told Urgyan-tendzin to make several coracles while we were away and to train some of the men to paddle them, for we would need them later on when we had to cross the Tsangpo, which is the name given to the upper reaches of the Brahmaputra in Tibet.

The spot chosen for our retreat was inspiringly beautiful, it lay beside a blue lake surrounded by high snow covered mountains; their peaks were glistening above the clouds and pine trees grew all around. The whole place was utterly different to the country about Surmang; it was more like Himalayan scenery.* Every evening we sat round the camp fire for our meal. Once we heard an aeroplane overhead and consulted whether we should cover the fire, though some said that the aeroplane was too far off to notice so small a thing. I took this opportunity to tell them how important it was in times of war never to show any sort of light. For a week all fires were carefully concealed, but when no further aeroplanes were heard we ceased to keep up this discipline. While waiting for a guide to materialize, all the camp busied themselves in repairing boots and making other preparations for the journey. We had expected that Akong Tulku would be joining us with Tsethar's group, however nothing had been heard of them. Our party was so large that Dorje-tsering undertook to organize the people into groups under separate leaders; he brought me a list with the names and ages of all the party. I was shocked at the numbers: about one hundred and seventy and among them men and women seventy and eighty years old as well as babies in arms, but very few able bodied men. I decided to explain to all of them the sort of journey we were facing and how very hard it was likely to be. I told them that we would not be able

---

* While in this place I wrote a poem an English translation of which, by my friend John Blackwood, appears on page 250 at the end of the book.

to visit any villages, so there would be no further opportunity to get fresh supplies of food; we must take all essential provisions, as from now. There would be many high passes and difficult streams on our route. It must be understood that we would be without tents and might have to sleep in the snow. We might well be captured before reaching the Indian frontier, for there were a great many Chinese in all this region. Finally I said to them: 'if any of you should be overcome by exhaustion, by long climbs and by trekking through rough country, it will be impossible for the others to stop and look after him. I want you all to realize what you are undertaking and if you think the hardships will be too great for you, now is the time to decide if you still wish to come with us.' I added, 'I do not want any definite answers for a day or two', for I knew that if anyone shouted that he wanted to come, all the rest would follow like sheep. After three days, they all said they wanted to come with me and that they would rather fall by the wayside than fall into Communist hands, for then at least they would feel that they had made all possible effort. I arranged meetings to explain to everyone what rules they must promise to follow, and concluded with these words: 'If we are attacked we must not kill any of the Chinese. We must not steal people's property on the way. There must be no disunity among ourselves; and if anything goes wrong I must immediately be told about it.' Everyone agreed to keep these rules, though Repön's party and those refugees who had their arms with them were not happy about the non-fighting clause. I told them that they must now provide themselves with the necessary food and train themselves to eat sparingly from the start. Everyone now sent their representatives to make these final purchases, bartering their tents and all superfluous possessions; the porters were sent back to Rigong-kha. I was very distressed at having to leave my books behind. Though the party disposed of their heavier goods, they still clung to their cooking pots and much spare clothing, these things in addition to their supplies of food made the loads very heavy; they amounted to almost twice as much as an average person would normally carry, the weight being chiefly due to the large amounts of food that had to be taken. Those of the party who were unable to carry all their own stuff arranged among themselves that if some of their stronger companions were willing to take a part of it, particularly gold and silver coins and jewellery, they would be given half of these things if they reached India. Since a supply of *tsampa* was vital, extra bags of it were entrusted to the strongest members of the party. Some people had bartered their possessions for musk which was light to carry and very valuable.

A message came from Kino Tulku that he had found a man who knew all about Lower Kongpo; he was prepared to act as our guide if I did not object to his bringing his wife with him. I gladly accepted their services provided that he was really aquainted with the terrain. He was due to arrive on September 13th but did not turn up on that or the following day. Meanwhile we had completed our preparations and I sent some men up the pass to clear the snow. They found that much of it had already melted and told me that everything was in good condition for the crossing.

CHAPTER SEVENTEEN

DAYS OF CRISIS

I DECIDED that if the guide and his wife did not arrive before two o'clock we should start by ourselves. This we did and reached the snow line without them. The weather was very clear; high up as we were, we could even see the mountains near Nyewo. For the first time I felt a conviction that we were going the right way and would reach India; I was aware of an inner strength guiding me and felt that I was not alone.

We waited in the cold till the next day and when I went round the various groups, I found that they were eating too much of their precious food; so I had to speak to them all very seriously, explaining that the food we were carrying would have to last a long time if we were to survive; also that they must be much more careful when camping to conceal themselves as much as possible and in no case to light any fires unless they could be screened from view. In future I myself would tell them if fires could be lighted at all. Furthermore I said, 'Our journey to India must be thought of as a pilgrimage; something that in the past few Tibetans have been able to make. Whether or not India has changed, the spiritual blessings imparted to that country by the presence of the Buddha remain: the places where he lived, freed himself from the bondage of *Samsara*, taught, and died have an eternal value. It is fortunate for us that our way is hard and that we are struggling against greater difficulties than the pilgrims of the past, for by this means we shall learn and profit the more from our journey. We should not be thinking only about the enemies threatening us from without. Each moment we should be aware of ourselves and of the forces of destruction that threaten each man from within. If we fail in this, we are indeed putting the spiritual object of our journey in jeopardy; each step along the way should be holy and precious to us.'

After this talk we all watched for the guide, but there was no sign of him, so I decided to go on without him the following day as the weather was now very good. At nightfall, however, he and his wife suddenly appeared wearing their Kongpo costumes. I had asked for him to bring some more of these garments, but he had not been able to obtain any. The guide's name was Tsepa, he was a nice fellow and appeared to be intelligent; above all, he had travelled all over the area and knew it from end to end. He said how sorry he was that he had not been able to reach us on the appointed day, but he had had to sell all his possessions; he brought a gun and ammunition with him. I explained to him the route we proposed to take following the suggestions of various local people and he agreed that it was feasible; indeed he considered our prospects hopeful. Early the next morning we set out in a scatter of snow. We found that the pass was not so steep as had been expected and the new snow had turned into ice, which made it easier to walk on. When we reached the top everyone shouted the customary Tibetan formula '*Lha gyalo!*' ('the gods are victorious!').

We were now facing towards India and beyond us lay the valley of Tong-gyug, which appeared to be empty, though we were still apprehensive lest some Communists might be lurking there. Our party was so conspicuous in their dark clothes against the white snowy background, I could only hope that they would not be spotted as they moved down. I told them that at least they must make as little noise as possible. The wind was against us and it was very cold; the sun seemed to give out no heat. If we could go further down the valley and cross over the mountain range towards Lower Kongpo it would be the easiest way, so I sent some of our people ahead to find out if this was possible. While they were away, we camped at the foot of the pass. On their return they told me that they had not seen any Chinese, nor anyone else, but there were a few footprints of Tibetans, obviously old ones. We had several days of pleasant walking through the valley, though always feeling a little uneasy lest our large party might somehow have been spotted by the Communists. When we camped at night we always chose a small secluded branch valley where there were herdsmen's huts, for this part was at a high altitude with very few trees and was used in the early summer as a grazing ground. Now, in late September, there were a lot of small yellow berries on the trees near the river which though acid could be eaten. As we went down the slope of the valley we came into a region of fir trees; seeing fresh footprints we decided to halt in the scrub under the trees. I sent Tsepa to investigate and told him to go into the villages pretending to be a messenger from relatives of some of the people there. The villagers gave him a lot of information about the number of Chinese in the vicinity of Lower Kongpo, and told him how strictly they were guarding the place; though people were still able to barter their barley in the surrounding districts the whole district was in a state of persecution, so they said. Anyone who had been sufficiently wealthy to have a servant was ill treated; servants were encouraged to wear their master's clothes and the masters made to wear those of their servants. The Communists had established working camps for their prisoners and forced them to labour on road making. A great number of Tibetans had died of starvation and other hardships, so the villagers lived in the utmost terror all the time. Tsepa managed to learn more about the lay-out of the land and what route we could follow; he also procured a small extra quantity of food.

From here I sent a second messenger to Tsethar's group to tell Akong Tulku where we were and the probable route that we intended to take. We went on down the valley and camped by a lake. It was so beautiful here that in spite of possible danger we could not resist choosing this site; the weather was however becoming colder. Our journey the next day was uphill; we gradually reached barer ground with more rocks and fewer trees, and the valley was becoming narrower; for several days the same sort of country lay before us. One morning we heard a man's voice; some of our party rushed off rifle in hand as far as a small bridge we had just crossed. It turned out to be bursar Tsethar with another monk. They told us that Akong Tulku was following close behind. Their party had sold most of their possessions and had been joined by about a hundred and twenty more refugees who had insisted on coming with Akong Tulku. Tsethar said that they all wished to join our party. He approved of our plans and agreed that we had chosen the right route; on the other hand, he thought that a rescue operation might be organized from the Indian side to include all the refugees, so perhaps it would have been better if we had waited for this to happen. Since the weather was still good, however, we decided to go on. The valley proved to be longer than we had expected and we camped again in the shelter of herdsmen's huts where we could have really good fires. We made the attempt to cross the pass over the high mountains very early the next morning, but were only able to get about a quarter of the way when it started to snow; the storm was so severe that we were brought to a standstill. However, we found some more huts where we could stop for a day and a night. In the afternoon some of our men struggled on to see how far up the pass they could go. They reported that the snow was terribly deep, much worse than the Tso-phu pass. I arranged that eight of our strongest men should hand over their baggage and try to make a track through the snow which we could follow. They found that they could make no headway when walking and the only way was for a man to lie prone so as to push the snow down with his weight. This was extremely exhausting and each man could only do this particular job five consecutive times, then it was taken over by the next man, and so on as each man's turn came round again; the others followed to tread down the track. The actual incline of the mountain was so steep that we almost had to turn back, for it did not allow of our making a zig-zag track. As it was, the rest of our party managed to struggle after the leaders. When we had nearly reached the top, we saw a large group coming behind us in the valley; we took it for granted that this must be Akong Tulku's party. By the time we reached a plateau, it was mid-day. We found ourselves surrounded by further rocks and making our way between them came suddenly upon a yet steeper gradient. However, at this great height the snow had hardened and this made the going slightly easier. It was difficult for the leaders to keep to the right track; several times they strayed off the path followed by the rest of the party, which meant that we all had to retrace our steps. However, at last we saw the prayer flag showing that we had reached the summit. The sun had already set and only a red glow remained; the wind was piercingly cold. The valley below seemed uninhabited, though we could not see very clearly as there were so many rocks in the way. Some of our party had fallen a long way behind; I felt anxious for the older people in case they had to spend the night in the snow. I knew that they could not have climbed any quicker, they had done magnificently by keeping up such a regular pace. We checked the list of families and felt sure that the younger members would look after their parents. All those who had reached the summit now started to walk down in the twilight. We saw a path of even ground below us, but had some difficulty in finding a way to reach it, being continually confronted with sudden rocky outcrops. A lot of loose stones got dislodged and the people in the rear had to shout a warning to those who were pressing ahead, for we had scattered in all directions, with each man trying to find his own way down. It was all but dark when the leaders reached a level piece of ground where we could stop for the night. There was an overhanging rock which offered shelter for some of us and my people insisted on giving me the best place; many others were forced to lie down in the snow. At sunrise we watched for the rest of the party. I feared that there might have been some casualties among the older members and was very happy to learn that everyone had survived. Once we were all together again we started down the valley, though everyone was pretty well exhausted after the hardships of the night before, but we felt we must struggle on since time and food were running very short. I sent a man ahead to see if the way was clear; he reported that he had not seen anyone and that the valley was a good one with no wild animals about. The wind had fallen and the sun was shining.

Now that we had crossed over the pass we were no longer in the Tong-gyu valley; we found ourselves on a plateau across which a river ran fed by streams from small surrounding valleys. Tsepa directed us to go by one of these valleys running south east. There were ranges of mountains on either side of it so we could only keep to the valley bottom until we found a turning point. One day, as we were travelling particularly slowly, Akong Tulku suddenly came striding along ahead of his party to overtake us. It was a most joyful meeting for us both: he said that the pass had not been so difficult for his people, as we had already trodden down the snow. The rest of his party soon followed and we all went on together and camped in herdsmen's huts. Akong had a great deal to report about happenings from the time when he received my letter telling of our intended departure from Nyewo with its details about getting rid of our animals and going on foot to Rigong-kha. Both his brother and bursar Tsethar had thought that there must be some way to Rigong-kha which could be taken on horseback with the baggage on mules and yaks, and they had managed to cross the Alado river at a point near their camp, after which they went south-east by a temporary bridge built by some of the Resistance. From there they changed direction and went across several very high passes towards Rigong-kha. The track was so broken up that in many cases they had had to put tree-trunks over chasms between the rocks, and once they had to build a whole bridge themselves. Hard work like this could only be done by the able-bodied men while the rest of the party waited with the

animals: it caused a lot of delay. In spite of all their care three of
their horses were lost on these fragile bridges, also owing to lack
of good feeding some of the horses were on the point of breaking
down, so those which seemed too weak to continue the journey were
sent back to Jigme Rinpoche's group to recuperate. The party
finally reached Rigong-kha with some three hundred yaks and
twenty horses, to the great astonishment of the inhabitants, for they
had never seen such animals before; and as there was little available
grazing the beasts had often to be fed on grain.

When Tsethar and his companions heard that we had left about a
fortnight previously for the Tso-phu valley, they arranged to leave
their horses and mules in the care of some of the villagers near
Rigong-kha. Some of the refugees, however, could not bring themselves to part with their animals, so when they started on the further
journey they took them with them, hoping they would be able to
swim over the river at the cable bridge; but the current was so
strong that many of the beasts were swept away by the flood.

By the time our friends reached the Tso-phu valley our own tracks
had become obliterated and some of the refugees, fearing that they
would never find us, decided to stay in the valley with what animals
they had left. Akong Tulku and Tsethar, however, were determined
to carry on; incidentally they were also able to visit Kino Tulku
whom they found to be very ill. He told them that he was very lonely
without us, but was glad that we had gone on, for he thought our
decision to try to get to India was a wise one, though it might bring
us into danger.

The following morning as I looked down on the camp I was
amazed to see so many people, for Tsethar's group had added some
hundred and twenty to our numbers, thus bringing the total up to
nearly three hundred. We all went on together and as I looked back,
it seemed more like an army on the march than a party of refugees.

The ground was still rocky with sudden steep slopes. At last we
reached the junction of two valleys where the local trading road
from the Powo valley to Kongpo runs beside the river. Our scouts
told me that they had seen a man with four loaded yaks going along
it, so we waited for two hours, hiding among the rocks, while two
of our men crossed the road and climbed the rocks above it, whence
they could see about three miles of the road in either direction. Once
they had given us the all clear the whole party crossed the road and
forded the river beside it. Here we entered a small valley where we

found several herdsmen's huts, though no-one was about. We spent a very disturbed night; several people thought that they heard men approaching and with so many women and children in the newly arrived party there was a great deal of noise in the camp with the babies crying a lot. At daybreak Tsepa and I held a consultation. He now recognized where we were and thought that we should leave the valley where we had spent the night in order to cross a high pass to the south; though he did not know what we would find on the farther side of it, he felt sure it would be in the right direction and we would be getting nearer to Lower Kongpo. No-one else in the camp had the least notion of our position; they simply put their trust in the leaders and said they would follow them wherever they went. I felt that we could no longer take any risks and should avoid the more open valleys with so large a party, not to mention the many noisy children. Few of these people had any idea of how to hide themselves in an emergency and they were mostly wearing light coloured clothes, conspicuous against a dark background. They had so little imagination that it never entered their heads that the Communists might capture us. However difficult it might be for the older and the very young members of the party to go over this rough ground, Tsepa and I agreed that it was the only safe thing to do.

Before we set off again, I called everyone together. I explained that we were now likely to enter more dangerous country, for the land here was more thickly populated. It was important for everyone to realize that the Communists had control of this area, so no-one could be trusted. If any of us should meet villagers it would be impossible to disguise the fact that we were a party of refugees. We must give them no clues about the direction that we were intending to take. Anything we bought must be paid for and everyone we happened to meet must be treated with the utmost courtesy. It was most important that we should make as little noise as possible, and if anyone felt ill, he must inform me at once.

We were still able to travel by day and crossed a low pass. Our guide was sure that from this point we should see some part of Lower Kongpo. We all felt excited about it. However, when we reached the top, all we saw was another range of rocky mountains, with no sign of life. Tsepa was puzzled, he did not know where to go next, but decided that we should proceed down to a little valley that could be seen below. When we reached it we found that there was no outlet, so that it was necessary to traverse another mountain. Beyond this we found that we had three more ranges to cross at the last one of which we were faced with a near precipice. It was covered with flat slippery grass; the descent was dangerous and some of the older people fell. Yet another chain of mountains lay ahead of us. We followed tracks made by wild animals and when we reached the summit of the next col we found a deep round hollow with trees growing in the grass, large enough for us all to camp there for the night.

Our guide realized that he had lost his way and was much distressed; Tsethar also was much disturbed and began complaining that none of us had any definite idea about the way we ought to take; he added that he was sure that by now the rest of the refugees would have been rescued by the resistance soldiers. I told him that we had no evidence of this and that I had been trusted to lead our party and we were all doing our best.

Next morning we followed a small track running across the shoulder of the mountain in front of us, which pointed in the direction of India. It sloped gently upwards and was an easy walk. Unfortunately the land was very bare without trees or rocks, so I was afraid that our large party would be seen. Towards evening we noticed some small rocky mountains with a high range of snow covered peaks behind them. People did not know what to think, some suggested that they were the mountains of Upper, others of Lower, Kongpo. As we mounted higher and higher the snow on the mountains reflected the dying sun and looked as if made of gold. We were afraid that if we went further we would be on yet higher ground, so we camped for the night. The frost was severe; there were no streams and our only water came from melted snow. Added to this we were limited in our use of fires, partly for the fear that they would be seen and also because of the difficulty of finding anything to burn. The next day we discovered that the track we had been following only led to the snow mountains which were not in the right direction, so we changed course and descended by a steep slope. Ahead of us we saw a pleasant looking valley with a river winding through it. There was some consternation in the camp when a black object was seen near the river which people thought was a man. Their uneasiness went so far that they imagined they heard voices. However, looking through my field glasses I could see that it was only a young yak, though there might well be a herdsman with it, even so, there was nothing to be done except to continue our downward course, for if we had stayed on the mountain we would have been still more conspicuous. We made our way through squat willows and found an empty hut. All who could went inside, while the rest of the party lay down in the open. Some of the younger members organized a scouting expedition in the evening; there appeared to be no-one about.

Some of the refugees were getting very short of food and came to ask me how long I thought it was likely to be before they would be able to renew their stocks. I had to explain that it was unlikely to be soon and they must ration themselves very strictly. They carried on for about a week and then came again to ask me if my party could spare some of their rations; unfortunately we had not much left, for the going had been so difficult that we had only been able to cover short distances each day. By now our guide had completely lost his bearings; he had no idea where we were, but we continued more or less blindly and after crossing several more ranges found ourselves in a large valley on quite low ground which we thought would probably be inhabited. It was decided that I should go on ahead with Akong Tulku, Yag Tulku, Yönten and our guide and if we found a possible way, we would signal to those behind. It was a great relief when we found that the valley was apparently empty. However, we did come across traces of dung and men's footprints; Yönten and the guide thought they might be about twenty-four hours old. We consulted among ourselves about the next step to be taken, but no-one had any positive suggestion. The party behind waited and watched us as we came back towards them. A lot of people wanted us to halt and make tea, but I thought this too dangerous, so we went on down the valley. After going about half way down it we saw a mountain, its slopes thickly covered with pines; I suddenly felt sure that this was the way we should go, though Tsethar was not of my opinion; he thought that to go ahead on the chance would be most unpractical. However, we all started to climb the slope, but when we had gone a mile or so Tsethar and several others suggested that it would have been much better to have continued along the valley. They grumbled that they had had no tea and were feeling tired, and now they were having to struggle up yet another mountain. I tried to explain that the valley they wished to follow led away from the direction of India, and it was also obvious that there were people living in these parts. Tsethar and the others were so annoyed that they began to argue with me. I told them 'If you want to go along the valley, you had better do so; in which case I can take no further responsibility for you. I myself am going up this mountain and when we reach a more remote spot we can stop and make tea.' Some of the refugees shouted, 'yes! that is the right thing to do' and finally they all decided to follow me. I understood how desperately tired everyone was feeling, yet I was confident that we must go this way. Personally, I felt a strange exhilaration travelling through such wild and unknown country; an inner strength seemed to sustain me. We walked on until we got above the pine level; here there was dense scrub, so that we lost our track again and again. It was a matter of battling through the undergrowth; those who had swords slashed their way through. Finally all of us reached the bare rocky mountain side beyond the scrub. In the distance, we heard sounds which seemed either to come from explosions and the rumbling of lorries, or, as some of the party thought, they might be sounds of actual fighting. On the farther side of the mountain we came to a dry valley. Since the decision to come this way had been entirely mine, our guide turned to me and asked where we should make for next. There were three gaps in the valley and he wanted to know which one we should choose. I said, 'the middle one' and when asked for my reasons I replied, 'One had to be chosen'—I added the two Tibetan sayings, 'A doubting mind will not fulfil one's wish', and 'Two needles cannot sew at the same time'. As we went through the gap I saw a cairn by the side of it; this cheered me, for it showed that others had gone this way before. Further on we suddenly felt a cold wind and found ourselves on the top of a cliff overlooking a lake which had black and red rocks reflected in it. My determination to take this way had not lessened and actually we found that the going was not too difficult, for we were able to move from rock to rock till we reached the farther side where we found tracks of wild animals. We now stopped for the night trying to screen our fires; however, it was impossible to disguise them from the sky and an aeroplane actually flew over. To add to my troubles I was told that one of the older men was very feeble; his relations were supporting him and other refugees carried his baggage. Beyond the lake the ground was flat and open, but ahead there lay a range of mountains, so that we were again faced with an arduous climb to a col, following tracks of hooves. Here the snow was deeper; we had to revert to the method we used over the previous high pass, with eight men again crushing down the snow under the weight of their prostrate bodies, though this time the gradient was not so steep as before. From the summit Tsepa thought that things looked more hopeful, we could again see far distant ranges in a southerly direction which we thought must be on the farther side of the Brahmaputra. Our present position, however, was anything but an easy one. The ground sloped downwards to a small depression and then rose again to an even higher range. Again we were faced with having to force our way through with the help of the eight men. This second climb proved to be very steep and I was exceedingly worried about the weakly old man. We decided that he must be given more food, though our own resources were already so slender; it helped him to carry on. I looked forward to reaching the top of the col, since our guide had been so sure that we were travelling in the right direction; but when we arrived there, it was only to see that we were surrounded by ranges, all under snow. Sounds of distant lorries or explosions were no longer to be heard. We appeared to be at the end of a range; the ground in front of us led steadily downhill to a series of lakes almost below snow level, though there were scattered patches of snow all around. We stopped to rest by one of the lakes and I looked through my field glasses at the valley beyond. It was very broad with a river winding through it between meadows and patches of pines, but I did not see any people there. Our guide thought that we must be somewhere near Tsela Dzong, the junction of the Upper Kongpo river and the Brahmaputra. I knew that the district would be likely to be dangerous, especially if we took the wrong pass, for this part of the country was certainly both more thickly populated and under fairly complete Chinese occupation; we had heard that the Communists were trying to indoctrinate the inhabitants which meant that some could not be entirely trusted. I asked the others for their opinion and they all agreed that if we were really near Tsela Dzong the wide valley would be very unsafe, so it would be better to turn eastwards towards Lower Kongpo. We therefore decided to go a little further down the mountain and then veer round to a south easterly course; this meant a longer route and led through a good deal of scrub. It brought us eventually to a series of valleys which we had to cross, a matter of continually scrambling up and down hill for about a week.

CHAPTER EIGHTEEN

TOUCH AND GO!

THOUGH I had frequently impressed upon all members of our party that they must inform me about any particular difficulties, I had been given no warning of an emergency, until some of them came to tell me that several of them had run out of food. They were actually beginning to boil the leather of their yak-skin bags; usually this leather is roughly cured with much of the fat left in it so it has some food value. I made enquiries among other groups and found they were having to do the same thing. The people had not wanted to worry me, since they knew that I had so many other grave anxieties.

At the same time we again lost our bearings and went too far in a north easterly direction, which compelled us to retrace our steps for three days. Tsepa's belief that we were near Tsela Dzong had evidently been wrong. We now followed a small valley running east until it also turned in a northerly direction and we had to leave it for another leading towards the south. Again there were more mountain ranges in front of us; the nearest ones were not very high and we were able to cross two each day for three days, but after this we were faced with much higher ridges each of which took more than a day's travelling to cross.

By this time many more of the refugees had consumed their last provisions, except for their leather bags and my own group had decided that they too must fall back on this fare, though some leather would have to be kept to build the coracles needed to cross the Brahmaputra, which meant we would have to go on very short commons meanwhile; it was now early November and there were no wild vegetables which could be used as a supplement. In spite of all their troubles the party was still cheerful and as soon as they found themselves in sufficiently remote places everyone would laugh and sing and individual groups would join with the monks in devotional chanting. They all seemed to have become acclimatized to the routine of travelling and the daily hardships.

Previously the weather had been good and usually sunny, but now winter was beginning with storms of rain turning into snow. It was taking longer to cover any distance over these high mountains and looking back we could often see the spot where we had camped the evening before. One day, after reaching the summit of a col, as we walked down on the farther side we could see open country with a broad river flowing through it which we thought must be the Brahmaputra. The landscape was clouded in smoke, but through my field glasses I could see Chinese lorries moving along the road beside the river. This came as a shock to all of us, for we had not known that there was a road-way through Lower Kongpo. Tsepa thought that this time we really must be near Tsela Dzong, where the river is too wide to be crossed using the limited means at our disposal; besides there was a large Chinese establishment there and a great many inhabitants. We were still travelling by day though taking great precautions. The land was much lower here and there were many secluded valleys where we could camp, so travelling was easier. People crossing these mountains had often built tall cairns to indicate the track; some of these from a distance looked alarmingly like human figures. As we turned further to the east, being still on high ground, we could see a number of villages beside the Brahmaputra; in the evenings lights were visible; they seemed to be brighter than house lamps and we took it for granted that they were the headlights of Chinese vehicles. Our guide said that we were near Temo Monastery; he recognized the bend of the Brahmaputra. Therefore we would still have to keep to the mountains for a time, and moreover if we followed the bends of the river the distance would be much increased; in any case we would not be able to light fires in the daytime, and only at night by using great care to conceal them by digging holes in the ground. By now we were feeling the shortage of food very acutely and came to the conclusion that we must try to find a shorter route. We thought that where we now were was too dangerous, so we retreated to a more remote area. Now we mostly had to travel between sunset and midnight, for there were few bushes or any sort of cover. Our guide was bewildered again and led us over col after col. The old man who had been so ill before finally dropped down and died; his son had done all possible to help him and had even carried his father over the worst passes. Suddenly another old man felt too exhausted to walk further and insisted on going down to one of the villages. He promised not to divulge our whereabouts nor to tell anyone about the escaping party.

The landscape was beginning to change to more rocky and bare ground. We came across local tracks which we had to avoid and it was often difficult to find a suitable place to camp. Most of the party were showing signs of extreme fatigue, but all the same they kept up their spirits. After several more crossings on high ground Tsepa realized that we were approaching the Temo pass on the Powo to Lhasa road. This meant that we must cross the road at the top of the pass and, in order to reach it, we must travel through the night. All the way lay under snow and it was impossible to avoid leaving tracks; unfortunately we could not reach the pass that same night and were forced to camp in the bitter cold hiding our fires with the greatest caution. Next evening we started off again; there were many animal tracks, but owing to the snow no people were travelling. At twilight we could see the pass beneath us, but we had to wait till it became dark and from our concealed position we watched and listened carefully for any possible travellers on the road. Though the snow was lying on the mountain side, the road itself was clear and we were able to cross it without mishap, though a man and horse must have passed earlier in the day, for their prints could be clearly discerned.

I had told everyone to walk in single file so that our tracks would not appear to belong to a very large party. We now needed to hurry on as quickly as possible to find somewhere where we could be concealed before daybreak; unfortunately the land here was very bare with little scrub and lay mostly under snow; it would have been easy for anyone to follow us, so we left a man to keep watch behind us and sent another scout ahead. The land was undulating and when we reached the higher places we could see for miles around, but the only thing to catch the eye was the track that we had made. Again we turned aside and found higher mountains in front of us, which appeared to be wild and uninhabited, so we could again travel by daylight. From the time that we crossed the road all the party had made a special effort to walk quickly; tired though we all were, we could not afford to stop and a few short rests taken at intervals had to suffice; the fact that everyone was on short commons made the strain all the greater. The all-important thing was to conserve our energies for the critical moment when we would have to cross the main Chinese highroad and, after that, the Brahmaputra. After several more days' travelling our guide again lost his way and we could only guess our direction. As we went we were faced with continuous ranges of mountains and valleys; there seemed no way to get through.

It has been mentioned before that people who were unable to carry all their own baggage often arranged for a stronger man to take the extra load by promising him half its contents at the journey's end. My own group now felt that they must fall back on their reserve of *tsampa*: to our dismay, we found that the man who had been carrying it had not only consumed his own share, but ours as well, and the same thing had happened in several other cases. Nevertheless, no-one ever attempted to kill any of the wild animals that we came across in our wanderings; this compassionate self-control displayed by a whole band of desperately hungry people moved me greatly at the time, and it remains a treasured memory of those heart-searching days.

We were now quite lost, surrounded by rocks on every side; there was nothing left for me to do except to resort to *tagpa*. The question that faced us was which rocks to choose for our next climb. Following the directions given by the *tagpa* and after climbing the particular rock it indicated we saw a high mountain with a col on its shoulder. The snow was very deep and the sun dazzled us, but fortunately most of the party carried either dark goggles or eye-shades. Actually, the climb up was easier than the rough ground we had been crossing before, where we had had to jump from rock to rock; but the descent on the farther side to a lower level was very steep and there seemed no indication where to go next. It was again left to me to make a decision, so I headed for a small lake surrounded by rocky ground which we bye-passed only to find ourselves confronted by three other ranges with rather steep cols leading gradually to lower ground. After this another line of mountains loomed ahead with a pass across which did not appear to be too steep. Tsepa and I always went ahead to direct the party and when we reached the top of this last pass we were amazed to see the Szechwan to Lhasa main road running along the mountainside below, less than a quarter of a mile away. I told everyone not to make any noise and to wait until I could find somewhere where we could all be hidden. This was not difficult on the boulder covered ground, so when everyone else was safely under cover Tsepa and I went out to investigate our surroundings. Through field glasses we could see the road leading through the Ser-kyem Pass which was actually the point that we had been aiming for; once across it we knew we would be very near Lower Kongpo and the spot where we should try to cross the Brahmaputra.

When we returned to the others we found them all preparing for this, the most dangerous part of our journey. The older people were nervous, fearing that travelling on the south side of the river would prove too much for them and that, should they fall out by the road side, the Chinese would be bound to find them and through them would trace the whole party. I told them that we must all cross over the road at the Ser-kyem pass together and that the younger ones must carry the luggage to enable the older people to walk more quickly. If a Chinese lorry should come along when they were about to cross, everyone must lie down in the fosse beside the road and make no movement. We waited till dark before approaching the road, but when we were some twenty yards away from it we suddenly saw the headlights of a lorry. Fortunately there were a lot of rocks close at hand behind which we all ducked. I had to be very severe with one woman who, to help herself control her fear, was chanting *mantras* in a loud voice; I told her that she must only whisper under her breath. Since the road went in loops round the mountain we had time to take cover while the lorry was still some distance away; as it came nearer and nearer we could hear the crunching sounds of its gear changes and soon its headlights illuminated the very rocks where we lay concealed. We held our breaths and the minutes seemed like hours, but eventually the lorry passed out of sight and earshot. Just as we were on the point of getting to our feet for the dash across—one man was actually standing up—we heard the noise of a second lorry. As it came near we heard the Chinese talking in high pitched and, as it seemed to us, excited voices; I was afraid it was because they had seen us; however, all was well and the lorry passed by. After a silence of about five minutes we all walked together across the road, leaving two men to brush out our footsteps. On the further side the ground was still rocky but became smoother as we worked our way down the valley; the air also felt much warmer. The discipline observed by everyone was beyond all praise; they looked very serious and no-one spoke a word. After some three miles we turned into a side valley which was thickly wooded. We could still see parts of the road and would have been able to spot any approaching headlights; however, there seemed to be no further traffic on it. We walked upwards through the valley to cross a pass in the mountains. The nun, who was the sister of the *chöpön* of Yag monastery, now completely broke down both physically and mentally; it would have been too dangerous for the whole party if we had stopped for her, so we gave her what little food we could spare and then left her: it was a horrid decision to have to take—it left a guilty feeling—but the safety of the whole party allowed of no other alternative. Generally speaking, the older refugees, by walking in a measured pace, had managed to save their energy for this especially dangerous time and they now walked in front, while it was the younger ones who lagged behind. I was feeling very exhausted myself; both Akong Tulku and Yag Tulku did their best to cheer me. The latter, however, was getting worn out by this continual going up and down mountains; he kept saying to me 'Rinpoche, what do you think we shall find behind this one?' I could only answer 'I don't know, perhaps we shall find a nice, warm, secluded valley.' At last to shut him up I said 'Probably we will find another still higher snow mountain': that stopped him worrying.

After climbing the next chain of mountains we walked along the ridge for about two miles in a southerly direction. My opinion was that we ought to bear south, but our guide was most emphatic in urging us to follow a westerly course. After a time we came upon a little rocky hollow covered in small scrub where it was possible to camp; the ground was too uneven for people to lie comfortably, but we were all thankful to have found a place where we could stop. Immediately fires were got going, care being taken to screen them from sight. There was now sufficient time to stew down some of our leather; other refugees had previously taught us how to do it. The leather has to be soaked for a day until it swells, then cut in small pieces and stewed for several hours till it begins to sizzle and looks like meat. We still had a little tea, salt and butter and after the first sip of our national beverage we all felt better. Yönten was the chief cook for our group and also did the serving. I was waiting to share the communal dish when he said 'we have kept a little *tsampa* especially for you': I asked him why, for I wished to share in everything on equal terms; he answered that leather was not suitable for his abbot to eat. I felt a little sad that this line had been drawn between me and the others; however, I discovered Akong Tulku and Yag Tulku's monks had done the same thing for them. By now, everyone seemed cheerful again and we slept in the hollow during the whole of the next day. Some of our men went up the mountain to spy out the land through field glasses; they could see the main Chinese road which we had just crossed and dozens of lorries full of soldiers travelling along it. Some of the refugees were becoming a little careless about allowing their fires to smoke during the day and I had to be very firm with them. Towards evening we started off again to cross another range; the ground was covered with short grass and sloped down in easy stages; however, the wind was very cold and sharp. In the far distance we could see villages and far behind them a snow covered range which we thought must lie on the farther side of the Brahmaputra. Starting off again next day we went further down the slope towards the Lower Kongpo valley through which the Brahmaputra flows, being much narrower at this point. This area was densely populated and there were villages half way up the mountain side on the narrow strip beside the river, besides others in various branch valleys. The land was thickly covered with holly trees. We did not see a road nor did we hear any sounds of lorries; this was reassuring, since it would make things easier for us when trying to cross the great river. Between us and it there was a succession of low hills and valleys where there would be villages and we actually could see smoke coming from some of them, so we looked for a place where the mountain went directly down to the water's edge. Ahead of us there was a small closed valley covered with brushwood, but to go down to it over such rough ground could not be done in the dark; hearing the sound of men's voices and a dog barking we thought it would be unwise to go further, so stayed where we were for the night. Next day I sent two men to investigate. They found a path leading downhill which, however, seemed to pass too dangerously near villages, so we changed our direction, fighting through thorny scrub until at last we found easier ground where only fir trees and holly grew; it was much warmer here. We went on until we noticed the smell of burning wood in the air; not daring to go further we camped among the boulders. Again I sent men to look round and in the daylight I went with Tsepa and Urgyan-tendzin to see for myself. We thought that if we followed a spur running below us, this would get us down to the Brahmaputra without hindrance. However, we could only see the slope of the spur which hid the river, and we could not tell if there were any villages on the bank. Here was another problem: we would need coracles to cross the river. We had brought the leather of the two we used to cross the Nyewo, but it had been kept folded up and had become stiff as a result; it needed to be soaked for a long time and there were few streams in the neighbourhood. I told my companions that we could at least go on for a few miles, for I felt sure that there were no nearby villages, so we started in the evening. The footprint of a man was suddenly spied in the track and we came upon a water-mill a few paces further on; fortunately the men who worked the mill had already gone home for the night. Some of Repön's people, who were desperately short of food, suggested that they should break open the door, and if they found anything eatable they would take it and leave some money. I told them that this would give a clue which could only lead to our discovery. Further on we came to a horse track and heard the sound of the bell on a passing horse. A murmur went through the party: they wondered if this was a Chinese or some villager; if the latter, they thought that perhaps he would sell them some food. Meanwhile the sound had ceased, so I said nothing. We crossed this local track; looking through my glasses, it seemed as if the rocky ground led straight down to the river, in which case it was time to get the coracles ready. We needed at least six more. We scouted round till we found a suitable place near a mountain stream where we were able to soak our coracle coverings together with other yak skin bags; the whole camp joined in the work of making the frames and sewing together the pieces of leather under the superintendence of Urgyan-tendzin.

By this time there was little else but leather to eat; people's health was becoming affected and symptoms of illness were beginning to show. I was much concerned and tried to think if there was any way to obtain further supplies. There was a possibility that we might approach the villagers in some remote spot and find out if the Chinese were in control of their whole area or if there was any chance of buying some food; there was always the danger that one of the villagers might act as a spy. I put the suggestion to the senior members of our party; some of them thought that we might try, others considered the risk too great. Everyone more or less agreed, however, that we must first get across the river.

Making eight coracles took two days; we set off at nightfall. By now there was little baggage left and whatever remained was taken over by others to enable three men to be allotted to carry each coracle. I warned everyone that we would now be going through villages; we must take the greatest care and make no noise, with everybody walking in single file. In spite of all these difficulties the whole party kept up their spirits; they were really excited at the prospect before them. I led the file with Tsepa, who proved of the greatest help. Though he did not actually know this part of the country, he was familiar with the general lay-out of villages and of the tracks joining them; there was no way of avoiding these, and though we saw lights in the houses, we met no-one. As we made our way down these minor paths the coracles had to be carried aloft and were apt to scrape against the hedges making a crackling noise; it was also difficult to keep the babies quiet, which added to our anxieties. The distance proved longer than we had expected, so there was not sufficient time, that night, to attempt the crossing, find somewhere on the further side where to hide, and dispose of the coracles. I, with Tsepa, Urgyan-tendzin, Yönten and several others carrying one coracle decided to take a path which led up the mountain side again. We waited and waited for the rest of the party who had lagged behind, but no-one appeared. We therefore went on uphill until we reached a place where we could hide our coracle among the holly trees and lie down ourselves. But sleep was impossible for me; I kept wondering why the rest of the party were lagging behind. At the first light of day we heard someone walking on the dry leaves; the sound came nearer and nearer. Tsepa had his gun ready; I jumped on him and said that there was to be no shooting. He asked me to make no noise. The footsteps came on and a man hove in sight; it turned out to be a messenger from our own party. He was delighted to have found us but said that he had also hoped to find two others of our men who were carrying a coracle, as they were not among the rest of the refugees who, having lost contact with us the night before, had found a hiding place in a holly thicket lower down the slope. His report on the way that some of the other people in the camp were behaving worried me greatly, for he told me that they had lighted fires and were not keeping sufficiently quiet. I sent him back with a message that rules had been laid down to save the lives of three hundred people and must be strictly adhered to. He was to tell everyone that as soon as it was dark we would join them and they must all be ready to start for the crossing.

From our hollow we could not see very far and did not know if there were any houses near, but as the sun came up it looked as if we had found a good hiding place. However, we could not discover any water in the vicinity and all felt very thirsty, so Tsepa decided to go down to the lower camp to fetch some; there would be no difficulty on the way as there was plenty of cover between the two camps. He suggested that he might visit some of the villages pretending to be a local man, since he wore the clothes of the district, but I told him that this might lead to danger. While he was away Urgyan-tendzin and I took field glasses and walked up the mountain to see how the land lay. We were at the end of the range and could see both banks of the Brahmaputra and the country on either side of it. At one point the river was fairly narrow but we would have to pass near a number of villages to reach it; we could see white-washed temples flying red flags, and these were also to be seen over most of the houses. A back-water ran beside the farther bank of the river downstream from the likely crossing place, with a narrow strip of dry ground between it and the main channel which, being wooded, could afford adequate cover; at the end of the back-water there appeared to be a dry passage onto the mainland. The ground here was level for about a quarter of a mile and then sloped uphill towards another range of mountains. The track led through a village some two miles away on the lower slope of the mountains; here too, red flags were flying on the houses and a very large one was displayed on a white temple building. There were fields all around where herdsmen were tending their flocks. Taking everything into consideration we still thought that our best plan would be to cross the river at the narrow part, walk along the strip between it and the backwater, and go out by the end passage. We would have to risk going through the village just beyond.

In the afternoon we were feeling very depressed, the sun was hot and we were longing for something to drink. About four o'clock a black mass of crows started to wheel over us; their shadows fell across the mountain as the sun was sinking and their raucous caws sounded very sinister. We went back to our small party in the hollow and found that Tsepa had brought some water. He told us that a few of the refugees from the lower camp had gone out on their own to try to buy food and the villagers had told them that they had seen two men in chains whom the Chinese had arrested alleging that they had stolen a bullock: these must have been the men of our party who had disappeared with the coracle. The local people had realized that the men asking to buy food were trying to escape and they had no intention of getting involved beyond receiving payment for their supplies; however they gave the information that at this time of year all the passes on the farther side of the Brahmaputra would be blocked by snow.

There was no other solution for us but to go on. We waited till dark and then went down to the lower camp. I had given strict orders that everyone was to be ready to start, but when we reached the camp I found that they had not finished packing up and told them they must hurry. As they were getting their baggage together my attendant found that a small bag of *tsampa* which had been kept for me had disappeared; his suspicion fell on a boy and losing his temper he started to chase him. Others tried to stop my attendant, unfortunately this angered him still more; everyone began to shout and to argue; the whole camp was in an uproar which further delayed the packing. I spoke very severely, for I saw that everyone was on the verge of hysteria. Catching my attendant by the arm I told him to control himself and explained that this was the most critical moment in our escape; every minute was valuable. The man was still agitated, but when he saw how very gravely I was looking at him, he calmed down and tried to explain that the boy had stolen my *tsampa*; I said 'I don't think that he has done so, but in any case, let him have it. At this time we all need strength, and I hope if he has taken the food that it will help him to work all the harder. What I am mostly concerned and distressed about is to hear that someone in the camp stole a bullock and that two innocent men are suffering for their crime.'

The Wheel of Truth

229

CHAPTER NINETEEN

ACROSS THE HIMALAYA

WE were now ready to start; it was the night of the full moon on December 15th. Akong Tulku was carrying a very heavy load on his back and I asked him if he could really take so much, adding cheerfully 'it might end in your collapse'. Laughingly, he replied, 'this is the decisive night and I can do it; please remember that I am tougher than you'. When we reached the level ground we could hear voices in the neighbouring village and dogs barking in the far distance; however, we got as far as the sandy approaches to the river and everyone was hopeful. I went from group to group to encourage those in the rear to move more quickly and as I was walking between them I saw a man in Kongpo dress in front of me behind a thorn bush; as I looked at him he disappeared, but soon afterwards I saw another man in the same costume who was carrying a rifle; I thought he might be Chinese as he had a very light skin. He too disappeared. I noticed that some groups of stragglers were going in the wrong direction so I had to rush after them to bring them back. At last my group reached the river and were the first to embark; eight of us got into one coracle with Urgyan-tendzin to paddle, followed closely by a second group. The full moon was just rising. It took some time to get across, though Urgyan-tendzin went as quickly as possible, and as soon as we disembarked he was ready to take the coracle back to fetch another lot of passengers. I heard a shout from the river from the man who was paddling another coracle; he was calling me by name and saying that he was unable to get across and they would all be drowned. I told him not to panic, it would be all right and he carried on and landed his party. As I walked up and down the bank talking to the three groups who had arrived, I suddenly heard gunfire. At first I thought it must have come from one of our party; then a second shot was fired and I could hear shrill shouts from Chinese voices. The firing became continuous and bullets came whizzing above us. Some of the remaining refugees jumped into coracles and were able to get across. The firing still went on, becoming even heavier. Altogether about fifty people reached our side and we rushed up the strip between the river and the back-water, expecting to find the dry passage at the end of the water, but no-one could locate it. Since the Chinese were evidently in force on the other side, we expected that there would also be some of them here, so all heavy baggage, such as bags containing coins and jewellery, was thrown into the water. Being unable to find the passage, we tried to wade across the back-water, but found it too deep, so some of the men went back to the riverbank to fetch the two coracles. These were now waterlogged and consequently very heavy and it took time to bring them. The men arrived at last and a few of us were paddled across. Everyone wanted to jump into the two coracles at once, so some had to be ordered to wait for the return journey, till finally all got across.

By this time it was near sunrise; many of the fugitives began to panic and rushed off on their own without waiting for me or anyone else to instruct them. Tsepa and his wife, Akong Tulku, Yag Tulku, Tsethar, Yag Tulku's and my attendants were the only ones near me and we started southwards towards the mountains. Yönten was still paddling people across the back-water, so I did not see him. Tsethar lost his temper and accused me of trying to save too many people. He said that our best plan would be to try and find a hiding place nearby; we could then go down the strip again and try to collect some of the baggage that we had left on the bank of the river, for the firing had now died down. I begged him not to attempt it, for I had already climbed some way up towards a village. However he was determined to go and said that he would return with Yönten. I told him that we intended to walk up the mountain until we found a suitable place where we would hide. Akong Tulku's younger brother and a nun joined us; we were all utterly exhausted, having eaten hardly anything and the climb took a long time; to add to our discomfort, our clothes, which had been soaked through when we tried to wade across the back-water, began to freeze on us. As light broke in the sky we could see the village in front of us. There were people on the balconies of the houses, some of whom looked like Chinese, and in the surrounding fields herdsmen were taking their animals out to the grazing grounds. But there seemed no better way than to creep through the village between the hedges and we succeeded in doing this without mishap. Beyond, a winding path led over a bare strip of chalky ground on which our dark clothing would be very visible and a herdsman who was driving his animals behind us seemed to be looking at us, but we took no further notice and simply went on in the same direction. From the higher ground we could see everything that was going on in the village and beyond it we had a good view of the river: a lot of people were still gathered beside the northern bank and had lighted fires. However, we pressed on and a little further up the slope found ourselves in a belt of holly trees; knowing that if we went higher we would come to more open ground we decided to stay under cover of the trees, for we were all very nearly at the end of our strength. The mountain faced north; no sun shone on it and it was bitterly cold; our frozen clothes clung to us. Throughout the day we heard firing and saw people walking about in all directions; it was obvious that the Chinese were looking for us, we could hear their steps coming nearer and nearer and then dying away again as they altered their course. From the village, there were no sounds of cheerfulness and the herdsmen instead of singing as they took their animals out now merely shouted at their herds. There were intermittent sounds of firing from below, and of blasting where the new road was being made. In our hiding place among the holly trees we still had to be very careful, for the dry leaves on the ground crackled whenever we moved; we tried several times to open our food pack, but each time we had to abandon the attempt because of a sound of footsteps and the thumps of a rifle being used as a walking stick. Akong Tulku's baggage had had to be jettisoned, so I teasingly told him that I, being more modest, had been able to bring along mine. My attendant suggested that it was now the time to practice the yoga of 'Inner Heat' (known as *tummo* in Tibetan), but Yag Tulku retorted that sitting down on the crackling holly leaves in order to take the cross legged position required for this *yoga* would make too much noise, not to mention the sound of the accompanying breathing exercises. I had to laugh and Tsepa whispered 'Hush! you must all keep quiet, someone is coming.' I whispered back 'perhaps this time, it is the spirits who are coming to protect us.' This bantering helped us to relax.

The day seemed dreadfully long. There were sounds of firing near the village and we were afraid that the Chinese might have found some of our party. It was slightly warmer around midday and then became terribly cold again towards evening. We dared not open our

food-pack and there was no water. We could only moisten our lips
with the hoar frost.

About an hour after dark there were no further suspicious sounds
to be heard, so we decided to walk on. Tsepa led the way in complete
darkness and we climbed for about five hours until we reached the
level of the fir trees. By this time we were completely exhausted and
the cold was intense. However we found a little *tsampa* at the bottom
of the food pack, and this, mixed with hoar frost, made us feel
slightly better; we could shelter in some hollow fir trunks and did
our best to sleep. My attendant was magnificent; he was lying close
to me and took this opportunity to talk about meditation. He said
that the experience that he had just gone through had been a spiritual lesson for him; he was now feeling at ease and believed that
our worst trials were behind us. I replied 'But what if we are captured tomorrow, one never knows? We are still in Chinese occupied
territory and their guards are hunting for us.' He begged me not to
speak about it. I said, 'this is only talk, we may actually have to go
through this experience and if so, will it still be a test of meditation
for you?' Then I raised my voice to ask Yag Tulku if he did not
agree. 'What are you talking about?', he said. 'We are talking about
meditation and whether this will help us if the Chinese capture us
tomorrow.' He answered, 'I am sure that the danger is over; what
do you think lies beyond this mountain?' I gave the usual reply,
'Another icy range, which will provide a still better opportunity for
us to practise the *yoga* of inner heat, for this time we will be able to
take up the correct posture'; this set everybody laughing. That night
none of us could sleep; just before dawn we dozed off only to be
awakened by a loud whisper from Tsepa 'wake up! wake up! someone is coming'. We all alerted. A voice was heard and the crunch of
frost under feet: we could see an advancing figure. Tsepa had his
gun ready; we others held our breath. I whispered to Yag Tulku
'You remember our conversation of last night.' The steps faded and
then came nearer again; Tsepa stood with his loaded rifle ready to
fire. My attendant and I implored him not to use it. Suddenly a
woman's figure appeared followed by others; they were the peasant
family who had joined us at Kino Tulku's monastery. Behind them
were Tsethar and Yönten; they had seen our footprints clearly on
the frost covered ground.

When Tsethar had gone back to the bank of the Brahmaputra to
try and salvage some of the baggage he had met Yönten. They

wanted to join our little group, but daylight overtook them, so they found a hiding place before reaching the village and remained there until the next night. They were only a few yards from the track between the village and the back-water and could see the villagers, and the Chinese going in all directions to hunt for the refugees. They could hear them talking to each other and saying that quantities of musk, gold and silver jewellery and sable skins had been found strewn along the back-water. They also spoke of having captured some of the refugees. Though they came quite close to where Tsethar and Yönten were hiding they failed to see them. It was quite warm in their hiding place so the two men were able to take off their wet clothes and dry them. They were very anxious about our group, and wondered if the talk about captured refugees referred to us. When night fell they started to go uphill again and, on the way, met the peasant family; all of them passed through the village in safety. Since they had found it so easy to follow our footprints, we felt it was hardly safe for us to stay any longer where we were.

It was now two days since we had crossed the river, and I will now follow my diary.

December 17th. We could now travel by daylight, though whenever we heard a suspicious sound we halted immediately; however, we soon realized that these noises came only from wild animals. Tsethar suggested stopping for tea; he was afraid that we might break down. We dug a hole for the fire. Fortunately, we had some tea and butter left, though little else. The drink seemed a meal in itself and everyone had a good night.

December 18th. Our walk today was over open ground; We could look down on the village and the river, but we felt that we ourselves were too far away to be spotted from below. Our party of fourteen started out together; but since we now thought that we were beyond pursuit by the Communists, discipline became somewhat relaxed, with Tsethar, the peasant family and my attendant lagging behind. From high up on the mountain we could see the many ranges that all our party had crossed together with such courage and determination, before we became separated at the Brahmaputra. We felt very sad, not knowing what had befallen our many friends and companions. We could clearly see both the river and its back-water, and through my field glasses I could distinguish a black patch which I took to be one of our coracles.

We did not stand for long on the skyline for fear of being seen, so the rest of us waited below the ridge while Tsepa went across to see what lay on the other side. He reported that it was a wild valley with no signs of a village, so we made our way down until we came to an obvious footpath which appeared to lead valleywards; on its surface we noticed prints of Tibetan boots which, however, on closer examination did not appear to be recent, so we followed the path down to the bottom. Here we espied a herdsman's hut where we thought we might shelter for the night, but when we reached it we were disappointed to find that it had fallen into ruins and no longer had a roof. Still it was a luxury to find a level field surrounded by rocks to protect us from the wind, with a stream nearby. This was our first opportunity to dry our wet clothes and to mend a few things: here at last we could all relax and wash. With approaching darkness we set to and collected wood for a fire by which we sat, lighted by the last rays of the setting sun.

Tsepa knew nothing of the country on this side of the Brahmaputra so we turned once again to the exceptional form of divination known as *prasena*, from which a clear vision came. It told us that we were to go up the mountain on our right, when we would see another range ahead; three cols would be visible and we were to make for the centre one: this would be the last high range that we would have to cross.

Yag Tulku was now convinced that we would reach India and gave a short talk of reassurance to our little party. In the evening with a good fire in this cosy valley we at last felt warmer, but at night it began to freeze again and by morning our clothes were stiff with frost.

December 19th. We now had to climb another spur and were soon at snow level. As we went up, we could see villages some three to four miles away. This made us anxious, for our dark clothes could be so easily noticed against the white background, though the sun was on the villages and we were in the shade on the north side of the range. The snow here was quite deep, in places dangerous as it had turned to ice and we were afraid of slipping. It took the whole morning to reach the top. On the southern slope there was no snow; the mountain was covered with short slippery grass dotted about with rocks. It was hard going with no indication of any path. A small valley now lay ahead of us and beyond it a high steep glaciered range of mountains where we could see three cols; we believed that the centre one was the col indicated by *prasena*; it looked quite near but the climb up was quite a long one. The higher we climbed the deeper the snow became. Tsepa and Yönten were the only really strong men in our party, so we could not adopt the method we had used before in very deep snow. Now these two men went first and the rest of us followed as best we could; the ascent was very laborious and took most of the afternoon. To make matters worse, a snowstorm burst over us towards evening, covering the ice with snow. We kept cheerful and eventually reached the top at an altitude of about 19,000 feet above sea level. Rising almost perpendicularly to the east of our pass was Mount Namcha Barwa or the 'Blazing Mountain of Celestial Metal'; its crest glittered far above the clouds, for this mountain is over 25,000 feet high (Photograph opposite page 190).

As we looked back along our path we saw that five cairns had been built at a lower level, so this track was obviously the right one.

The storm had now passed and the sun was shining again. When we looked down on the south side we saw that we were surrounded by snowy peaks with behind them range after range of lower mountains reaching into the far distance in every direction; these looked a smoky blue colour as if covered by a jungle of trees; we thought that the most distant ones might be in Indian territory.

At our feet the ground looked very rough; it appeared to be a moraine with a series of rocks showing deep patches of snow between them. There was no way of bye-passing this stretch, we had to go straight down it. The whole place seemed completely desolate, without even traces of wild animals. The surface was appallingly slippery; Yag Tulku slid down in a sitting position for about fifty yards and was only stopped by a small rock within a few feet of a sheer drop. Further down the gradient became, if anything, even steeper; we seemed surrounded by cliffs and could see no way of getting by them. Looking back we could see that had we attempted to cross either of the other two cols it would have been disastrous, for glaciers fell away steeply on this side of them; so though our own position was far from pleasant, any other way would have been worse. It was getting near nightfall and dislodged stones were falling on the people in front. We decided to get out of line and to search individually for any possible pathway. Tsepa suddenly shouted that he thought he had found a way down. It led downwards through a slight depression between two almost perpendicular rocks. Following in Tsepa's track we came to a cave surrounded by bushes. By now it was quite dark and since we felt that we were safe from any possible unpleasant encounters we made a glorious blaze and spent the evening in devotional chanting. The nun still had some butter, Akong Tulku's young brother some tea, and both Yönten and the peasant family a little *tsampa*, so we had all the basic necessities. This was the first night since the beginning of our escape that I slept really peacefully.

December 20th. We were desperately short of food, so we could not afford to delay. As we walked down in the morning we looked at a stretch of snow-covered ground surrounding a large lake. We made our way beside it and a little further on suddenly found ourselves at the edge of a steep escarpment which at first appeared to be impassable. However there was a crack running down it which, though abrupt, had an uneven stony surface affording a reasonably firm foothold; the younger people among us helped those who found it too difficult. Once we got to the bottom everything looked easy, for we were in a small valley with a frozen stream running through it and there was much less snow. The country was completely deserted with no sign of human habitation, the only living creatures being wild animals such as deer, foxes etc. We chose a sheltered camping place among rocks, from where we could see distant woods of holly and fir.

December 21st. In the morning we noticed a large patch of green which we took for a field of grass, but when we reached it we found to our horror that it was a large muddy swamp which could not be crossed. We tried to walk round it; this presented further difficulties, for the whole land was covered with a very prickly kind of thorn bush which had to be hacked through with every available knife or sword. This was particularly arduous work and took a long time. Towards evening we reached the junction of two rivers. There was evidence here of recent footprints. We thought that this might be a track leading to Doshong pass and that Chinese might be in the neighbourhood, though the footprints were clearly of Tibetan boots. That night we camped among reeds and trees beside the river.

December 22nd. As we went on I felt more and more puzzled, for everything looked somehow strange. It was all utterly unlike anything I had known hitherto; the air was much warmer and there were so many unknown trees. We were obviously getting near to an inhabited part of the country. That evening, as we sat round the fire, we held counsel together. The question was whether, if we were within reach of a source of food supplies, we could now allow ourselves to consume more of the slender remains of our food, or whether, if the Chinese were in the district, we must ration ourselves yet more severely. Someone suggested that if the Chinese were indeed here, it might be best to surrender, for we were in a poor state of health after so many acute privations and were near starvation. However, most of the party felt sure that there were no Chinese in the vicinity and, even if there were, they said that at all costs we must not surrender but must still make every effort to escape. That night, while trying to sleep, we heard many strange noises and at first were greatly disturbed, until we realized that they only came from the wild animals around us.

December 23rd. We had been continuously going up and down the mountain slopes and now hoped to find easier ground. However, with every step the way seemed to become more difficult; the ground was again rougher and the mountains steeper; the trees here grew much taller. In places we had to negotiate great rocks, only able to be crossed by narrow foot-holds, with rusty chains for support, which reminded me of the track to Rigong-kha: the streams merely had log bridges of the most primitive kind. It was so tiring jumping from rock to rock that I was beginning to feel at the end of my tether, hardly knowing how to go on; but I dared not tell this to anyone for fear of discouraging them. We camped in a little cave and again saw traces of the same footprints as before. Our *tsampa* and butter were now all but gone, though we still had some tea; Tsethar remarked that we would have to reach a village within a day or so, otherwise we would all die. A voice called out 'Be a strong Khampa and don't lose heart' and everyone laughed.

December 24th. Our journey now took us through yet stranger country; there were all sorts of trees forming a dense jungle with no level spaces; a tangle of mountains with continual rain and mist. For the first time we saw banana trees, but did not know that the fruit was edible and dared not experiment. The rain poured in torrents all day, splashing up from the ground as it fell. Towards evening we found quite a nice cave with many signs that travellers had used it before. We now had nothing left except tea and a few leather bags. However, we could make a good fire and really enjoyed this meagre fare. I was touched to find that Yönten had still kept a small quantity of *tsampa* for me. After we had eaten, Tsepa volunteered to go down to see if he could find a village where he could get some food; he and the peasant husband went off together. He

said that if he could find a village that night he would return to us
with supplies, but if no village was near, we were to come on next
day and he would meet us on the way. About an hour after he left,
we heard the report of a gun; then nothing further. We felt very
anxious.

December 25th. We stayed in the cave all day and kept up our spirits
by chanting as we cooked our leather; it was such a luxury to have
a fire and we stayed on in the cave that night.

December 26th. With the morning light we started off and walked
down the slope and as we turned uphill again we met the peasant
husband carrying a large bag of *tsampa*. To our amazement he said
that he and Tsepa had overtaken Akong Tulku's elder brother in
company with Dorje-tsering's wife and three nuns and they had
given him the *tsampa* to tide over our immediate needs. They told
him how they had been captured by the Chinese near the back-
water, but managed to escape from the headquarters where they
were being held and had afterwards joined up with some Kongpo
peasants who were also escaping. The party had heard Tsepa's gun
the night before and had been so frightened that they had rushed
away. It appeared that the gun had only been fired to scare a wild
animal which seemed as if it might attack. Tsepa had sent the
peasant husband back to us while he himself went up to the village
on the mountain side to buy provisions. He sent us a message saying
that we were to go to a cave below that place where the other party
were waiting for us; he would join us there later with the food. We
soon reached the cave and spent a very happy morning telling each
other of our experiences. They told us that a group of them had
crossed the river and the back-water and had tried to follow us;
however, they had lost their way and after lying hidden in the long
grass for a time they reached the village. When the Chinese discovered them, there was no fighting; all the refugees were taken
prisoner and removed to a village which was a local Chinese headquarters, on the south side of the Brahmaputra. Their baggage was
thoroughly searched; all the contents of their amulet boxes were
thrown out and all religious books were immediately destroyed.
Each person was privately questioned to find out if their stories
tallied; they were asked where they came from and where they were
going. Most of them said that they were trying to escape to India,
though a few said that they were going on pilgrimage to that
country. The lamas and leaders were separated from the rest and put

under guard to be interrogated more closely. They were given the most menial work to do, such as cleaning out latrines. One of the lamas despaired and hanged himself; he had already escaped from one prison camp in Derge and this was the second time that he had been captured. As other prisoners were brought into the camp all our party were relieved to find that no members of our little group were among them; but when the Chinese could not trace Akong Tulku, Yag Tulku or me among the senior prisoners, they thought we might be lurking disguised among the crowd, since they knew that we had been the leaders of the party; so the prisoners were checked again, especially the younger ones.

At night everyone was locked up together in a single room, but women and the less important men were allowed to go out into the village during the day: they were, however, called in for individual questioning from time to time. The Chinese would then tell them that now that Lhasa was liberated they could go there whenever they wished to, there would be no trouble on the roads; but of course there were more useful things to be done than wandering off on pilgrimages, which were indeed only superstition. The prisoners were even told that should they wish to go to India for this purpose, the Chinese administration were quite ready to let them out; however, such a journey would be exceedingly dangerous, for anyone might die of starvation or fall ill from the hot climate there.

When a rumour went round the camp that all the able bodied refugees were shortly to be sent north to join labour camps on the other side of the Brahmaputra and that the senior people and those too old for work were to be sent to concentration camps, one of the nuns contrived to buy food for herself and Akong Tulku's brother; she also obtained information about the best way to reach Doshong Pass. Dorje-tsering's wife and two other nuns were also able to procure some food and all five managed to escape together. They stopped in a wood the first night and crossed the Doshong Pass the following day. Here they met the family from Kongpo who knew the country and were also making their escape, so they joined forces.

The Kongpo family were camping in a valley below our cave and the man came up to see me, bringing a jug of soup made of meat and barley which we much appreciated. He told me how he and his people had escaped: it had been very difficult to get out of their village as permits were only given to visit friends in the near neighbourhood and when the visit was over the holder had to apply to the local authorities for permission to return to his own home. Having obtained the permits to leave his village, our friend and his family took the opposite direction towards the mountains to the south. A number of the villagers had wanted to do the same thing, but knowing the danger they would have to encounter in crossing the snow-bound Doshong Pass, they had not dared to undertake the journey.

Some refugee lamas from Lower Kongpo were sheltering in the small monastery in the village above our cave. A monk came down with Tsepa to request me to conduct a devotional service for them as well as for the villagers. I was surprised to see him wearing a long dagger which looked somehow wrong for a monk. He was particularly friendly and invited us all to stay in the monastery. However, we felt that this village was too near Lower Kongpo and might not be a safe place for us so, seeing that one could not get to the monastery and back again that same afternoon, we stayed where we were in and around the cave. We had an excellent meal with some pork the villagers had supplied and made dumplings with their wheat flour which they also gave us. We tried the local dish of millet, but found this difficult to swallow.

December 27th. Some of our party had bought roast corn from the villagers, which we nibbled throughout the day; unfortunately we had not realized that it would swell up inside us and this, followed by a meal of fat pork, gave us all severe stomach aches, so that none of us were able to sleep that night. However, we were all feeling comforted, for we thought that this part of the country was too wild and unproductive to be of much interest to the Communists. A year later, however, the Chinese occupied these frontier regions, including this part.

December 28th. The Kongpo refugees remained in the vicinity, while we resumed our journey. There are a great many holy mountains in this district which is called Pema-kö; Guru Padmasambhava used to meditate in its caves and Tibetans have often come here as hermits and pilgrims to practise meditation.

There were many small villages dotted about and we passed through wild valleys and crossed streams by very primitive bamboo bridges. That night we camped on the bank of a stream.

December 29th. Today it was very hard going, for our way led up and down slopes covered with large rocks; in some cases rough steps had been hewn, in others, it was the old story of narrow nitches cut in the rock faces. There were trees and undergrowth everywhere and we could not see anything of the country around us. To add to our discomfort it was raining very hard and we were wet through before we could stop for the night.

December 30th. In one of the villages which we passed we stopped to rest and some of the villagers, who appeared to be very poor, welcomed us bringing small rice cakes cooked in oil as well as a local beer also made from rice; as the drink was fermented we were unable to accept it and this rather upset their sense of hospitality. We were much interested when one of the peasants took us up the hill to show us how he grew his corn. This required immense labour, for there were only small patches among the rocks on the mountain side where it could be sown, and it was always in danger of being eaten by the many wild animals about the place; to protect it he had built small well-thatched sheds from where he could keep watch against them. We spent the night on a little hill where there was water.

December 31st. When we woke up in the morning we could see our next objective, a village high up on the slopes on the other side of the river. We crossed this by a slender bamboo bridge and, beyond it, found ourselves on steep hard ground. There were no rocks, but footholds had been cut on the stony surface in a zig-zag pattern to make the climb easier. As we went further up we could see the Brahmaputra again, now on its south-westward course: the ranges on its south side looked very beautiful with patches of cloud and little groups of houses dotted about. These foothills of the Himalayas have a continual rainfall and everything looked wonderfully green. We could not recognize most of the plants here for they were utterly different from those which grow in East Tibet. We later learned that this is the best time for travelling, for in the winter there are no snakes nor leeches about. Our climb was very arduous and from the time that we had crossed the river there was no water to be had anywhere until we reached a village called Pedong late in the afternoon. I had sent a messenger ahead of the party to ask if we could be given accommodation for a couple of weeks; when we arrived we received a warm welcome and were able to rent rooms in various houses.

I, together with my attendant, Yönten, Tsepa and his wife and the peasant family stayed in the headman's house; our host gave me his best room and that evening he himself cooked our meal. Some of the dishes were made of stewed leather, which is largely eaten in this area; being now nicely cooked with spices and vegetables I did not even realize that it was leather. For drink he gave us an alcoholic liquor made from wheat and, when I asked for tea, he told me that no water was available that night and that this drink would be good for us after our long journey, since we must be worn out and in need of rest. As monks do not touch alcohol we did not drink it, however, and pretended that the soup had been enough to quench our thirst, which disappointed our host. He was a very gentle and friendly man anxious to help us in every way; moreover he knew Tibetan and acted as interpreter to all our party, for the villagers only spoke the local dialect.

January 1st. I took a walk in the country outside the village and was shocked to see some little boys hunting birds which they took home and roasted in their kitchens. When I spoke about this to our host he said it was difficult to stop people from doing it as it was the custom. Akong Tulku and Yag Tulku had had the same experience as ourselves in refusing the alcoholic drink, but after we had walked round together and seen for ourselves the scarcity of water, we understood the position better, for the villagers had to walk a long way down to the valley and then dig a hole, into which water would slowly trickle. This work was generally done by the women. The villagers' chief industry was very fine and artistic basket work coloured with beautiful vegetable dyes.

During the following days I had many talks with the local people; they considered themselves to be Buddhists, though all this area still showed traces of the ancient Bön religion. There were temples in the villages, but the priests in charge were singularly lax; they had never received any training, and the way to celebrate the rites had merely been handed on orally from father to son. They were all married and led more or less worldly lives. For the devotional ceremonies, the fathers of the household and their sons joined with the priest in charge, while the women and children looked on, and these assemblies generally included the serving of alcoholic drinks to all by the women. Though this part of the country had been considered holy since the eighth century, latterly pilgrims who came to meditate in the neighbouring caves rarely went near the small villages so that the indigenous people seldom had any contact with instructed Buddhists.

In the eighth century when Buddhism first began to spread into

Tibet practices such as the worship of nature spirits and the animal sacrifices of the Bön religion were forbidden and many Bönpo adherents emigrated to the outlying regions of the Himalayas, both to the Pema-kö district and to parts of Nepal, for they could not go to India which at that time was largely Buddhist. However, after Buddhism had become universal in Tibet the inhabitants of the Pema-kö area took shelter under the name of Buddhism, though still practising some of the Bön rites. On the other hand in the eastern province of Kyungpo the people still call themselves Bönpos, though their practice is Buddhist in effect; they are known as 'White Bönpos'.

In 1950 Dünjom Rinpoche, a renowned teacher of the Nyingmapa Order or 'Order of the Ancients' came to Pema-kö. He had already established a monastery in Upper Kongpo and wished to found a second one here with a good library, his chief object being to train monks so that they might instruct the local people in the real teachings of Buddhism; in their isolation they had sadly lapsed and reform was necessary. Among other things he introduced cows, so that the villagers need not be solely dependant on hunting wild animals for food. He knew the local dialect and could mix with and teach the people himself.

The villagers told me how much it had meant to them having his monastery there to take a lead in this much needed work of reform. At one time they had had a Tibetan monk-official as administrator of the district; later, the Chinese had also established a headquarters in this area, but had withdrawn after two years; they had made very little impression on the people. All were now very anti-Chinese and were prepared to fight for their liberty, if only with primitive bows and arrows. They had made plans to build bridges in such a way that they could be demolished at the very moment when the Chinese would be crossing them.

There was no possibility of getting any milk and, since it was winter, vegetables were in very short supply; there was nothing left for us, therefore, but to fall in with the local custom of drinking beer, of which the villagers had large quantities. This, combined with better food and rest, certainly renewed our health. When our fortnight was up we were ready to go on with our journey.

January 14th. After about four hours' walking we came to the next village. We had already met many of the inhabitants and they had prepared accommodation for all of us. Here the houses were brighter and more cheerful and the people wore better clothes. I met a lama who had escaped from Upper Kongpo with a number of peasant refugees. His account of the Chinese persecution was the usual sad one. This party had travelled by a different route to the one we had taken.

January 15th. The next village lay further away. Mostly we were following the Brahmaputra, but all the villages were situated on the slopes of the mountains. A bridge that we saw over the river was different from any we had yet seen; it was made of very wobbly bamboo wattle; bamboo hoops placed at intervals round it served to help the passenger to keep his balance. This village had some contact with the Indian side of the Himalayas, and consequently there were certain Indian goods to be seen, I was amused to meet men wearing pyjamas. Indian coinage was partly in circulation here and cuttings of Indian pictures from newspapers were often stuck on the walls. The speciality of this village was making a particular poison to put on their arrow heads which paralyzed the animals they hunted. The women sat on their balconies all busily engaged in spinning and weaving. The majority of the inhabitants only spoke the Mön dialect; however, some of the older ones knew Tibetan and we were welcomed and put up for the night. We were told that a detachment of Indian guards had been stationed near the village who had invited all the villagers to join in their New Year festivities on January 1st, and the people had been very interested to see Indian aeroplanes in the vicinity.

I met the priest who was living with his family in the local temple; he could speak Tibetan and was proud of the fact that he had visited many places in Tibet. He told me that he had been in retreat and that its chief benefit had been an increase of magical power. We had an argument and I pointed out to him that Buddhism teaches that one must go beyond selfish aims: a retreat should be to increase spiritual awareness; one must start with the five moral precepts. He courteously agreed, after which we both remained silent. Yag Tulku, who had been much scandalized by the corrupt habits of these people was delighted that I had had an opportunity to expound a truly Buddhist way of life. He said that, had he been talking to this priest, he would probably have lost his temper and said something rude.

January 16th. We started on a long trek, passing several villages until we came to the last one on Tibetan territory where we camped by the river bank. We were delighted to have water to drink and I now made it a rule that in future no beer was to be taken; I was afraid that some of the younger people were growing too fond of it. *January 17th.* Our party of nineteen started out very early. It was impossible to keep close to the Brahmaputra as the bank was too rocky, so we had to walk along the mountainside above it. The top of the next pass was the boundary between Tibet and India. We were still uncertain how we would be received by the guards there. There was a big noticeboard facing us painted in the colours of the Indian flag, with large letters in Hindi saying 'Bharat' and English letters saying 'India'. Below, we saw a newly built *stupa* made of concrete and whitewashed; its presence was encouraging. The two men on guard showed their welcome as they shook hands with us though we could not speak each other's languages. We felt intensely happy at this moment and particularly so in seeing the *stupa*, symbol of Buddhism, on Indian soil.

We walked down a further mile to the check post. The soldiers there confiscated Tsepa's gun and my field glasses and in sign language indicated that we should go further down the mountainside and not stay where we were. There were various soldiers travelling on the road and we heard an aeroplane overhead. Feeling tired after our long day, we camped beside a small stream. In the middle of the night a soldier came with an interpreter to see what we were up to. He merely woke us up, looked round, and went away. *January 18th.* Early in the morning another soldier came to our camp and, seeing our warm fire, sat down beside it. He was smoking and offered us some of his *cheroots*; we accepted them because we did not like to refuse his kindness, but none of us smoked. We watched him with the greatest interest; he was so different from any Tibetan type, with his pointed nose, deep set eyes and moustache. Not long after a second soldier arrived; he looked more like a Tibetan and could speak our language; he said he was a Bhutanese. He had heard of Gyalwa Karmapa and told me that his party had arrived in India before the Dalai Lama left Lhasa and, to our great sorrow, he added that Chentze Rinpoche of Dzong-sar had died.

A messenger came from the army camp, which was about a quarter of a mile away, to tell us to go on to the camp where we would be looked after. When we reached it we were shown into the *dak* bungalow which was entirely built of bamboo and the walls were covered with basket work. Everything was beautifully arranged with bathroom etc. and a fully equipped kitchen. We were told that we must rest and were given rice and tinned food. We discovered that it was the adjutant of the Indian regiment stationed there who was personally looking after us; he spoke Tibetan fluently and asked for all our names. He understood that we had been abbots of important monasteries and told me that he had been privileged to meet many lamas who had come by this pass and that he himself was a Buddhist.

January 19th. In the morning the adjutant came with his senior officer. They made a list of everything that we had brought with us and asked particulars about the route that we had taken and at what date we had left our monasteries.

January 20th. The adjutant brought us temporary permits to show the Indian authorities at the airport. He explained that they had little food to spare at the camp as they were rather short themselves; but he gave us what he could and told me that we should always stay in the local *dak* bungalows. Before leaving he asked for my blessing.

January 21st. The road here was much better; and the bridges more strongly built with steel cables. On the way, we met an Indian official travelling on his district rounds, with no less than five porters to carry his baggage. He was very sympathetic about our having had to leave our own country and assured us that the Indian government would look after us, just as they were looking after the Dalai Lama and other Tibetan refugees. His interpreter, the headman of the local village, looked very proud of himself in his uniform. This was the country of a primitive tribe who worship nature spirits and the whole atmosphere here seemed quite different from anything we had known before, with no obvious influences either from Tibet or the Indian side. There was much greater poverty in the villages and the *dak* bungalow where we stopped for the night was very small. There were, however, a few people here who had worked in India among Tibetans, and I asked them to teach me a few useful Hindi words.

January 22nd. We reached the town of Tuting round about midday and were shown a bamboo shelter where we could stay the night. Due to the rainy weather, here too there was a shortage of food and we were told that if we could manage on our own small supplies it would be a good thing. In the town there was a large camp of different races, all engaged on building houses for the army and the government officials in the area. There were quite a number of shops and small restaurants, and we were able to buy a few necessities, changing our Tibetan coins into Indian currency.

January 23rd. No-one knew how we could get to India proper, for there was a waiting list for the few aeroplanes flying to and fro. However, we no longer felt anxious: we were free at last and were able to wander about the town at will. I was struck by the fact that people here were much gayer and more cheerful than in the Communist-controlled Tibetan towns. As we were having our midday meal, a messenger came to tell us to go down to the airport, as there was every possibility that we would get a lift that same evening. A tractor arrived with a trailer behind it, into which we all bundled. The winding road led through a valley and we came to the gate of the airport. It was built in decorative Tibetan style, surmounted by the Asoka emblem. We disembarked and waited. No-one knew of any aeroplanes likely to arrive that day. The evening drew in and it was quite dark. A jeep came to take me to see the local district administrator; he gave me a bag of rice and a few vegetables and apologized that supplies were so scanty and the accommodation so limited. However, he was sure that the plane would come the next day. He asked me to leave my blessing in the place, that things should go well. I thanked him and presented him with a white scarf. We spent that night in the hut.

January 24th. In the morning an official came and read out a list of our names. He told us that we would be given priority on the next plane. It arrived that morning and, since it was a transport plane, its cargo of building material was first taken off and seats screwed in afterwards. There was only room for six of us: myself, my own attendant, Yag Tulku and his attendant, Tsethar and Yönten; the rest of the party followed in a second plane that same day.

This, our first flight, was a strange new experience, skimming over cloud covered mountains, seeing far below us the small villages and footpaths leading up to them; only by the moving shadow of the plane on the ground could we gauge how fast we were travelling.

We thought about the teaching of impermanence; this was a complete severance of all that had been Tibet and we were travelling by mechanized transport. As the moments passed, the mountain range was left behind, and the view changed to the misty space of the Indian plains stretching out in front of us.

URGYEN-TENDZIN had waited until he had taken the last fugitives across the Brahmaputra back-water; then he escaped himself. It had been easier for him to travel as a single man and he had followed the Brahmaputra all the way and reached India about a month later. Some of Repön's party, including himself, succeeded in getting away from the Chinese camp and arrived in India some months later, where he is now.

A few of the refugees from Drölma-Lhakhang, after crossing the back-water, managed to escape capture and they also made their way to India.

Lama Riwa's party who had stayed at Rigong-kha and went on by the Yigong valley were all captured by the Chinese, but escaped, reaching safety after a very difficult journey.

Nothing has been heard of Karma-tendzin, the Queen of Nangchen and her party, nor of Lama Urgyen's group of monks who went to the pilgrimage valley.

The Banner of Victory

249

SONG OF THE WANDERER IN POWO VALLEY*

To the one greater than all the gods, beyond compare,
O Padma Trime, remembering your deep kindnesses,
Sad songs of love and irresistable devotion,
Among the rocks and snows and lakes, well up in me.

I see the snowy mountain reach to heaven
Pagoda like, the clouds are its necklaces;
But when the red wind of evening scatters them,
How sad to see its body naked and bare.

This lake of liquid sky, the earth's great ornament,
The measure of the fullness of my mind—
When fish and otter fight there for their lives,
How many drops of blood are spread upon it.

Mortal, yet once we enjoyed the masquerade;
Now we see clearly all things perishing.
The Powo valley is a charnel ground,
I, Chögyam, will leap and dance towards the east.

The red headed vulture on the graveyard tree,
The crocodile who sleeps in the graveyard waters—
How brave they are, devouring human corpses,
Not knowing another preys on their own dead flesh.

In this dark age, when nephew slaughters uncle,
And neighbours all are barbarous enemies,
And everywhere the poison fog seeps irresistably;

I call time and again upon my Guru Father,
And his face of kindness, real beyond alteration,
Unborn, undying, rises from my heart.

Out of all time, he utters the highest teaching,
And I go forth to freedom, his only son.

---

* The Powo valley is the name given to the whole surrounding district; Padma
Trime is the personal name of my *guru*.

EPILOGUE

PLANTING THE DHARMA IN THE WEST

SEVENTEEN years after my departure from Tibet, I am writing this in Land O' Lakes, Wisconsin, where I am conducting the 1976 Vajradhatu Seminary for 130 advanced students, instructing them in meditation and the journey of the three yanas. Looking back, my thoughts are filled with appreciation for my teachers and tutors and the powerful world of Tibet. There is some sense of desolation, of aloneness, but I would not call it nostalgia. I have never felt nostalgic about anything. What I feel now is a sense of maturity.

My stay in India from 1959 to 1963 was filled with fascination and inquisitiveness. By contrast to the medieval world of Tibet, India was a very modern place. Here for the first time I had contact with Westerners, and I realized that it was absolutely necessary for me to study their language in order to spread the Dharma. During this period I served as spiritual advisor to the Young Lamas Home School, a role to which I was appointed by His Holiness the Dalai Lama. Forced from their homeland, many of my people seemed to have scattered their spirit and dignity; without the presence and activity of His Holiness' Tibetan government-in-exile, things would have been much worse.

While in India, I had the opportunity to meet with Prime Minister Nehru as well as President Radhakrishnan. Both were impressive men, philosopher-statesmen who combined, with no incongruity, spiritual quality and political ability. Outstanding among the many Westerners I met was Freda Bedi, now Sister Karma Kechog Palmo, who worked with the Central Social Welfare Board of the Indian government overseeing the Tibetan refugees. She extended herself to me as a sort of destined mother and saviour. In Kalimpong I met John Driver, a man who impressed me both by his insight and brilliance as well as by his remarkable devotion to Dingo Chentze Rinpoche. He tutored me in English and definitely inspired me to go eventually to Europe to teach. At the same time, I realized there was much more to learn about Western culture. Through John Driver, Freda Bedi and the Tibet Society of the United Kingdom, I received a Spalding sponsorship in 1963 to attend Oxford University, with Akong to accompany me. We sailed from Bombay to Tilbury aboard the P & O Line, an exciting journey made even more so by being completely surrounded by Westerners.

My first impression of England was that it was very clean and orderly and, on the whole, very strange—unlike anything I had ever seen before. Arriving at Oxford was a moving experience. Coming from Tibet and India, one's preconception of the West was of a stark modern realm, but it turned out to have its own dignified culture, which I began to appreciate while living and studying at Oxford. My stay there was quite good, apart from the air pollution, and I learned a great deal. Among other subjects, I studied comparative religion and philosophy; with John Driver's help, the reading of Plato and other Western philosophers became fascinating, in spite of my difficulty in following some of the lectures. The fine arts in particular intrigued me. The manner in which recent Western art cut through all hesitations to freely express whatever strange things came out of one's head was certainly different from the oriental tradition in art. Occasionally, I visited London and the museums.

But there was also a sense of dissatisfaction. My ambition was to teach and spread the Dharma. I was strongly encouraged by visits to Prinknash Monastery and Stanbrook Abbey, which demonstrated that the contemplative life could be carried out in the West. With the great help and inspiration of Esmé Cramer Roberts, the first edition of *Born in Tibet* was published in 1966. Nevertheless, there was as yet no situation in which I could begin to make a full and proper presentation of the teachings of Buddhism. This now began to change. Ananda Bodhi, senior incumbent of the English Sangha Vihara and founder of a Buddhist contemplative centre in Scotland called Johnstone House, proposed turning the direction of the House over to myself and Akong. The Johnstone House trustees invited us up to conduct a retreat. At once the fresh air and beautiful rolling hills of Dumfriesshire invigorated me and filled me with joyous expectation. After a series of further visits, Johnstone House was finally turned over to us and we moved in, giving it the name of Samyê-Ling Meditation Centre. This was a forward step. Nevertheless, it was not entirely satisfying, for the scale of activity was small, and the people who did come to participate seemed to be slightly missing the point.

In 1968 I was invited by the royal family of Bhutan to pay a visit— I had been providing tutoring in Buddhism to the young Crown Prince, Jigme Wangchuk, now the King of Bhutan, who was then studying at Ascot. Before reaching Bhutan, I stayed for a few days at the Central Hotel in Calcutta where I had the good fortune to meet Father Thomas Merton. He was in Calcutta attending some kind of collective religious conference, and he was appalled at the cheapness of the spiritual values that various of the conference participants were advocating. Father Merton himself was an open, unguarded and deep person. During these few days, we spent much time together and grew to like one another immensely. He proposed that we should collaborate on a book bringing together sacred writings of the Catholic and Vajrayana Buddhist traditions. Father Merton's sudden death shortly thereafter was a tremendous loss, to me personally and to the world of genuine spirituality.

Travelling on to Bhutan, I was warmly greeted by Her Majesty the Queen. Throughout my visit Her Majesty, who is now the Queen Mother, accorded me overwhelmingly kind hospitality. Also, the royal family had selected as their spiritual advisor Dingo Chentze Rinpoche, whom I now met again with a very full heart.

Of tremendous significance to my future activity were the ten days of this visit which I spent in retreat at Tagtsang. Tagtsang is the place in Bhutan where, over a thousand years ago, Guru Rinpoche (Padmasambhava) first manifested himself in the wrathful form of Dorje Trollo and subjugated evil forces before entering Tibet. Since I had never been to central Tibet or seen the great holy places of Guru Rinpoche or of the Ka–gyü forefathers, this visit to Tagtsang was very moving for me. The place is spacious and awe-inspiring, and one can still feel the presence of Guru Rinpoche. During my retreat there I was able to reflect on my life and particularly on how to propagate the Dharma in the West. I invoked Guru Rinpoche and the Ka–gyü forefathers to provide vision for the future. For a few days nothing happened. Then there came a jolting experience of the need to develop more openness and greater energy. At the same time there arose a feeling of deep devotion to Karma Pakshi, the second Karmapa, and to Guru Rinpoche. I realized that in fact these two were one in the unified tradition of Mahamudra and Ati. Filled with the vivid recognition of them and their oneness, I composed in two days the *Sadhana of Mahamudra*, of twenty-four pages. Its purpose was to bring together the two great traditions of the Vajrayana, as well as to exorcise the materialism which seemed to pervade spiritual disciplines in the modern world. The message that I had received from my supplication was that one must try to expose spiritual materialism and all its trappings, otherwise true spirituality could not develop. I began to realize that I would have to take daring steps in my life.

Returning from Bhutan through India, I was delighted to meet again with His Holiness Karmapa and also His Holiness the Dalai Lama. I also made the acquaintance at this time of Mr James George, the Canadian High Commissioner to India, and his wonderful family. Mr George is a wise and benevolent man, an ideal statesman, who holds great respect and faith for the teachings of Buddhism.

I returned to Samyê-Ling, reflecting on the experience of Tagtsang. One positive message which awaited me was the approval of my application for British citizenship. This I felt very good about, as a confirmation of my appreciation for English culture and, on my side, as a gesture toward working with the occidental world and its own valid traditions. I was proud to become a British subject and resident of Scotland, and I was in fact the first Tibetan ever to become Her Majesty's British subject.

Nevertheless, there remained some hesitation as to how to throw myself completely into proclaiming the Dharma to the Western world, uprooting spiritual materialism and developing further compassion and affection. I went through several months of ambivalence, of feeling pushed forward and pulled back simultaneously, unable to respond clearly in spite of a series of small warnings. Then driving one day in Northumberland, I blacked out at the wheel of my car, ran off the road and smashed through the front of a joke shop. I was brought to Newcastle General Hospital. In spite of the pain, my mind was very clear; there was a strong sense of communication—finally the real message had got through—and I felt a sense of relief and even humour. Twenty-four hours later, awakening suddenly, I found that my left side was paralysed.

When plunging completely and genuinely into the teachings, one is not allowed to bring along one's deceptions. I realized that I could no longer attempt to preserve any privacy for myself, any special identity or legitimacy. I should not hide behind the robes of a monk, creating an impression of inscrutability which, for me, turned out to be only an obstacle. With a sense of further involving myself with the sangha, I determined to give up my monastic vows. More than ever I felt myself given over to serving the cause of Buddhism.

I decided at this time to marry a young lady of the Pybus family, a very devoted Buddhist who inspired me in my work. She, with her problems of departing from her culture to become a full-fledged Buddhist practitioner, and I, also desiring to transcend cultural boundaries, both felt it a good idea to be married and provide a united front in devoting ourselves to the cause of Buddhadharma. Her name was Diana Judith, innocent and cheerful. We were married at the Registrar's Office in Edinburgh, to the consternation of her mother and other family members. Her father had died a few years earlier, but apparently he had been an open-minded man who was intrigued with Buddhism and had given Diana a few hints about the existence of Buddhist wisdom before his death. (Recently Mrs Pybus, Diana's mother, moved to the United States and, meeting her for the first time, apart from a brief encounter before the marriage, I found that she is a magnificent woman of tremendous energy and insight. We now enjoy a close relationship, and her dignity and breadth of vision have enhanced my world.) After our marriage, Diana took my family name of Mukpo, which is the name of one of the six major tribes of Tibet. My family is descended from the famous Lord Mukpo, Gesar of Ling.

The marriage stirred up a great deal of conflict among students at Samyê-Ling, who were unable to understand the significance of it. The conflict became intense. One individual, by the name of Christopher Woodman, showed particular delight at this conflict. Mr. Woodman was so inspired by the prospect of jealous warfare against myself and Diana that he attempted to convince the London Buddhist Society and other Buddhist organizations in Britain that my sense of dedication should be regarded as that of a neurotic criminal.

Matters having reached such a point, I invoked again and again the inspiration of Dorje Trollo Karma Pakshi. I even consulted the *I Ching*, which indicated that one should cross the great water. I did not want to waste further time in waging war, but rather felt determined to proceed in my work of propagating the Dharma. In view of this, and the meagre potential for genuine Buddhism in Britain at this time, I decided to journey to the American continent.

America was fresh and unknown territory for me, although there were some people there to whom I was known. *Born in Tibet* had been published in the United States in 1968. In 1969 *Meditation in Action,* drawn from a series of talks at Saymê-Ling, was published by the English firm of Stuart and Watkins. A young American bookseller by the name of Samuel Bercholz saw it during a visit with the publisher and was immediately inspired to bring it out in America. *Meditation in Action* appeared in the United States as the first book published by Shambhala Publications, in the autumn of 1969, just a few months before my arrival. The response to it was very positive. One indication of this was an invitation from a group at the University of Colorado to come to Boulder and teach. Also, a number of American students who had been at Samyê-Ling had left for the United States before me as a vanguard to prepare for my arrival. They had purchased a 434-acre farm in northern Vermont, to which they gave the name Tail of the Tiger.

With the invitation from Boulder and the news of the establishment of Tail of the Tiger, added to the growing inhospitableness of our situation in Scotland, Diana and I departed for America. My physical disability and her youth made the journey, and what lay ahead of us, all the more exciting. On the aeroplane from Glasgow to Toronto, we talked of conquering the American continent, and we were filled with a kind of constant humour. As we did not yet have a visa to enter the United States, we proceeded to Montreal, where we spent the next six weeks living in a small apartment. Students from Tail of the Tiger came up to visit, and I also responded to several requests to teach in Montreal. In May of 1970, we obtained our visa and entered the United States.

At Tail of the Tiger we found an undisciplined atmosphere combining the flavours of New York City and hippies. Here too people still seemed to miss the point of Dharma, though not in the same way as in Britain, but in American free-thinking style. Everyone was eager to jump into tantric practices at once. Travelling to California on a teaching tour set up by Tail of the Tiger and Mr Bercholz, I encountered many more free-style people indulging themselves in confused spiritual pursuits. The saving grace of this visit was the warm hospitality offered me by Mr Bercholz and his

Vajracarya the Venerable Chögyam Trungpa, Rinpoche,
February 1977

Vajra Regent Ösel Tendzin

Trungpa Rinpoche, His Holiness the XVIth Gyalwa Karmapa, (*Photo:* James (
Jamgön Kongtrül of Pepung

Diana Mukpo riding dressage

colleagues in Shambhala Publications, which was located in Berkeley. At the same time, I realized that the energy behind people's fascinations was beginning to lighten and that America held genuine possibilities for receiving the Dharma. Meeting the students of other teachers was especially disappointing. These students seemed to lack any understanding of discipline, and purely to appreciate teachers who went along with their own neurosis. No-one seemed to be presenting a way of cutting through the students' neurosis. One outstanding exception to this situation was Shunryu Suzuki-roshi and his students, whose presence felt like a breath of fresh air. I would have more contact with them later.

I returned to Tail of the Tiger where I presented my first long seminar in this country, consisting of seventeen talks on Gampopa's text *The Jewel Ornament of Liberation*. This was followed by a similar seminar on the life and teachings of Milarepa. During this period Diana returned to England to try and fetch my eight-year-old Tibetan son, Ösel Rangtrol, who had remained behind in the care of Christopher Woodman. To our surprise, Mr Woodman refused to let him go, deciding to hold him as a captive. A court case followed which resulted in Ösel being temporarily sent to live at the Pestalozzi Children's Village in Sussex. Here I visited him for ten days in the autumn of 1970. It was not until the following year that we were able to bring Ösel to live with us in America.

From England, I flew directly to Denver, Colorado, where I was received by the University of Colorado group. They provided initial hospitality, putting me up in a cabin in Gold Hill, an old mining town in the mountains above Boulder. After a few weeks, I moved to a larger house in Four Mile Canyon near Boulder, where Diana joined me. Both of us took a strong liking to the city of Boulder, its fresh air, its manageable size and of course its mountains. I began to teach and a community of students began to gather, renting a house on Alpine Street to which I gave the name Anitya Bhavan, 'House of Impermanence'. Gradually the feeling of the students was changing and I saw definite potential for transforming them from home-grown dilettantes into genuine disciplined people.

As the enthusiasm for meditation practice and study grew, so did our membership. A group of students of Swami Satchidananda's Integral Yoga Institute first hosted us, then joined us, and we took over their practice facilities on Pearl Street in downtown Boulder.

One California disciple of Swami Satchidananda, a young American of Italian background, came to me with an invitation to attend a 'World Enlightenment Festival'. He was known as Narayana, a colourful personality with lots of smiles, possessing the charm of American Hindu diplomacy. From the first, I felt some definite sense of connection with him.

In March of 1971 Diana gave birth to a son. Witnessing the birth, I was filled with a sense of delight and of the child's sacredness. His Holiness the Dalai Lama gave him the name of Tendzin Lhawang, and I added Tagtrug, meaning 'tiger's cub'. Later he was recognized by His Holiness Karmapa as the rebirth of one of his teachers, Surmang Tendzin Rinpoche.

The energy and openness of the students now began to unfold quite rapidly, and we formally established a meditation centre in Boulder under the name of Karma Dzong, 'Fortress of Action'. In addition, after a certain amount of searching, we purchased 360 acres of land west of Fort Collins, Colorado, which we called the Rocky Mountain Dharma Center. The first students who moved on to this land were a group of young and quite innocent hippies who called themselves 'The Pygmies'.

During this period I travelled a great deal. On my second visit to California, I was able to spend more time with Suzuki-roshi, and this proved to be an extraordinary and very special experience. Suzuki-roshi was a Zen master in the Soto Zen tradition who had come to America in 1958 and founded the Zen Center, San Francisco and Zen Mountain Center at Tassajara Springs. He was a man of genuine Buddhism, delightful and profound, full of flashes of Zen wit. In the example of his spiritual power and integrity, I found great encouragement that genuine Buddhism could be established in America. His students were disciplined and dedicated to the practice of meditation, and on the whole presented themselves as precise and tidy. Mrs Suzuki also I found to be a wonderful woman who was very generous to both myself and Diana.

When Suzuki-roshi died in December of 1971, I was left with a feeling of great lonesomeness. Yet his death had the effect on me of arousing further strength; his genuine effort to plant the Dharma in America must not be allowed to die. I did, however, feel especially keenly the loss of the possibility of exploring further the link between Tibetan and Japanese culture. Since coming to the West,

I have become increasingly fascinated with aesthetics and the psychology of beauty. Through Suzuki-roshi's spiritual strength and his accomplishments in the arts of the Zen tradition, I felt I could have learned much more in these areas.

During this period my presentation of the Dharma to students was based on the practice of pure sitting meditation, the traditional shamatha-vipashyana technique presented by the Buddha. Students maintained a daily sitting practice, as well as taking intensive solitary and group meditation retreats. The other major element in my teaching was continual warnings against dilettantism, spiritual shopping and the dangers of spiritual materialism. The enthusiasm and trust of students all over America continued to accelerate, with the result that local centres for study and practice sprang up in different parts of the United States and Canada. To all of these centres we gave the name Dharmadhatu, meaning 'space of Dharma'. Now, inspired by the strength of my encounter with Suzuki-roshi and by the genuine friendship of my own students, I decided to establish Vajradhatu, a national organization with offices in Boulder to oversee and unify the present and future Dharmadhatus. Narayana became an early member of Vajradhatu's board of directors.

Alongside the traditional teachings and practice of Buddhism, one of my principal intents was to develop a Buddhist culture, one which would transcend the cultural characteristics of particular nationalities. An early step in this direction was the establishment of the Mudra theatre group. It developed out of a notorious theatre conference which we hosted in Boulder early in 1973 bringing together our students and members of various experimental theatre groups from around the country such as the Open Theater, the Byrd-Hoffmann and the Provisional Theater. Amidst the variety of demonstrations and exchanges taking place among the participants, my personal style and uncompromisingness had both positive and negative effects; in any case, all of the participants became highly emergized. Following this conference, I presented to our own Mudra theatre group the notion of training body, speech and mind rather than immediately embarking on conventional performances. I introduced a series of exercises based on Tibetan monastic dance and the oriental martial arts which focused on the principles of centre and space and their mutual intensification and diffusion.

Members of the Mudra group have maintained a regular practice over the years and are now at the point of presenting performances to the public, which they have begun with two short plays of my own composition.

The Mudra approach to theatre has a parallel in the Maitri project, which also got under way at this time. The idea for it arose from a discussion that Suzuki-roshi and I had had concerning the need for a therapeutic facility for disturbed individuals interested in meditation. The Maitri approach to therapy involves working the different styles of neurosis through the tantric principles of the five Buddha families. Rather than being subjected to any form of analysis, individuals are encouraged to encounter their own energies through a meditation practice employing various postures in rooms of corresponding shapes and colours. A major facility for these practices, the Maitri Center, is located on a secluded, 90-acre farm outside of New York City.

In May of 1973 my third son, Gesar Arthur, was born. We named him after the two great warrior kings, of ancient Tibet and England. Later he was recognized by Chentze Rinpoche and His Holiness Karmapa as the rebirth of my own root-guru, Jamgön Kongtrül of Sechen.

As students became more completely involved with practice and study, I felt there was a need for more advanced training in the tradition of Jamgön Kongtrül the Great and of the Ka-gyü contemplative order. A situation was needed in which a systematic and thorough presentation of the Dharma could be made. Accordingly, I initiated the annual Vajradhatu Seminary, a three-month intensive practice and study retreat for mature students. The first of these seminaries, involving eighty students, took place at Jackson Hole, Wyoming, in the autumn of 1973. Periods of all-day sitting meditation alternated with a study programme methodically progressing through the three yanas of Buddhist teaching, Hinayana, Mahayana and Vajrayana.

This progress through the three yanas was also manifested in the development of the community itself. Through the strict discipline of sitting practice, students were encouraged to develop warmth and a greater compassion toward themselves. Beyond this, it was necessary for them to have compassion toward their world and to share what they had learned with others. Working for the benefit of others is at the heart of the Buddhist approach, particularly that of the Mahayana. I began to appoint some of the older students as meditation instructors to work with newer ones. These individuals are instructors in a very strict sense; their role is not to theorize or analyse but just to transmit what they themselves have learned and understood.

Going further in our effort to expand communiation with others, we evolved the plan of establishing the Naropa Institute. The purpose of this Institute is, first of all, to provide a vessel for the development of Bodhisattva activity among both teachers and students. It emphasizes the discipline of learning and the appreciation of our heritages of both the Orient and the Occident, grounded in meditation practice and commitment to personal development. The first session of the Institute in the summer of 1974 attracted over two thousand students. Among other prominent teachers who participated, perhaps the most colourful was Ram Dass; the interplay between the two of us during the course of the summer was delightfully humorous. After a second highly successful summer in 1975, Naropa Institute adopted a year-round degree-granting programme.

By this time my relationship with my students had become entirely natural, and the flow of communication between us was effortless. There was a need, however, for them to witness other teachers of our lineage. In the autumn of 1974, with perfect timing, His Holiness Karmapa made his first visit to the West. Arriving in New York, he travelled across the country visiting each of our main centres. While at Tail of the Tiger, at my request he gave it the new Tibetan name of Karme-Chöling, 'Dharma Place of the Karma Ka-gyüs.' In spite of a certain amount of uncertainty and clumsiness on the part of the students, His Holiness was extremely pleased with them and with what I had accomplished. Many people had the great fortune of participating in the Vajra Crown ceremony as well as several abhisekas which His Holiness performed. The visit served as a landmark to confirm that the Dharma had actually taken root in the soil of America. His Holiness issued a proclamation confirming the existence of Buddhism in America and the fulfilment of my role as a Vajra Master, further empowering me as Vajracarya, a spiritual master of the highest level.

Following the first Vajradhatu Seminary I had transmitted to a small group of close students the preliminary practices of the Vajrayana. With the introduction of these practices, along with the enormous inspiration to devotion aroused by the visit of His Holiness, the true Vajrayana style of surrender combined with complete discipline began to show through in our sangha. One example of this was that the contingent of voluntary bodyguards who had served His Holiness requested after his departure to remain active on a permanent basis, to assist me personally and to prevent any interruptions to our work.

By now Vajradhatu had become one of the foremost Buddhist institutions in America. Its growth had been natural and unforced, but in order to accommodate such large-scale work, it became clearly necessary to employ a number of the students as a permanent staff. In the beginning most of these administrators were complete amateurs. Coming to their work purely as practitioners of meditation, they learned from their experience, step by step, and developed increasing administrative capabilities, combining efficiency with a wakeful sense of humour. Narayana has been an outstanding example of this process. Another is my private secretary, David Rome, who has been a reliable companion and confidant to me for the last four years and has helped a lot in inspiring my work.

During all of this time my wife Diana has been a considerable source of encouragement to me, as she has involved herself with Dharma practice and the care of our children. Also, she has revived an interest from her own childhood in horses, which has led to her becoming a student of the classical school of equitation known as dressage, exemplified by the Spanish Riding School of Vienna. She has made extremely rapid progress in working up to the level of Grand Prix, and the two of us share a keen interest in the art of horsemanship.

All in all, my sense at each point on the way has been one of trying very hard at first, then relaxing and thinking to the future. By now, I feel, the major obstacles have been overcome and there is a sense of having achieved what was envisaged. No doubt there is much more work and many adventures still awaiting me, and for these I feel prepared. Whatever I had done has been guided by the blessings of Jamgön Kongtrül, and his presence is closer now than ever before. There is a constant sense of gratitude to my tutors and of appreciation for the Tibetan wisdom which was imparted to me,

Dingo Chentze Rinpoche

(*Photo:* Blair Hansen)

The Sakyong Mipham Rinpoche

(*Photo:* William Karellis)

Dingo Chentze Rinpoche and
the Sakyong Mipham Rinpoche

(*Photo:* Lee Weingra

Karmê-Chöling in Barnet, Vermont

(*Photo :* Jane Coh

everything from how to pitch a tent to the attainment of enlightenment. I feel young and old at the same time.

In order to impart this wealth to so many people, and to ensure that everything will not stop at my death, it is necessary to have one person as an inheritor, someone whom I can train and observe over a period of many years. For a long time it was in my mind to appoint Narayana to this role, and in the summer of 1976 I did so, empowering him as Dorje Gyaltsap, Vajra Regent. Assuming the refuge name which I had given him several years before of Ösel Tendzin, 'Radiant Holder of the Teachings', he took on his heavy responsibility, feeling burdened by it but tremendously inspired. Six hundred people attended the ceremony of his empowerment. There was a wide range of reactions; mostly, people were deeply moved that a future holder of the lineage could be an American.

Ösel Tendzin himself is arrogant and humble, resourceful and impatient, and always willing to regard his position as a further training process. Working with him takes no struggle, and he is quick to apply what he has learned. My training of him is primarily through close and critical observation. My approach to administration and the community in general has been to give more and more responsibility to people but to hold the nerve centre in my control, and I am teaching Ösel Tendzin to do likewise.

For their part, community members are taking on more and more duties, contributing their full or part-time energy. A large number of authorized meditation instructors throughout the country work personally with newer students. In a few cases early leaders in the administration have fallen out through ambition and lack of vision, but they have remained as faithful practitioners. On the whole I find that all of the members of the community are becoming mature people committed to working on themselves and for others. They begin to feel at home in their new Buddhist world. In their manner of respecting and helping each other there is no need for big brothers, yet they have a genuine affection for leadership and sense of constant forward vision. They begin to present themselves with confidence and even elegance, although there could still be problems of exclusivity and self-satisfaction.

Throughout this time I have been conducting numerous seminars and public talks, making regular visits to the east and west coasts, and each year there have been more people in attendance. The size of our centres, as well as of the Vajradhatu Seminary, has grown accordingly. In the autumn of 1976 we completed a major construction project at Karme-Chöling, including a large shrine hall, halls for Vajrayana practice, classrooms, dining hall, library, staff quarters and dormitories for visitors. In Boulder we purchased a large older building to accommodate the expanded office needs of Karma Dzong and Vajradhatu. Community members did extensive renovation work on the building, to which we gave the name Dorje Dzong, and the top floor was converted into a handsome shrine hall capable of accommodating six hundred pepole. Other projects are in the planning, including a major group retreat facility at the Rocky Mountain Dharma Center.

We have also had more wonderful visits from teachers of the lineage. Dingo Chentze Rinpoche made an extensive visit in 1976 which was personally very moving for me. The response of our students and the progress in their practice have certainly contributed to prolonging his life, and he has promised to visit us again. His Holiness Dudjom Rinpoche, head of the Nyingma order, also paid us a visit, and his teachings have greatly benefited many of our students.

As I conclude my writing of this chapter, His Holiness Karmapa is with us again on his second visit, accompanied by the 22-year-old Jamgön Kongtrül of Pepung, whose previous incarnation ordained me when I was eight years old. This time the hospitality and genuineness of His Holiness' reception have been spotless, reflecting the maturity of the students, their lack of resistance and their fearless devotion. Consequently His Holiness is enjoying himself thoroughly, as if coming to America were returning home rather than travelling to a foreign country. He has given his confirmation and blessing to Ösel Tendzin as Vajra Regent as well as to my son Gesar as the rebirth of Jamgön Kongtrül of Sechen. He has also requested me to act as one of the principal organizers of an international affiliation of Karma Ka-gyü institutions.

At this point, for the purpose of reviewing what has been achieved and what needs to be done further, as well as to devote time to practice, I have decided to set aside the year of 1977 for a personal retreat. During this year all of my students, headed by Ösel Tendzin, will have the opportunity to continue on their own. I have no doubt that they will be able to carry out the vision of the golden sun of Dharma, energetically extending themselves for the benefit of beings and arousing the authentic dawn of Vajrasattva.

APPENDIXES

APPENDIX I

THE ADMINISTRATION OF THE KA-GYÜ MONASTERIES OF EAST TIBET

Trindzin ...... The Supreme Abbot.

Gyaltsap ...... The Regent Abbot.

Khenpo .... Master of studies, in charge of academic work. He conducts both the Hinayana and the Mahayana rites.

Dorje-lobpön .. Master of Rites. He conducts the Vajrayana rites. (Both the *khenpo* and the *dorje-lobpön* officiate at these rites in the absence of the supreme abbot).

Drupön .... Master of Meditation, head of the retreat centre.

Gekö .... Senior monk in charge of discipline. Head of the administrative body. He receives visitors to the monastery and keeps lists of the monks and novices.

Kyorpön ...... Senior tutor under the *khenpo*.

Chandzö ...... Senior Secretary under the abbot.

Umdze .... The Precentor, in charge of music and chanting and of the time-table of assemblies.

Chöpön .... In charge of the arrangement of the altars and shrines and of their proper upkeep, including the decoration of votive offerings.

Champön ...... Master of Dancing; trainer of the dancers in the 'Mystery plays' of which each monastic Order has its own particular form.

Nyerpa .... Bursar, in charge of the personal finance, lodging and food of the supreme abbot. He also manages his property.

Tratsang	The Collegiate Council for the monastery, working directly under the *gekö*. In charge of all the finances of the monastery outside the supreme abbot's obligations and all the festival properties.
Tra-nyerpa	A lay treasurer. All donations to the monastery which come under the charge of the *gekö* and the *tratsang* are received and administered by the *tra-nyerpa*.
Junior tra-nyerpa	In charge of catering and domestic work; he can be either a monk or a layman.
Geyö	Title given to a number of men with authority to keep order among the monks, who also attend to the general tidiness of the monastery.
Chöyö	Assistant to the *chöpön*, who attends to the assembly halls, shrine rooms, altars etc.
Machen	Head of kitchen.
Ja-drenpas	Members of the domestic staff.
Jamas	Cooks.
Chumas	Water carriers.

Except for the supreme abbot, the regent abbot and the senior secretary, all other members of the monastic administration hold office for three years but can be re-elected.

All young monks on entering the monastery, from whatsoever background, must begin with the more menial tasks, rising later according to their abilities.

MONASTIC FINANCES

The organization of Tibetan monasteries was somewhat different from that practised in other Buddhist countries.

The Tibetans have always lived for and in their religion and from the time that Buddhism was introduced their religious centres have been the pivot of the community. Large and small properties were continually being donated in order to establish monasteries; the produce of these lands became a source of monastic income while at the same time increasing the means of livelihood for the inhabitants of the district.

The tenure of monastic land, including domicile, cattle, horses, implements, seed and incidental expenses, was granted to a peasant on a three yearly lease, which might be renewed. In return he had to provide the monastery with a contracted return in kind and labour; any profits above the contract he could keep for himself. When his lease was up he was obliged to return the same quota that he had taken over and in equally good condition. The leaseholder had to provide the monastery with such items as meat, silk and its products, grain etc. and, by trading, to supply the monastery's requirements of tea. Certain properties were allocated to meeting the expenses of particular annual celebrations. There were other less wealthy tenants whose contribution to the monastery was to provide fuel, consisting of wood and dried dung; transport animals such as yaks, horses and mules were allotted under similar conditions of return at the end of the contract period.

Every peasant owned his own small holding and was usually self-supporting. He was free to dispose of his land inside his own area but seldom did so. He was, however, expected to farm a given plot of the monastic estate every so many years.

The abbot or, in cases when more than a single monastery was involved, the supreme abbot was responsible for renovations and alterations of the monastery. The income for this came from the personal donations that he received. The senior secretary directed the disbursement for the major projects, but the abbot's more personal expenditure such as his clothes, table, travelling expenses, guests and petty cash or, in the case of a minor, his educational expenses was all under the management of his bursar. When he received large gifts of brocade or cloth the abbot would hand over most of these to the monastery.

There was also the matter of farm land belonging personally to the abbot; the produce from this went to the monastery.

Thus monasteries and peasants were always interdependent and in cases of tenants falling into financial difficulties the abbot would give them assistance.

To understand the doctrine of '*Tulkus*' in Tibet, it is necessary first of all to understand the Buddhist attitude to 'rebirth'. It is true that the Buddha spoke of an undergoing of countless existences by each one of us, and almost all Asian people envisage life in this sense: naturally, one has always to distinguish between popularized versions of this doctrine and its proper understanding by those who do not confuse the issue through overvaluing their individual selves. In fact, the Buddha's message was not that these countless lives possess an intrinsic reality, but that there is for all of us the possibility of a release from their illusion. He saw that a stream of suffering pervades the lives of men and other beings and that their desire to perpetuate their own individuality is one of the strongest forces keeping them wedded to suffering. He taught that to abandon the sense of 'I' leads to release from all those tendencies that bring about successive birth and death; as Tilopa, an Indian sage, put it: the spiritual quest is like a snake unwinding itself.

While we remain more or less enmeshed in a selfhood regarded as our own, past and future lives are continually being produced by those forces which still bind us to worldly existence. In the case of a *Tulku*, however, the forces which produce his existence are of a different order. Something, or someone, that has no 'individuality' or *ego* in the ordinary sense decides to work on earth for the sake of all beings. He (or 'it') therefore takes birth over a certain period of time, in a series of human individuals, and it is these who are named '*Tulkus*'.

The influence in question may emanate from any of the archetypal sources of Wisdom, which is the stable essence of the Universe, or else of Compassion, which is Wisdom in operation throughout countless world systems. So it may be said of a *Tulku* that he is an emanation of Manjusri, the Bodhisattva of Wisdom or of Avalokitesvara, the Bodhisattva of Compassion; the Dalai Lama is known as an incarnation of the latter. In Tibet, a great sage such as Milarepa, known to have passed quite beyond the bondage of created things, is said to extend his influence over various lines of such incarnations. In the present book one finds Lamas, such as Gyalwa Karmapa, Chentze Rinpoche and Jamgön Kongtrül Rinpoche who are recognized to be embodiments of particular spiritual influences. One such influence may in fact manifest itself through several individuals at once, as was the case with the five incarnations of the Jamgön Kongtrül.

These are high Incarnates; but not all known *Tulkus* are of this kind. In some instances a man of advanced spiritual development, but short of final liberation, dies before accomplishing a certain task and returns to complete it. Another kind of incarnation is known as a '*Tulku* of benediction': when a certain well beloved Lama dies, his disciples will ask another Lama who has been closely associated with the deceased (the latter, as often as not, will be the presiding Lama of their school) to locate his spirit; as a result of this, the Lama, though he does not return in person, confers his blessing upon the one who is to carry on his teaching; the person thus designated for the task will then reincarnate the departed Master in the sense of perpetuating his spiritual influence.

Multiple incarnations, of which an example was given above, most frequently occurs in fives, of which one in particular will embody the visible presence of the departed Lama, another his powers of speech, and yet another his powers of thought; again, one will represent his activities and another his qualities.

Readers who are interested in this oft misunderstood aspect of Tibetan spirituality may also consult with advantage the chapter on the Dalai Lama and his function in a book entitled *The Way and the Mountain* by Marco Pallis (who contributed the foreword to the present book) published by Peter Owen, London; that chapter contains much information on the subject of *tulkuhood*, both factual and technical. The same book also contains two other chapters treating respectively of Compassion and Gnosis from the point of view of the Tibetan tradition.

GLOSSARY

Amrita ...... *ambrosia*, food of the gods; the Elixir of Immortality; also a metaphor for spiritual healing.

Atiyana ...... 'the Ultimate Way'; the last and highest vehicle of spiritual instruction.

Bardo .... the indeterminate state intermediate between death and rebirth.

Bhikshu ...... a Buddhist monk who has received the higher ordination; a full member of the *Sangha*.

Bodhisattva .... one who is on the way to attaining Buddhahood; transposed into a higher dimension, this term indicates one who has been entirely freed from self and thus is qualified to work for the freeing of all beings still in bondage to the world and its illusions.

Bön .... the old religion of the Tibetans prior to the coming of Buddhism: a form of 'Shamanism'.

Buddha ...... 'the Wake', who has won the victory over Ignorance (here likened to a sleep full of dreams good and bad) and attained Enlightenment.

Buddha-mandala a symbolical representation of various levels and aspects inherent in Buddhahood.

Chakra .... a wheel or circle. Used in certain centres or focal points of the human body, with their special subtle and spiritual correspondences, which figure in various forms of *yoga*.

Chöten .... see *Stupa*.

Dakini .... a feminine aspect of divinity; a 'goddess'.

Dharma ...... the religion founded by the Buddha, his Doctrine; the law or 'Norm' governing all existence; any particular entity, thing or being. The *dharmas* are the innumerable things composing the Universe. (*Dharma* comes from a root out of which a whole series of related meanings can be drawn.)

Dharmakaya ..   the 'Body of Quiddity' or 'Essential Body' of all the Buddhas; the 'body of the Norm'; the inexpressible reality underlying everything.

Drogpa ......   a Tibetan highlander; an alpine herdsman.

Düdsi ....   see *Amrita*.

Gelugpa ......   the latest of the four schools of Tibetan Buddhism, founded early in the fifteenth century by Lobsang Tragpa, surnamed Tsong Khapa. In this school great emphasis is laid on scriptural study and learning generally. Both the Dalai and Panchen Lamas belong to this school.

Genyen ......   one who has received the primary ordination; this is imparted at one level to lay adherents and at another to celibates training for an eventual monastic ordination in the full sense.

Geshe ....   the highest scholastic qualification in the Gelug and Sakya Orders; a 'doctorate' in religious studies.

Getsül ....   a novice monk.

Gönkhang ......   'house of the Protective Divinities'; a special temple reserved for certain rites.

Gönpo ....   a protective aspect of Divinity.

Guru ....   a Spiritual Master; one's personal teacher.

Gyalwa Karmapı   the head Lama of the Karma Kagyü Order. *Gyalwa* is a title meaning 'Victorious'; *karma* means 'action' and here refers to the activities of a Buddha.

Hinayana ......   the 'Lesser Vehicle', contrasted with *Mahayana*, the 'Greater Vehicle'. The former corresponds to the preliminary stages of the spiritual Way. (This particular terminology belongs to the northern schools of Buddhism, in China, Japan and Tibet; the southern schools of Ceylon, Burma and Thailand do not use these terms).

Kadampa .... the school founded by the Indian saint Atisha Dipankara who came to Tibet towards the middle of the eleventh century; in this school special stress is laid on scriptural instruction and on the practice of loving kindness. The Gelugpa school (see above) was a later revival of the Kadampa.

Kagyü .... the 'Oral Tradition', the second oldest school of Buddhism in Tibet; whence also *Kagyüpa*, a follower of this school. Its characteristic teachings go back to Marpa and Milarepa, two saints who lived in the eleventh century; the former obtained his doctrine from Naropa, the head of the great Buddhist centre of Nalanda, in what is now the Indian province of Bihar. The *Kagyü* Order has numerous subdivisions of which the *Karma Kagyü*, to which the author of this book belongs, is one. Its present form was given to the whole Order by Gampopa, a direct disciple of Milarepa.

Kalung ...... 'ritual authorisation' allowing one to engage in a particular method or to read the books relating thereunto; sometimes *kalung* indicates permission to recite a certain *mantra*.

Karma .... literally 'action'. In Buddhist parlance this word usually refers to 'action and its concordant reaction'', cause of successive rebirth in ever varying states of existence, according to the merit or demerit thus incurred. *Karma* may be said to correspond to the 'immanent justice' of the Universe. In relation to any given being, *karma* is the 'fate' that being has inherited from past causes and modified in its present state of existence, thus determining the nature of a future existence in the world. Suffering is the recurrent price of this process: Buddhahood is deliverance therefrom through an understanding of the real nature of things, including that of the karmic process itself.

Lama .... literally 'superior', by derivation a 'spiritual teacher', the equivalent of *guru*; such a teacher may be a monk or a layman. Not all monks ate 'lamas', therefore, though in India and the West the title is often loosely applied in that sense. (Concerning 'incarnate Lamas' or *Tulkus* see Appendix II.)

Mahamudra .... the 'great symbol', which transcends expression and contains the Universe; the most profound form of Tantrik meditation.

Mahayana .... the 'Great Vehicle' or 'Great Way' that leads beings to Enlightenment, to the final awakening.

Mandala ...... a symbolical design, usually circular in shape with an inscribed square, meant to serve as a 'mnenonic key' for those who practise yogic meditation under one of its many forms. Such a *mandala* may be painted or merely pictured in the mind; in connection with certain rites *mandalas* are sometimes carried out in coloured sand upon the ground.

Mantra ...... sonorous form expressive of Buddhahood under one or other of its aspects; formula pregnant with the influence of a particular Bodhisattva or Sage. The language of *mantra* is Sanskrit, the words are never translated. Such *mantras* play an important part in various rituals. Chiefly, they are 'invoked', with or without the aid of a rosary, as a means of concentrating attention and as an element of initiatic method.

Mudra .... a symbolic gesture, used both in rites and yogic exercises; an essential feature in the sacred iconography of divinities and saints.

Nyingmapa .... the earliest of the four schools of Tibetan Buddhism—the word itself means 'ancient'. The patron of the Order is Padma Sambhava who brought the Buddhist tradition to Tibet.

Nirmanakaya.... the 'Emanation Body' of the Buddhas; the earthly form of the Buddha in this, or any other world cycle; also symbolical manifestations of the Doctrine, such as sacred images, paintings and books.

Prasena ...... exceptional form of divination only practised by initiates.

Rinpoche ...... literally 'precious one'. A title given to Incarnate Lamas, senior abbots and occasionally even to kings.

Sakya .... the third in date of the monastic foundations of Tibet. The chief centre (whence the name) lies some seventy miles to the north of Mt Everest, but this Order also has many adherents in Eastern Tibet.

Samadhi ...... a state of spiritual concentration; a yogic trance; also used of the death of any spiritual person.

Sambhogakaya the 'Fruition Body' or 'Body of Bliss' of the Buddhas; the link between the inexpressible Essence and its manifestation in the visible Buddhas; the various aspects of wisdom, compassion and other divine names or qualities.

Samsara ...... the Round of Existence; the indefinite play of interacting cause and effect which expresses itself in the birth and death of beings, with its incidental suffering.

Sangha .... the 'Congregation' founded by the Buddha; his dedicated followers; the whole Order of Buddhist monks. In the Mahayana this term embraces the whole company of Saints, in all states of existence.

Serto .... a golden crest ornament to indicate dignity, placed on the roofs of sacred edifices and houses; people of importance also put it on the heads of their horses. See illustration opposite page 89.

Shramanera .. A monk undergoing training: many monks remain at this degree and do not take the higher ordination for bhikshuship.

Stupa .... symbolical monument, roughly bell-shaped, common to the Buddhist world since early times. In its Tibetan and kindred forms, the tiers and other details of a *stupa* denote various stages of spiritual realization.

Sutra .... a book of the canonical Scriptures; also a theoretical treatize not directly concerned with methodic realization, accessible to all the faithful without restriction.

Tagpa .... elementary form of divination.

Taisitu .... Chinese title confered by one of the Ming emperors on the abbots of Pepung.

Tanka .... a sacred painting, usually carried out on cotton cloth primed with plaster and mounted on Chinese silk so as to form a scroll that can, if necessary, be rolled up. Patchwork *tankas* occur, but more rarely; also a few have been embroidered, mostly by Mongol artists.

Tantra .... a treatise relating to methods of spiritual concentration; a book of instruction concerning particular forms of *yoga*. As compared with *sutras* (see under that heading), *tantras* remain relatively 'secret' documents, for the use of initiates only; a *kalung* is required in order to qualify a person to study one of these, while a *wang* (empowerment) is required in order to practise the method in question.

Togden .... a term used in the Kagyü school indicating one who has actually experienced reality in a high degree.

Torma ..... a symbolical cake, usually conical in shape, to be used in rituals. (The Sanskrit equivalent is *bhalinta*.)

Tulku.......... see Appendix II.

Upasaka ...... see *Genyen*.

Vajra .... a symbol of the nature of reality indicating its eternal or 'adamantine' quality; a ritual sceptre, shaped like the thunderbolt of Jupiter. (In Tibetan it is called *dorje*, meaning the 'noble stone').

Vajra posture .. the cross-legged meditation position associated with the Buddha and with *yogins* generally.

Vajrayana .... the highest of the three Vehicles or Ways. The way from which there is no turning back until Enlightenment is reached.

Varshka Vihara place for the traditional 'summer retreat' carried out by monks ever since the time of the Buddha.

Vihara .... originally a Sanskrit word meaning 'a dwelling'. In Buddhism it is used for a religious building, usually a monastery.

Wangkur ...... literally 'empowerment'; an 'initiation', conferred privately or sometimes also to groups, enabling those receiving it to practise a particular meditation or yogic method under a qualified Spiritual Master. In Tibet (as elsewhere) all teachings aiming at a supra-individual realization follow this pattern, though forms and rites will vary considerably as to detail.

Yoga .... literally 'union', the same root as the English word 'yoke'. It denotes any specific method (including its theoretical premisses) of which the aim is to release the unitive Knowledge latent in the heart of man, by bringing under control the various dispersive tendencies of mind and body. A *Yogi* is one who practises such a method and, more especially, one who in virtue of the Knowledge thus awakened has qualified as a Master of this spiritual art.

INDEX

279

INDEX